The IRS Ha
Compete
law and practice

General Editor:
Neil Rankin

Legal Editor:
Paul Epstein, Cloisters

Members of the LexisNexis Group worldwide

United Kingdom	IRS, member of the Eclipse Group Ltd, 18-20 Highbury Place, London N5 1QP
Argentina	Abeledo Perrot, Jurisprudencia Argentina and Depalma, BUENOS AIRES
Australia	Butterworths, a Division of Reed International Books Australia Pty Ltd, CHATSWOOD, New South Wales
Austria	ARD Betriebsdienst and Verlag Orac, VIENNA
Canada	Butterworths Canada Ltd, MARKHAM, Ontario
Chile	Publitecsa and Conosur Ltda, SANTIAGO DE CHILE
Czech Republic	Orac sro, PRAGUE
France	Editions du Juris-Classeur SA, PARIS
Hong Kong	Butterworths Asia (Hong Kong), HONG KONG
Hungary	Hvg Orac, BUDAPEST
India	Butterworths India, NEW DELHI
Ireland	Butterworths (Ireland) Ltd, DUBLIN
Italy	Giuffré, MILAN
Malaysia	Malayan Law Journal Sdn Bhd, KUALA LUMPUR
New Zealand	Butterworths of New Zealand, WELLINGTON
Poland	Wydawnictwa Prawnicze PWN, WARSAW
Singapore	Butterworths Asia, SINGAPORE
South Africa	Butterworths Publishers (Pty) Ltd, DURBAN
Switzerland	Stämpfli Verlag AG, BERNE
USA	LexisNexis, Dayton, OHIO

© Eclipse Group Ltd 2001

A CIP Catalogue record for this book is available from the British Library.

ISBN 0 406 946345

Typeset by Letterpart Ltd, Reigate, Surrey
Printed and bound in Great Britain by Hobbs the Printers Ltd, Totton, Hampshire

Visit Butterworths LexisNexis direct at www.butterworths.com

Contents

Preface

Welcome. The *IRS handbook on competencies – law and practice* appears at a uniquely important time in the use of competency frameworks. Today, we have available a rich store of experience from two decades of employers' use of competencies. Instead of the challenge facing the early pioneers, who had to find their own solutions to the many pitfalls and costly mistakes they encountered, modern-day developers of competencies and those engaged in renewing their existing frameworks can learn from this experience and save time, money and effort.

But today's developers and users of competencies face a fresh challenge. Society has changed; there is greater emphasis on fairness at work, a greater awareness of individual rights, and an increased willingness to assert them through legal action. New laws from Brussels and Westminster, and the social agenda of the Labour Government, are combining to extend the reach of legislation further and further into the workplace and day-to-day personnel practices.

Competencies now provide the basis for employers' decisions in areas that have a major impact on individual rights at work: recruitment, access to training, selection for promotion and individual pay awards. The fairness of these decisions in terms of unfair discrimination and other laws will increasingly be challenged in tribunals and the courts. Competency frameworks that are flawed in themselves, or have been misapplied or assessed, could prove the weak link when employers seek to defend such actions.

This handbook brings these two worlds of law and practice together. The *law*, where the challenges are still emerging, is expertly analysed by our legal editor, Paul Epstein, a barrister who specialises in discrimination issues at Cloisters Chambers. His active involvement in the latest cases means that we can present the law at its most recent stage of development.

The *practice* in the handbook's title highlights the key issues connected with the design, introduction and revision of competency frameworks. A team of expert advisers and researchers draws on the collective experience of employers to identify the factors that require strategic decisions, the options when designing, introducing and using competencies, and the ways in which they have addressed problems and difficulties.

The structure of the handbook has been designed to make it as accessible as possible. Each chapter is accompanied by a set of Learning Points, highlighting the issues covered by it. There are three further checklists (to be found in chapter 1); the first brings together the key factors involved in initiating a project to design a framework; the second summarises the factors that should be considered should problems occur. The third relates law to practice.

Chapter 1 provides an overview of the design, introduction and use of competencies, and illustrates its points with extracts from a baker's dozen of employers' own competency frameworks. The next three chapters explore some of these issues in further depth, so that readers can target those areas that interest them most. Chapter 2 provides greater detail on the key issues that greatly influence the success or failure of competency initiatives, while chapter 3 addresses technical aspects of competency design. Chapter 4 follows up the points made in chapter 1 about the importance of establishing a business need for the introduction of competencies.

Chapters 5 and 6 provide detailed information on the law, and the issues concerned with unfair discrimination where competencies are used.

Chapter 7 also covers a fast-moving and emerging area; in this case, this is the concept of "emotional intelligence". In many respects, this is a rebranding and reinterpretation of the main interpersonal competencies, and great claims are being made about its potential contribution to raising performance at work.

In chapter 8, we give special attention to the single most important practical issue connected with the use of competencies: what is known in the jargon as "buy in" – gaining the acceptance and active involvement of employees and line managers.

Chapters 9 and 10 are devoted to some specialised topics. Chapter 9 provides in-depth coverage of competency-related pay, an issue that attracts interest and heated controversy in equal measure. Chapter 10 examines another controversial issue: the development of international competency frameworks that attempt to span cultural and geographical divides.

Finally, in chapters 11 and 12 we turn to practice once competency frameworks are in place. Assessment, the subject of chapter 11, brings competencies to life. Unless individuals are assessed against their competencies, the framework will be of little but academic interest. And, in chapter 12, we consider the crucial issue of ensuring the continued existence and relevance of competencies after the hard work involved in their initial development.

Neil Rankin

Contributors

Neil Rankin (General Editor) has edited IRS's *Competency &
Emotional Intelligence* series of products since their launch in 1993,
and has researched and written extensively in the area of
competencies and other personnel management practices. He
conducts the annual benchmarking survey of employers' use of
competencies. Neil has also edited another IRS journal, *Employee
Development Bulletin*, since its launch in 1990, and is an associate of
IRS Research, the contract-research division of IRS. Previously, he
has worked as a researcher for both *IRS Employment Trends* and the
Pay and Benefits Bulletin. Neil has a postgraduate degree from the
School of Industrial and Business Studies, University of Warwick and
a professional qualification in information studies.

Paul Epstein BA Hons, Barrister (Legal Editor) was called to the bar
in 1988. He is an employment and discrimination law specialist
whose areas of practice include individual and collective rights,
unfair and wrongful dismissal, sex, race and disability discrimination,
equal value, TUPE, collective redundancy, union legislation, breach
of contract and injunction applications. He is a member of the
ELAAS Scheme and represents litigants under the Bar Pro Bono
Scheme and for FRU. He lectures regularly, including to the Law
Society, Liberty, Justice and the Employment Lawyers Association.
He teaches advocacy for the Middle Temple. He has appeared as a
legal expert in Television Education Network programmes, and on
national radio and television. Paul Epstein is a member of the
Employment Law Bar Association and Employment Lawyers
Association. He is an author of Tolley's *Working Time*, Bullen &
Leake & Jacob's *Precedents of Pleading*, and Butterworths'
Employment Law Guide. Paul Epstein has appeared in: *Care First v
Roffey* (whistleblowing), *Dickinson v Rushmer* (oral partnership
agreement), *Edmonds v Lawson* (pupil barrister and minimum wage),
Riniker v UCL (issue of proceedings), *Hale and Clunie v Wiltshire
NHS Trust* (compulsory rotating shifts for nurses), *MOD v Lowe*
(armed forces pregnancy termination), *Ojjeh v Waller* (liability of
director for representations), *Hornsby v CKL* (liability for fraudulent

employee), *HM Attorney General v Sunday Newspapers* (contempt action arising out of Grobbelaar match-fixing prosecution), *Sita (GB) v Burton* (TUPE), and *Marcel v Metropolitan Police* (police power to use seized documents).

Katherine Adams was the research officer with *Competency & Emotional Intelligence Quarterly* for more than two years prior to her move to the USA in 2000. She has many years' experience as a researcher and writer in the fields of competency, vocational qualifications, human resource management and equal opportunities. Before joining the journal, she worked for three years at the Scottish Vocational Education Council, where she was involved in developing standards of competence. Katherine has also been a research officer with IRS's *Employee Development Bulletin* and a freelance writer, editor and communication skills trainer.

Sharon Atchley manages the360.co.uk with Jane Coomber and Peter Goodge. It is a provider of internet-based 360-degree feedback systems that is run as a partnership of IT professionals and business psychologists. Sharon graduated in mathematics from Kings College, Cambridge in 1985, and has worked in IT for 16 years. She began her career with RAE Farnborough, where she was involved in mathematical modelling, and moved on to work on real-time blast-furnace control systems. She now specialises in mathematical modelling, database applications and the statistical analysis of questionnaires.

George Boak is an independent consultant specialising in management and personal development. He develops and adapts competency models and work-based learning systems, and advises on their application. He was the programme director for the Northern Regional Management Centre from 1987 to 1995, where he led a competency-based executive MBA programme, and led the team that developed the Management Charter Initiative's personal competence model for senior managers. Recent publications, based on practical experience, include *A complete guide to learning contracts* (Gower) and, with David Thompson, *Mental models for managers* (Century). He is a visiting lecturer at Newcastle Business School and at the College of York St John.

Dr Mee-Yan Cheung-Judge founded Quality and Equality, a consultancy specialising in organisation development and equal opportunities, in 1987, following an academic and business career.

She is an organisational development practitioner and diversity expert, and has worked with hundreds of clients from all sectors in the areas of organisational renewal, change management, equal opportunities and human resource management.

Jane Coomber manages the360.co.uk with Sharon Atchley, and Peter Goodge. Jane has a postgraduate Diploma in Computing and has 10 years' experience in IT in a commercial environment. She was involved with the pioneering "real-time" patient administration and nursing personnel systems at the London Hospital, Whitechapel. Further career moves provided experience in developing information systems and in programming database systems. In partnership with Sharon Atchley, she has spent recent years working exclusively on website development for a variety of clients in business, education and the arts.

Professor Adrian Furnham is Professor of Psychology at the University of London and founder director of Applied Behavioural Research Associates, which is a management consultancy specialising in research into corporate evaluation and design, performance appraisal, assessment and selection. A broadcaster and writer, his recent books include *The incompetent manager*, *The psychology of money* and *Assessing potential*. He has written 35 books and 400 academic articles, and writes regularly for the *Financial Times* and the *Daily Telegraph*. He is a Chartered Occupational and Health Psychologist and Fellow of the British Psychological Society.

Peter Goodge manages the360.co.uk with Sharon Atchley and Jane Coomber. He is a Chartered Business Psychologist, and has designed and run 360-degree feedback systems for Brewers Fayre, Centrica, Co-operative Insurance, Dell, Prudential, Standard Life, TGI Fridays, Whitbread and many others. He writes extensively on 360-degree feedback, and is a frequent conference presenter. His consultancy work also covers development centres and competency research. Peter is perhaps best known for his work with Peter Griffiths on "third-generation" development centre design. Prior to consulting, Peter worked in training and development in pharmaceuticals and the health service.

Lionel Laroche is founder and President of ITAP Canada, based in Toronto. Born in France, he obtained his Diplôme d'Ingénieur Polytechnicien from the Ecole Polytechnique in Paris and his PhD in chemical engineering from the California Institute of Technology in

Pasadena. Focusing on cross-cultural consulting and training, he established ITAP in Canada in 1998, following a 15-year career as an international engineer working with people from all over the world. Lionel has lived in eight different countries (France, Germany, Italy, Belgium, Denmark, the Netherlands, Canada and the USA), working in senior roles with multinational companies such as Xerox, Procter & Gamble, British Petroleum and Jeumont-Schneider.

Stephen Martin is founder and managing director of Kimball Consulting, a consultancy focusing on competency analysis, and integrated human resource development and organisational development applications. Stephen is also President of ITAP Europe, the combination producing a unique blend of broad-based HRD and cross-cultural management development, training and consulting capabilities. Stephen's career of more than 20 years spans international executive and consultancy roles in global financial services and manufacturing, and includes direct experience in the USA, Latin America and Europe. Based for three years in New York, he was vice president, global staffing, mobility and development for the Chase Manhattan Bank, and has wide experience of all major areas of human resources management.

Clare Muhiudeen is a partner at Watson Wyatt and head of the UK human capital team. Since joining the company in October 1985, Clare has had responsibility for a number of clients, covering reward strategy, competency design, reward management and compensation surveys, attitude surveys and organisational analysis. She has experience in a variety of organisations, both private and public sector, working in multi-union environments. Clare holds a BSc in Psychology from University College London and an MSc in Industrial Relations and Personnel Management from the London School of Economics.

Anand Shukla is a researcher and writer specialising in workplace emotional intelligence issues. Anand also researches and writes on politics, e-commerce and the single European currency. He is currently Development Manager at IRS.

John Warner is a regular contributor to *Competency & Emotional Intelligence Quarterly* and a frequent contributor to other IRS publications. He is a freelance writer in the fields of HR, management, communications and learning strategies. John is often called upon by professional bodies, companies and government departments. Originally a teacher, he later became a director of a national organisation which sought a better understanding of business. He has been working independently for the past five years.

Louis Wustemann is a freelance journalist with 12 years' experience of research and writing on employment issues, and is a frequent contributor to *Competency & Emotional Intelligence Quarterly*. Louis also researches and writes on facilities issues and was the editor of the Eclipse journal *Flexible Working* for four years. Formerly, he was a research officer on IRS's *Employment Review* for eight years, specialising in employee consultation procedures and company communications, and also researched and wrote on remuneration topics for IRS's *Pay and Benefits Bulletin*.

Chapter 1

Methods of designing frameworks

Introduction

Neil Rankin

Competency projects often have a lot riding on them. They are
frequently sponsored by an individual or team – often from within
personnel or training departments – and the success or failure of the
initiative will reflect on their credibility within the organisation. If
the high stakes involved were not enough, competencies are
technically demanding to understand, develop and implement. Faced
with what is effectively a blank sheet of paper, the obvious and
easiest solution is to turn to external sources of expertise. Yet, it
would be unwise to pass over the entire project to a team of
consultants. Competencies are merely the means to an end – a
technique (often described as a "language of performance";
"corporate DNA"; or more prosaically the articulation of "how we
do things around here") – rather than a self-contained system that
can be bought in and bolted on.

For a competency framework to justify the time, effort and expense
of developing and implementing it, it must contribute to the
business. It acts as a bridge between corporate ambitions, goals and
values, on the one hand, and individual effort and activity, on the
other. This means that a successful framework will be measured by
the extent to which it raises the performance of individuals and the
teams they work in. The higher levels of performance may lead to
greater profits, productivity, levels of service, improved quality, or
whatever the organisation decides is of importance to it.

But whatever the precise outcomes may be, a competency framework
can only be effective if it has been found to be relevant to the
organisation that will use it – and that managers and employees
perceive that it possesses this relevance. This demands the active
involvement of internal personnel in situations where external

11

advisers are brought in. And, in turn, this places an onus on these personnel to gain at least a basic appreciation of the nature of competency, and how a competency framework is designed.

So, this chapter provides an overview of the various ways in which competencies are developed, and the ways in which the results of this development work can be presented – the formats that competency frameworks can adopt, in other words. Beyond this introduction, chapter 1 engages with the key issues that those involved in introducing or revising a framework should bear in mind. It delves into the design phase of a competency-development project: how this should be managed and conducted, and the equally crucial issues of piloting and validating the framework. Finally, it deals with the tactics that can be adopted when, rather than if, problems occur. The two checklists accompanying this chapter bring many of these issues together for the benefit of those leading a competency-development project, and those actively involved in it. Chapter 1 ends with some real-life examples of employers' competency frameworks, selected to illustrate the different approaches currently being taken.

Chapters 2, 3 and 4 are closely linked to the areas covered in this chapter. Chapter 2 sets out the key issues that deserve careful, and early, consideration by those intending to introduce or update competency frameworks. It is based on the invaluable experience of two experts, George Boak and Professor Adrian Furnham. Chapter 3 concentrates on technical issues. Katherine Adams explains the workings of three of the best methods of identifying and defining competencies. She then provides a fuller explanation than given in this chapter of the different types of competencies, and traces back these differences to their American and British origins. Chapter 4 follows up the point made in this chapter that competency initiatives need to contribute to organisational effectiveness. Stephen Martin and Lionel Laroche draw on their own experience of making such a business case and give a worked example of how competencies' contribution can be demonstrated.

First principles

Neil Rankin

As definitions of performance, the development of competencies inevitably involves an analysis of *what* individuals do at work (technical/functional competences) or *how* they go about it (behavioural/emotional intelligence competencies) – or, increasingly, conducting an analysis that encompasses both approaches.

These distinctions are explained in depth by Katherine Adams in chapter 3. But, in essence, analysing the "what" of an individual's activities, or the demands of the job they do, will usually produce a set of what are variously known as "technical skills", "functional competences" or "hard skills". By their nature, these competences or skills are specific, rather than broad-ranging, and often tied to a small group of related jobs (sometimes called "job families"). There also tends to be a great many of them, as they describe the various facets of technical knowledge, activities and, perhaps, behaviours ("concern for health and safety", for example) that each job entails. In most organisations, these "what" types of competences are kept separate from the "how" types of competencies, often being found as appendices to a general set of "how" competencies, or incorporated in customised versions provided for each job family (where, for example, marketing staff will have a set of competencies tailored to their needs, as will IT specialists, personnel staff, and so on).

Conversely, analysing the "how" – the way that individuals go about performing their jobs or roles – will lead to a set of competencies that are variously known as "soft skills", "behaviours" or "personal competencies". Unlike "what"-type competencies, these are broader ranging, as they describe how a job or role should be tackled in a general way – for example, approaching each specific task from the same standpoint of "concern for customer care", "business orientation" or "showing initiative". These "how" competencies are usually identified by analysing the values and priorities that the organisation requires for its success (it may require a high level of customer care, for example) and the ways in which successful performers tend to conduct themselves at work (for example, generally showing a concern for quality, or for the value of teamworking as opposed to being a "lone ranger" intent on achieving personal results at any cost).

Taking a step back, though, is vital before such distinctions become of overriding concern. Whoever is leading or involved in the process of developing a competency framework must begin by identifying the ultimate purpose of their efforts. This should involve an identifiable (and, if possible, measurable) business benefit, and must be capable of winning support from key individuals in the organisation, as well as line managers and other end-users.

As other employers have painfully learned, competency development projects require careful management to keep them on track. The pitfalls that leaders and project teams should beware of include:

Timescales: The investigation stage when competencies are being identified and defined can become seductively all-important; ever-greater amounts of time and energy are consumed to create the ultimate in an exhaustive and seemingly well-designed set of competencies. The result is a huge overrun in the time and resources required to develop the framework, leading to demotivation among employees and managers as the project slips from sight, and their initial enthusiasm and familiarity change to boredom and alienation.

Complexity: Competencies are meant to touch every aspect of an organisation's operations. There is a danger, therefore, that they will raise many obliquely connected issues and problems during the design phase. Those involved in designing the framework will find themselves stretched too thinly to complete their main task, with the danger that no issue is tackled satisfactorily. Again, careful project management is required to maintain a focus on the prime goal.

Allied to this, the extensive research and consultation required to develop competencies will put the designers into contact with a wide range of potential stakeholders. The danger here is that many stakeholders will expect their own priorities and needs to be explicitly incorporated into the framework, leading to duplication, a loss of simplicity and focus and, ultimately, something that is too unwieldy to be of practical use. The design of the framework can help to reduce these pressures, if the competencies and definitions can be shown to be relevant to stakeholders' needs. It may be, though, that the best way forward is to create a series of competency frameworks, each specifically addressed to the needs of a particular department, "job family" (a group of staff in related grades, roles or other criteria held in common) or other interest group.

Priorities: Each stage of the design process should be incorporated into a project plan, with its own deadline, resource needs and the person responsible for it identified in advance. Overall, though, employers' experience shows that most find, with hindsight, that their priorities were wrong. Instead of investing most or much of their time, effort and emotional energy in the design phase, they should have given at least equal weight to, first, the process of involving and communicating with their workforces and, second, the point at which the competencies were introduced through the provision of briefings, motivational meetings, publicity and training. Project leaders could learn from this feedback and plan accordingly.

Employers' experience also reveals that timing is crucial in a further way over and above the practice of classic project management. They have found that competency projects are usually most successful when they can take advantage of a business "lever" – some key event or development that the competency project can use as a means of winning support and resources. A new set of business objectives often provides such a lever, where the organisation wishes to become more customer-oriented, quality conscious or international in outlook, for example. Or there may be a more general desire to achieve some form of "cultural change", perhaps by developing a culture of individual contribution and responsibility.

These and other basic considerations that a team or individual may wish to evaluate before starting on the road to a competency framework (or revising their existing one) are set out in Checklist 1.

Checklist 1. Planning the introduction of competencies

1. Identify an end-result for the introduction of competencies. The essential criteria for this end-result are that it must: be high profile; demonstrate the contribution of HR/training department; support one or more key business objectives; and show how it will make line managers' work easier.

2. Identify a business-related lever to help gain support for the introduction of competencies, such as: a reorganisation; cultural change programme; new business direction; takeover/merger.

3. Ensure that there is sufficient support for the introduction of competencies. At minimum, this requires one project champion and several active implementers. Criteria for project champions: one or two key people who are respected and influential; who will give backing; and provide resources. Criteria for implementers (the project team): a small team of respected, influential people; mainly line managers; from most/all areas to be covered by the competency initiative.

---

4. Consider whether you have ready access to the necessary expertise in-house for this project. If not, find an external expert – criteria: known to relate their expertise and advice to clients' actual needs; known to be a convincing advocate for competencies; known to be convinced of need to involve and communicate meaningfully and constantly.

5. Decide whether you want to pilot the use of competencies (there are pros and cons). If so, identify a section/department whose head is: respected and influential; who will give active support to the pilot; give you/the project team honest feedback on the bugs and problems.

6. Decide what your own involvement will be.

7. Assemble a *small* project team (based on (3) implementers, above). Are there others who unavoidably must be included (due to internal politics, etc)?

8. Work out an initial action plan, with deadlines for each stage. Review this with the team; aim to complete development work within three to four months, maximum.

9. Do detailed planning: What has to be done? Who in the team will be responsible for different components? Who else needs to be involved? Re-check the timescales. Check that the project has not become over-elaborate: keep it simple. Above all, work out in practical terms how employees and managers will be actively involved in developing, piloting and implementing the competency project. Involvement, involvement, involvement is the key to success. Try to build in to your plans for the competency initiative a few important measures of success (metrics/benchmarks), and a simple means of keeping the competencies up to date.

10. Consider nominating a member of the project team as internal publicity coordinator.

11. Training is essential for all those covered by the competency initiative (employees as well as their managers). Identify: who will deliver the training; and when it will take place; then slot these details into your project work plan.

12. How will the requirements of the law and good practice be addressed? Ensure the team has the expertise, or access to external advice, about legal requirements. Ensure that good

practice is covered via one or more of: literature reviews; benchmarking; site visits; networking.

13. Maintenance: evaluate the initiative after the pilot phase, if a pilot has been used, or, if not, after one year of use. What works? What doesn't? What do line managers want changed? Check the relevant results of applying the competencies (eg appraisals; training provision; pay awards) for unfair discrimination, and for indications that only lip-service is being paid to implementing the initiative.

14. Longer-term maintenance: set up a mechanism to review the initiative every two years thereafter, particularly to check that: it continues to support the business, takes account of any important developments (such as new business goals); and does not discriminate unfairly.

The design phase

The design process is usually managed by either a small project team or a single project leader. The team or individual then gets feedback on the "what" and the "how" of jobs from the jobholders, their managers and those leading the organisation.

Current practice among employers favours using teams, rather than placing what can be a heavy workload on a single individual (see box 1.1). Even then, the teams are seldom left without further resources, and most organisations also retain an external adviser to give them expert assistance. A project team offers a further advantage, beyond spreading the work among several people. Its membership can also begin what is the most crucial aspect of any competency project: ensuring the commitment of employees and managers to the introduction and use of competencies. In fact, two-thirds of employers deliberately involve line managers at the design stage – either in a project group or as active participants in the research efforts used to develop the competencies. Employees, numerically if not politically, are more important end-users, and many – albeit slightly fewer – organisations also involve them in the process of designing competency frameworks.

1.1. Employers' ways of developing competencies

The processes used by employers to develop and design competencies, based on 113 organisations.

	% of employers
Set up a project group	64%
Involve line managers at the design stage	64%
Use an external consultant (with or without internal input)	58%
Involve employees at the design stage	56%
Pilot the competencies in one department, work group, etc	44%
Deliberately check or validate them for possible unfair discrimination	22%

Source: Rankin (2001).

The specific techniques used to gain this feedback vary from employer to employer. In most cases, though, one-to-one interviews are one of the methods used. These are time-consuming, and may be restricted to the most important stakeholders and most influential individuals in the organisation. The interviewee's status may dictate that one-to-one interviews should be used, rather than group meetings, questionnaires or other larger-scale methods. Their importance as sources of information and insights may also be a determining factor. A main-board director, for example, may represent a rich source of material on corporate strategy and the likely future direction of the organisation, and it would be inefficient to gather this information by any other means.

Many employers' competency projects also or alternatively use focus groups at the design stage – where a small meeting led by a facilitator discusses issues and develops ideas based on a creative interaction of the participants. These can be particularly helpful in assisting participants to crystalise and articulate their views on what may be difficult or unfamiliar issues. For example, the competency project may wish to identify the characteristics of people who are seen as successful in a role or activity. A facilitated focus group discussion can help individuals identify the type of person who would qualify as being defined as "successful", and provide a framework to help them think through the technical or behavioural skills that they believe contribute to this success.

In fact, group meetings are one of the most common ways that employers use to develop their competency frameworks. But there are other techniques that are also often employed, but that offer the prospect of greater rigour and consistency to the project – and, therefore, the possibility that the resultant competencies are more accurate, relevant and clearly defined. These methods are repertory grids, the critical incident technique and a variant of this called the behavioural event interview. In brief, these methods usually involve one-to-one interviews, but use a structure that attempts to focus the interviewee's attention on important aspects of their work and the competencies underlying the ways that they approach them (these methods are explained in depth in chapter 3).

Benchmarking

Missing from box 1.1 is a method so universally practised that it seldom warrants specific mention: the practice of benchmarking an organisation against one or more comparators. Almost all of the employers that are the subjects of case studies in *Competency & Emotional Intelligence Quarterly* incorporate some form of external monitoring in the process of designing their own competency frameworks. At minimum, this involves an examination of other organisations' frameworks, involving no more, in some cases, than simply reading the lists of competencies and other documentation. More commonly, though, one or more of the design team will visit other organisations, discuss these contacts' experiences and be given an insight into the structure and content of their competencies.

True benchmarking, as understood in manufacturing industry, is rarely practised in the competency area. Here, highly effective comparator firms are researched and make up a group that the company compares itself against. Key measures (metrics) are identified and compared against the current performance of the company conducting the research, with a view to raising its own performance to their levels and learning from practices that are more efficient than its own. One example of this approach is found at BNFL, the nuclear energy company. Attached to all its behavioural competencies, with the exception of "working in teams", is an external performance benchmark based on a group of world-class companies. The benchmarks indicate the level at which outstanding individuals in the benchmarked companies are performing. BNFL's aim is that the benchmarks will encourage all employees to develop to this level in the medium term (Warner, 2001a).

Piloting

Once the draft framework has been produced, employers have two choices: to attempt a full implementation or to use a pilot exercise in one department, group or grade of staff. A pilot programme has several advantages. It presents a further opportunity to involve employees and managers in the system at a formative stage (and, thus, increase their commitment to the end product). And, of course, it can provide a trial ground to identify areas for improvement at a stage where mistakes and problems will be restricted in scope.

The ability of a pilot implementation programme to lend a greater measure of control is the key to its popularity. Finding a group of staff and an open-minded section head or line manager is crucial. Competencies are controversial in most organisations. While some staff and managers will be all too ready to point to problems and weaknesses, others will remain silent when it would have been more helpful for them to have raised their concerns. A pilot programme that will give a fair trial to the use of competencies should, hopefully, avoid these extremes, containing problems but ensuring they are identified and resolved with minimal fuss and side-effects.

It is no coincidence, therefore, that many pilot programmes in the past have involved personnel and training departments, where these specialists have been centrally involved in managing and designing the competency frameworks. By definition, though, specialist departments have less in common with the main functional structures of an organisation and may not be as effective in "de-bugging" the new framework. Politically, line managers and their staff may not be convinced that those involved were truly impartial and committed to looking for faults and problems. They may see it as yet another initiative that has been imposed from "outside".

On the other hand, there may be a difficulty in using a pilot programme before a full roll-out of a competency initiative. We have seen above that many employers believe, with hindsight, that they took too long to develop their frameworks. A pilot programme will require six months to a year to be effective – the minimum being one round of development planning, performance-management reviews, or whatever assessment cycle is relevant to the use of competencies – and this can only further extend the period of delay.

According to an analysis by John Warner of current practice among employers using pilot programmes (Warner, 2001b), most pilots involve a group of employees within the workforce, such as:

- one level or grade;

- one occupational group, for example: a group of nurses in an NHS trust;

- one site;

- a vertical slice/team, for example: employees sharing responsibility for the same service outcomes in the same department – from top to bottom – in a London borough; or

- a representative sample, for example: South Lanarkshire Council chose a small representative sample of employees from seven different "resources" (divisions of the council);

However, a pilot can also be based on the use of competencies for a particular personnel process (such as performance management or training) instead of being introduced across several personnel processes at once. For example, the Commonwealth Secretariat has piloted the use of competencies in one of its human resource processes: recruitment and selection. In other cases, the pilot programme may be limited, not in terms of the number of employees covered or the range of personnel processes involved, but by virtue of having a fixed time frame, with the initial use of competencies in the workforce being subject to a review after a predetermined period. For example, Smith and Nephew Wound Management set a time period of one year during which employees could comment on the competency framework, and modifications could be made based on their feedback.

Current practice finds that around four in 10 employers (44%) with competency frameworks incorporate a pilot stage in their development process – although private sector services firms are noticeably less likely to have a pilot stage that other organisations. While 54% of public sector bodies, and 52% of manufacturing firms, introduce competencies by using pilot programmes, only 30% of private sector services firms do so (Rankin, 2001).

Validating for equality

Discrimination law is having a progressively greater impact on personnel management practices in the UK. Any personnel process, such as the use of competencies, should routinely be validated to ensure that it does not breach any legal requirements and, ideally, that it conforms to all the tenets of good practice. As box 1.1 shows, though, such compliance checking remains very much the exception, rather than the rule: less than a quarter (22%) of employers check or validate their competencies for possible unfair discrimination.

Detailed research conducted for the 1999/2000 benchmarking report (Rankin, 2000) shows that most of the work conducted by employers to uncover adverse impact occurs during the stage of designing their competencies, and very few organisations undertake a post-implementation validation study. Even fewer implement both measures.

The employers tackling potential bias do so in many different ways. The most frequently-used method involves ensuring that competencies are developed from representative samples of employees. In addition, or alternatively, many employers active in promoting equality of opportunity will review existing competency frameworks for potential bias or stereotyping. These will be frameworks already in use in the same organisation – in other departments, for example, or existing sets of competencies that are under revision. Or they will be frameworks in use in other organisations, where equal opportunities issues make up part of the agenda for the benchmarking that the employers conduct. Many employers active in the equality area also ensure that managers are trained in bias-free assessment. A smaller proportion of organisations train those involved in developing the competencies, so that they are aware of equal opportunities issues in competency design. Many such organisations also monitor managers' assessments in order to ensure that bias is not occurring once the framework is in use. Chapters 5 and 6 provide further information on legal requirements and equal opportunities issues.

Apart from equal opportunities considerations, competencies should be validated in more general terms. Pilot programmes, by their nature, are intended to test out the operation of a competency initiative. Many of them concentrate on practical matters, such as ease of use, acceptability and relevance. But there is also a need to investigate, and *demonstrate* to others within the organisation, that the application of competencies has resulted in a contribution to the business – for example, that the level of individuals' skills has increased, that flexibility has been enhanced, productivity has risen, labour turnover has fallen and (the Holy Grail) that profits have improved. Processes that ensure competencies are up to date (covered in chapter 12) and produce business benefits are usually based on some form of informal feedback from line managers and other users, and the personal knowledge of those managing the review process.

There is little evidence, though, that formal validation is practised by review teams or that it is often built into the process of designing the competency frameworks in the first place. There are exceptions, including the notable one involving a validation study undertaken for Rothmans International. Its existing frameworks of competencies for managers had been in use for six years by the time that it was recognised it needed to be updated and revalidated. Consultants from Wickland Westcott were involved in a project team whose remit involved evaluating the content of the competencies against the future needs of the business, simplifying the competency approach to make it more user-friendly and, significantly, validating the competencies so that they could be used in all the countries where this multinational company had a presence. The cross-cultural validation involved conducting focus groups with line managers and personnel specialists who were working in China, Hong Kong, Malaysia, Singapore, Japan and Korea, conducting a benchmarking exercise against other multinational organisations, and reviewing relevant research and literature (Boutet, Milsom and Mercer, 2000).

The format of competencies

The results of the design and validation processes take the form of the competencies and their definitions. There are many ways that this information can be structured and presented.

By their nature, "how" competencies are more general in scope than job-specific technical skills, and are often brought together in a single list or framework that applies to a large number of individuals in the organisation. Some employers, such as Alliance & Leicester, favour one single, universal list (a "core framework") – see the next section, "Examples of employers' frameworks".

Other employers have encountered problems with this approach and many now prefer to produce a series of frameworks that address the needs and interests of specific groups (often based on "job families"). Examples include Abbey Life Assurance and Parkside Health NHS Trust. The main difficulty for some employers in this approach lies not so much in the inflexibility of a core framework, but its perception by employees and managers as being so, and of having ignored their own priorities and needs. The trend gives as much priority to presentation as it does to the initial design and development. In a growing number of cases, each job family, or other group of related jobs, is, in effect, given a competency framework that is ostensibly unique and entirely based on its own needs. Individuals in this group see only their own framework for day-to-day purposes, although those aspiring to gain promotion or move sideways to another role will be able to use the relevant competency framework as a useful guide to what they will be expected to achieve in the role in question.

However, because the strategic aims of the organisation generally apply to all job families, and most jobs are inter-related in essential ways, the underlying competencies are less diverse than their presentation will suggest. For example, if the organisation sees customer service as a key means of achieving success, then most, if not all, job families will need to give this priority, and some form of a "customer service" competency will apply to each one. And if most job families use the same computer system, for example, then "computer literacy", "IT savvy" or a similar such technical competence will be found in their separate lists of competences.

Building in flexibility

There are various ways of taking account of these similarities, while, at the same time, observing the essential differences (and, more importantly, being seen to take account of them). First, some employers develop a single set of competencies, then identify exceptions that only apply to some jobs or roles (for example, employers with a core framework often include a few additional competencies for managers to take account of their responsibilities for people, budgets and results). Examples include Electrolux and Hanover Housing Association.

Second, some employers differentiate their competencies through responsibility or seniority levels. For example, most or all roles may be found to require a "customer care" type of competency, yet individuals in senior roles may have to deploy their skills at more demanding or more strategic levels. The result is a set of definitions (often supplemented by some examples of how performance can be observed, known as "behavioural indicators"). At British Waterways, for example, "customer care" has five levels of performance, ranging from "sets clear national policy for customer care . . ." at level five, down to "can explain who the customers are . . ." at level one.

This is a popular approach adopted by many employers, as it offers a considerable degree of flexibility within a reasonably structured format provided by a small group of competencies. Some organisations vary the number of responsibility/seniority levels according to the competency in question – at First Data Resources, for example, five is the upper limit on the levels, but there can be fewer than this. Others, more ambitiously, attempt to create a form of conceptual classification that they apply to all competencies in the same way. The Commonwealth Secretariat, for example, has 14 competencies, each of which is divided into the same four levels, ranging from mainly routine and predictable demands at level 1, to "the application of a significant range of fundamental principles and complex techniques across a wide and often unpredictable variety of contexts" at level 4.

Both these first two approaches lend themselves to the current trend towards *presenting* competencies as being unique to each job family or other group. The basic work has already been done, in terms of identifying additional competencies and/or responsibility/seniority levels. Using computer software (and often, these days, using an intranet to disseminate the results), the relevant competencies and/or levels can be grouped together for a particular group, whose members see only this snapshot of a much larger, and more complex whole.

Third, while some employers have developed a single core framework, others have gone to the other end of the spectrum. Instead of a table d'hôte, these employers offer an à la carte. All the competencies that the development work has identified as being relevant to the organisation are brought together as a menu, and an individual and his or her manager jointly decide which of them are relevant to the individual's job or role. To prevent chaos or absurdities (such as finding that 20 competencies are relevant, or none at all), employers that follow this approach often set guidelines on how this selection should be made, and on the number of competencies to be chosen (often, within a range).

For example, Westminster City Council has adopted a menu consisting of 14 competencies, of which four or so are jointly agreed by the postholder and their manager as being relevant to the demands of the job. To add a further dimension of flexibility, each competency has been divided into three levels: "directs" (applicable to the top two or three tiers in the organisation); "manages" (covering middle and junior management levels); and "delivers" (applicable to front-line staff). Similarly, the ambitious competency initiative being rolled out to a quarter of a million public sector employees in the Republic of Ireland takes the form of a menu of 17 behavioural competencies. The competencies are arranged in four clusters: "personal effectiveness"; "thinking style and problem-solving"; "group and interpersonal effectiveness"; and "managing for results".

Fourth, some employers do not attempt to develop any commonly-held competencies, but take specific groups, departments or sites in their workforces as the focus for developing different sets of entirely bespoke competency frameworks. In these cases, even competencies with essentially the same orientation and approach may be differently labelled and defined. "Customer care", for example, may also appear in parallel frameworks as "concern for customer service", "customer obsession" or "external and internal customer focus". Organisations with group-specific sets of competencies include the Edinburgh International Conference Centre.

Current pattern

These, then, are the main options for the structure and presentation of competencies. Current practice, based on the 2000/01 benchmarking survey (Rankin, 2001) among 113 employers, shows that the most common approach involves presenting the competencies in the form of a series of specific frameworks for different groups or grades of staff (adopted by 48% of employers). Two related options follow in terms of popularity: a core framework for the whole workforce (22% of employers), and a core framework supplemented by technical competences for specific jobs (20% of employers). Finally, some employers use a core framework that is supplemented with behavioural competencies for managers or other groups/grades (10% of employers).

Numbers of competencies

The many different ways that employers can construct their competency frameworks obviously makes it difficult to analyse in any meaningful way the typical size of a framework. However, with this limitation in mind, the latest benchmarking survey (Rankin, 2001) analysed 52 frameworks used by employers that have either a single core framework applying to the whole workforce, or have introduced frameworks where all the competencies apply to a specific grade or work group. (In other words, the analysis omits frameworks that offer a long menu of optional competencies, and those that have a core list supplemented with additional competencies for particular grades or groups).

The analysis found that many frameworks involve a considerable number of competencies (ranging from three to 26, with one in four employers having 12 or more competencies). The median (midpoint in the range) is 10 competencies, and the average is 11 competencies. The most common number of competencies (the mode), though, is 8.

A separate research project for the Chartered Institute of Personnel and Development took a slightly smaller sample of employers' competency frameworks (44 organisations), but tracked their development over time to provide a longitudinal perspective, rather than a snapshot (Miller, Rankin and Neathey, 2001). This produced a similar result in terms of the median number of competencies (12 against 10 in the benchmarking study), but also found that the median had *not* changed between the earliest and latest versions of each employer's framework. While 62% of the sample had conducted at least one review of their frameworks (to keep it up to date, for example), this shows that most of the reviews did not involve a reduction in the overall number of competencies in use.

Commonly used competencies

Critics of the competency approach frequently make the point that many employers' frameworks appear indistinguishable from each other. This, they argue, means that there is no advantage in developing tailor-made competency lists; any other organisation's framework would do just as well. Indeed, criticism often takes this a step further and argues that the similarity of employers' frameworks means that the whole competency approach offers little or no competitive advantage. They ask: "How can an organisation gain an edge over its rivals through the use of competencies if both it and its competitors use fundamentally the same competency frameworks?".

It is certainly true that many frameworks look remarkably similar. Box 1.2 gives the analysis of 40 employers' core frameworks, containing a total of 433 competencies (Rankin, 2001). This shows, for instance, that a third contain a "decision-making" competency, two-thirds have one that relates to "communication", and over three-quarters include a trait connected with "team orientation". >p.31

1.2. Commonly used competency names

This box classifies 40 employers' core frameworks, involving 433 competencies in total, according to the competency names they use. The results are ranked in descending order of prevalence. Note, however, that factors specific to each organisation will affect how a competency name is understood; the names are not always a reliable guide to their meaning.

%*	Competency	Typical alternative names
78%	Team orientation	Working in a team; Team leadership; Teamwork and cooperation; Teamworking; Building and leading a team
65%	Communication	Communicating effectively; Oral communication; Written communication; Interpersonal communication
65%	Customer focus	Customer obsession; Customer service orientation; Client focus; External/internal customer focus
58%	People management	Managing and developing individuals; Managing others; Appraising staff; Attracting talent; Creating and inspiring commitment
58%	Results orientation	Results focus; Achieving results; Goal orientation; Determination; Drive for results; Passion for results; Delivery

55%	Problem-solving	Solves problems; Developing solutions; Analytical thinking and judgment
48%	Planning and organising	Planning and reviewing; Operational planning; Organisation and work planning
43%	Leadership	Leading people
38%	Business awareness	Business and marketplace awareness; Business orientation; Commercial and financial awareness
35%	Decision-making	Taking sound decisions; Coming to decisions; Decisiveness
35%	Technical skills	Underpinning knowledge and understanding; Technical skills and knowledge; Job expertise and professional competence; Professional ability; Professional judgment; Specialised expertise; Specialist skills and knowledge
33%	Developing others	People development; Developing staff; Developing talent
33%	Initiative	Taking initiative; Tenacity and initiative
30%	Creativity	Think and act creatively/innovatively; Innovative and creative thinking; Innovativeness; Driving innovation
30%	Influence and persuasion	Influencing and negotiation; Influencing others; Winning agreement
30%	Quality focus	Quality orientation; Concern for quality; Drive to deliver quality results; Improving quality of services
30%	Relationships	Relationship-building; Relationships with colleagues; Relationships with the public; Building effective relationships
28%	Change orientation	Managing change/strategic thinking; Responding positively to change
25%	Information management	Using information effectively; Managing information

25%	Interpersonal skills	Interpersonal sensitivity; Interpersonal understanding; Active listening; Working with customers; Working with others; Working with people
25%	Strategic orientation	Global vision; Using a strategic approach; Vision and strategic direction
23%	Self-development	Managing and developing yourself; Personal development; Personal learning
20%	Commitment	Display personal commitment and courage; Tenacity and initiative
20%	Self-confidence	Self-confidence; Assertiveness; Self-projection and assertiveness
18%	Managing	Management skills; Managing budgets and resources; Managing the provision of services; Using/managing resources
15%	Flexibility	Flexibility and response to change; Flexibility/adaptability
15%	Personal effectiveness	Personal impact; Efficiency and effectiveness
13%	Coaching and counselling	Coaching and developing; Coaching/mentoring
10%	Working with others	Cooperation
10%	Listening	Listening and understanding
10%	Self-control	Self-management; Managing self
8%	Continuous improvement	Improvement focus
8%	Delegating	Delegation
8%	Enthusiasm	–
8%	Organisational awareness	–
8%	Responsibility	Sense of responsibility
8%	Valuing differences	Valuing diversity; Achieving equal opportunities
5%	Anticipation	Anticipation/prioritisation
5%	Behaving ethically	Integrity
5%	Financial awareness	Financial/business acumen
5%	Numeracy	Numeracy and data handling

* Percentage of employers' frameworks using this, or a similar, competency name.

Source: Rankin (2001).

But, there are two vital points to remember. First, the names chosen to describe a behaviour or skill are not necessarily reliable guides to what people within each organisation understand by the terms – "the devil is in the detail". It is the definitions and sets of behavioural indicators accompanying each competency name that serve to interpret and explain its meaning and contribution to performance.

Second, the presence in employers' frameworks of similar competencies is not a source of weakness, as critics maintain, but a validation that the competency approach is attuned to organisational requirements. Take the top four competencies from the analysis – "team orientation", "communication", "customer focus" and "people management" – what modern organisation is not vitally concerned with customer care, effective communication or the use of teamworking? It is the way that these priorities are put into practice within the specific context of each organisation that is important.

While the comparison of competency names is of limited value, it is useful in that it can provide a final "reality check" to ensure that those developing or revising an employer's framework have not overlooked any important behaviour or skill. The analysis in box 1.2 confirms the importance that organisations place on how work is performed, and the role that people play in organisational success. Most of the top competency names are of the behavioural and, particularly, the interpersonal type. Also noteworthy is the fact that many of the competency names cover skills and behaviours that Daniel Goleman and others argue occupy the area of "emotional intelligence", such as the following (the percentages are taken from box 1.2 and show their prevalence among employers' frameworks):

team orientation (78%);

communication (65%);

aspects of people management (inspiring others, for example) (58%);

aspects of results orientation (determination, for example) (58%);

leadership (43%);

creativity (30%);

influence and persuasion (30%);

relationships (30%);

interpersonal skills (25%);

self-confidence and assertiveness (20%); and

flexibility (15%).

Resolving problems

No initiative or process that involves people will be problem-free, and competencies are no exception. The latest benchmarking survey report shows that almost all (93%) of employers that have introduced competencies have encountered one or more difficulties with them. A glance at the specific types of problem reported by employers (see box 1.3) will show that most of their difficulties have three possible causes:

- poor project management of the development phase;
- faulty design; and/or
- insufficient buy-in from line managers and/or employees.

1.3 Problems experienced by employers

Type of problem	%*
The language used to define or describe competencies	65%
Employees' understanding	65%
Line managers' understanding	63%
Assessing the competencies	59%
The time, resources and/or costs involved	53%
Defining the competencies	48%
Gaining commitment	46%
Keeping the competencies up-to-date/relevant	45%
Relationship between the competency framework and corporate culture	44%
Complexity and/or the paperwork involved	42%

Incorporating emotional intelligence concepts in the framework	25%
Attitudes of trade union(s)	10%
Other	4%

* Percentage of employers.

Source: Rankin (2001).

These three themes, and the specific areas of difficulty shown in box 1.3, can provide valuable insights for project leaders and teams as to the main pitfalls that their competency frameworks should avoid. The feedback from employers' experience will be of most use if it is considered as early as possible in the whole project – at the initial planning stage before any mistakes are made, or the organisation is committed to a course of action.

But it is unlikely that even the best-designed and implemented competency framework will be entirely free of difficulties and controversy. Pilot programmes, as we saw above, can help to address many of them, provided that the root cause of the matter has been correctly diagnosed. Later on, when the framework has been introduced more widely, the initiative will greatly benefit from the attention of a politically-astute troubleshooter who can make tactful enquiries about problems, and identify where the trouble lies. Their intervention can help to tackle initial problems that could permanently undermine the successful adoption of competencies – long before any process of revising and updating the framework could hope to address them.

At their most successful, competencies provide a bridge between the work of those directing the overall strategy of the organisation and the day-to-day activities of each member of the workforce. Competencies do this by articulating the aims and attitudes that the organisation requires for success, and then incorporating this information in key processes that influence the performance of each employee and manager – such as recruitment, appraisal, training and promotion (and, sometimes, reward). Almost inevitably, the far-reaching nature of the use of competencies in this way will give them maximum exposure to vested interests, discontented groups of staff and managers, internal power politics, trade union-management frictions and all other areas where there could be a reaction against them.

Moreover, competencies are tools that must be used by personnel management processes; they are a means to an end. So, the processes themselves could be sources of friction or faulty design, and this could rebound on the competency initiative itself. If the performance management system is disliked because it is seen as a distraction from the "real business" that line managers should be concentrating on, or because its flawed design leads to unfair ratings and unsatisfactory appraisal meetings, then the competencies that are assessed through the system will be seen as guilty by association.

All of this is meant as an explanation why it is important to get to the root cause of any apparent problems connected with the introduction and use of competencies – and not to discourage their use. In fact, it is the scale of competencies' potential contribution to raising performance that presents the greatest argument for their introduction, and the challenge of managing difficulties as they arise should be seen in that context. Small-scale initiatives usually incur no more than small-scale difficulties, but their impact on the business will also be minor.

Checklist 2 brings together the possible reasons for problems being experienced with competencies, the ways that they can be investigated, and some lines of action that could be taken.

Checklist 2. When things go wrong

1. Problems with your competency initiative are bound to occur. How serious are they? The saying insists that there is no smoke without fire, but are some staff actively fanning the flames?

2. If there is a lot of "noise" surrounding the competency initiative, try to establish its causes. Is this a sign that people were not adequately involved in designing, piloting and implementing the initiative? Were the principal stakeholders and the influencers in the organisation given due attention and consideration? How effective was your champion (see Checklist 1, point 3) in keeping the dissenters in line, and helping to win them over?

3. Use your contacts to sound out people about the initiative. Use, too, more formal monitoring processes that you should have incorporated in the design of the competency initiative (see Checklist 1, points 13 and 14). And use existing mechanisms to get additional feedback from staff and managers, such as

---

attitude surveys, exit interviews/separation questionnaires, points raised during appraisal/performance management reviews, and so on.

4. How serious do you judge the problems to be? Are the root causes concerned with the initiative, or merely symptoms of other or more general problems?

5. Consider honestly how the problems can be addressed. Has the competency initiative been fatally compromised? If so, it may be best to abandon it; its continuation may cause more damage to your and your department's reputation than attempting to "tough it out". If a decision to withdraw is taken, ensure that a record is made of what went wrong, and consider carefully whether the competency approach still offers your organisation a business benefit. If so, bide your time until a better opportunity arises to introduce competencies (see Checklist 1, point 2), and learn from your mistakes.

6. Conversely, you may decide that there is a reasonable chance of remedying the flaws and restoring credibility for the initiative. This does not mean, though, that this will be cost-effective in terms of the time and effort required – so, factor these into your calculations.

7. Establishing the root cause of your difficulties is vital; the solutions will vary accordingly. The most common problem experienced by employers is the result of a failure to obtain buy-in from users. Consider whether line managers/team leaders, and the people they supervise, were fully involved in designing your competency initiative, piloting it (if applicable) and providing feedback on the experience of implementing it. Were they given full, frequent and honest communications? Were they given training in understanding and using the competency initiative?

8. Motivational problems are also often caused by poor planning: the design stage consumes too much time or too many resources. This means that people lose interest as the project drags on and on. And taking too long over the design often means that the organisation has neither the emotional energy nor resources to devote sufficient time and money to the crucial introductory and implementation stages.

9. The other main cause of employers' difficulties relates to the design of the competency framework and associated initiatives.

Is your framework too complicated for day-to-day use? Does it contain competencies that people find irrelevant or hard to apply to their own situation? Conversely, if a single core framework has been adopted, does a one-size-fits-all approach really work for your organisation? If levels of performance are used, are they easy to apply by a manager when assessing someone's performance?

10. Competency initiatives that have been in use for a couple of years or more are also often beset by the problem of being overtaken by events: the organisation may have revised its business objectives, or corporate values, or reorganised or merged, for example. Consider whether the competency initiative was designed for ease of updating (see Checklist 1, point 9), and that a process was built in to ensure that it was revised regularly. If these are in place, has anything actually been done to keep the competencies in line with business developments?

11. The remedies must fit the root cause of your problems. If lack of buy-in is the cause, it will almost certainly involve your organisation repeating the development and implementation stages – but with fuller involvement of staff and managers – although fast-track versions, based on revisiting the current competencies, may be acceptable.

12. Remedying design flaws, such as over-elaborate or one-size-fits-all frameworks, often involves the same type of solution. The framework, provided it is basically sound, can be shaped into a series of parallel versions, each one for a particular work group or "job family". Users see only their version, and can be fully consulted on its relevance and refinements. This clarity of focus immediately simplifies and adds relevance to the competencies and the processes based on them, helping to win people over. Underlying all these personalised frameworks, though, is a basic structure of a set of core competencies, definitions, performance levels, and so on, that does not vary sufficiently across the organisation to undermine consistency and fairness in application, or its business relevance.

13. Longer-term, even the best competency initiative needs not only maintenance but a spurt of renewed emotional energy. Consider using your staff newspaper, presentations and other forums to publicise the successes of competencies. Use case studies of individuals who have benefited; they may have gained

promotion, boosted their self-confidence or discovered new skills and abilities. The use of competencies may (and ought) to have improved the fairness and consistency of people management – find examples of how this has benefited people in your organisation. And it ought to have improved equality of opportunity. Again, find the evidence and publicise your successes.

Examples of employers' frameworks

Abbey Life Assurance

Financial services, 1,500 employees. Format: sets of behavioural, emotional intelligence-type and technical competencies for different groups of staff. Each competency has an overall definition and a definition for up to eight levels of performance.

Clerical and secretarial jobs

Efficiency and effectiveness

Quality and accuracy

Customer-service orientation

Interpersonal understanding

Anticipation/prioritisation

Assertiveness

Teamwork

Personal development

Managerial and technical jobs

Achievement and action

Interpersonal influencing

Leadership and direction

Thinking environment and use of expertise

Personal effectiveness

AIB Capital Markets

Financial services, 2,000 employees. Format: core framework of behavioural, emotional intelligence-type and technical competencies, currently being extended to the whole workforce.

Example definition: Influencing

Definition: Influencing, persuading or negotiating so that other people commit to a point of view, agree an outcome, change ideas or take a course of action.

Level 0

Not applicable/not demonstrating required behaviours at any other levels.

✓ Uses direct logic to influence.

✗ Unsystematic when persuading.

Level 1

Recognise the need to persuade/negotiate.

Identify own preferred range of objectives and outcomes beforehand.

Clarify current situation and required final situation.

Have a fallback position.

Clarify areas of agreement, focus energy on areas of non-agreement.

Explain the benefits and rewards of acting, and impact of not acting.

Present a well-reasoned and well-prepared case clearly, leading to a logical conclusion.

Demonstrate enthusiasm for outcomes, and ask for commitment.

✓   Plan and tailor approach.

✗   Approach is unplanned or inappropriate.

Level 2

Anticipate how others will respond; plan and tailor approach accordingly.

Anticipate the impact of own actions or words.

Structure the approach and agenda for the interaction to gain step-by-step commitment.

Build rapport before attempting to persuade.

Seek and clarify other person's needs, wants and concerns, and build into the outcomes.

Adapt own objectives to obtain a win–win outcome.

Tailor arguments to appeal to the needs, wants, interest or perspective of others.

Use a friendly and supportive approach when others are insecure or in a new situation.

Keep negotiations issue-focused, never person-focused.

✓   Use multiple approaches to influence.

✗   Approach is inflexible or too simplistic.

Level 3

Actively control the course of the interaction to move towards the agreed outcome.

Calculate an approach to make a specific impact.

Use advanced verbal and non-verbal behaviours to gain uncontested agreement.

Methods of designing frameworks

Assess the reactions to the approach, and flexibly adapt style and language to gain agreement.

Have a win–win approach so that all are seen to gain.

Take bold, creative or unusual approaches to make a point or get through to other people.

Anticipate the most likely objections in the structure of information presented.

Handle objections by clarifying and rephrasing more positively.

✓   Use indirect influence and involve other people.

✗   Influencing approach is not sufficiently subtle.

Level 4

Structure situations to influence others' behaviour.

Accept objections as valid and use them to improve.

Involve key people to identify and support own case with other groups.

Involve people in the outcome by ensuring they participate in the process.

Take a long-term view of who, why, what, how and when to influence.

✓   Demonstrate constructive use of political skills.

✗   Misuse political skills.

Level 5

Create and sustain political coalitions to gain support and influence outcome.

Use third parties and experts to influence and mediate.

Alliance & Leicester

Banking, 9,000 employees. Format: single set of behavioural and emotional intelligence-type competencies supplemented with sets of technical competences for specific groups of staff. Each of the 10 competencies has a definition and is described under five levels. The framework applies to all staff in the Group. There is a single set of negative indicators for each competency as a whole.

Customer obsession

Drive

Team focus

Personal impact

Thinking

Committed achiever

Managing development

Business understanding

Leadership

Innovation

British Waterways

Inland waterways, 1,900 employees. Format: single set of 10 behavioural competencies. Each behavioural competency has a general statement of its importance, and sets of behavioural indicators for each level of performance. The indicators are grouped into "expected" and "advanced" sub-levels.

Example definition: Customer care

Level one

Expected indicators:

1.   Can explain who the customers are.

2.   Applies the correct procedures when dealing with customers.

3.   Provides a friendly, helpful service.

4.   Avoids confrontation by remaining helpful and polite.

5. Knows when and to whom to pass comments and queries.

6. Shows that customer care is an integral part of the job.

Level two

Expected indicators:

1. Promotes the achievement of Customer Charter standards.

2. Resolves complaints and confrontation constructively.

3. Regularly adapts the way that tasks are performed to meet customer needs and preferences.

4. Adjusts behaviours and processes to promote an effective response to customers.

5. Focuses team on developing and achieving clear customer-service standards.

Level three

Expected indicators:

1. Creates a positive commitment to Customer Care.

2. Develops plans to meet customer needs at optimum cost.

3. Strives for partnerships, rather than traditional customer/supplier interface.

4. Identifies and leads implementation of improvements in customer service.

Level four

Expected indicators:

1. Plays an integral role in the development of national policy for Customer Care to meet the needs of internal and/or external customers.

2. Provides expertise in Customer Care.

3. Anticipates major changes in customer demands and recommends action.

4. Proactive in the generation of policy.

Level five

Expected indicators:

1. Sets clear national policy for Customer Care to meet the needs of internal and external customers, and drives the business to meet them.

2. Identifies the policy and future direction of Customer Care issues for BW.

3. Develops national risk framework.

Centre for Management & Organisation Development/Irish Civil Service

Management development (Centre; 70 employees); central government (Civil Service; 30,000 employees); ultimately, 250,000 employees in Irish public sector. Format: a framework of 17 behavioural competencies, linked to a performance management and development system, being gradually introduced throughout the Republic of Ireland's Civil Service and, eventually, to all parts of the public sector. The framework acts as menu from which the behavioural competencies that are relevant to each department or office are chosen.

Personal effectiveness

Self-confidence

Achievement/drive/commitment

Initiative

Teamworking

Communication

Thinking style and problem-solving

Analytical thinking

Conceptual thinking

Decision-making/judgment

Specialised expertise

Group and interpersonal effectiveness

Networking/influencing

Interpersonal understanding

Customer service

Managing and developing people

Leadership

Managing for results

Managing budgets and resources

Information-seeking and management

Concern for clarity and work quality

Commonwealth Secretariat

Inter-governmental organisation, 300 employees. Format: recently developed framework still being implemented to all groups of staff, and consisting of eight clusters of 14 competencies. Each competency has a definition, and four levels of performance. These are based on job demands, ranging from mainly routine and predictable demands (level 1) to "the application of a significant range of fundamental principles and complex techniques across a wide and often unpredictable variety of contexts" (level 4). The levels for each competency also have their own definitions, supplemented by "benchmarks" – behavioural indicators for some of the levels.

Example definition: Problem-solving and decision-making

[From the Managing change cluster.]

Level 1

Needs to work on own initiative in receiving, assessing, forwarding or responding to incoming mail.

In the absence of team members, needs to handle and respond to enquiries, seeking guidance if necessary. Maintains regular contact to ensure that matters of priority are drawn to their attention and followed up.

Level 3

Required to develop programmes and projects targeted at solving problems with technical, economic and socio-cultural dimensions. Attempts resolution of these multi-dimensional problems.

Identifies and obtains information and advice from other experts.

Analyses and presents solutions/options to governments, industry and research/academic institutions.

Edinburgh International Conference Centre

Conference centre, 62 employees. Format: sets of behavioural and technical competencies for different groups of staff.

Team leader profile

Customer focus

Commercial and financial awareness

Performance results and accountability

Management of people – leadership, motivation and coaching

Teamworking

Continuous improvement

Inspires trust

Electrolux

Manufacturing and sales, 700 employees. Format: a framework of behavioural competencies, which includes both core competencies common to all roles and additional competencies for specific roles. There are also sets of technical competences for different groups of staff. The framework shows all possible competencies, grouping them into five clusters. Each competency has a definition and sets of behavioural indicators for four levels. These accord with responsibilities, ranging from "level one (foundation)", applying to "staff who operate within restricted and well-defined areas of responsibility", to "level four (directional)", which applies to roles with strategic responsibilities and high levels of autonomy.

Methods of designing frameworks

Customer focus

Customer partnership

Electrolux ambassadorship

Quality orientation

Solves problems

Management of work

Numeracy and data handling

Measurement

Planning and organising

Profit awareness

Setting and sharing goals and objectives

Knowledge/experience

Business and marketplace awareness

Specialist skills and knowledge

Technology awareness

Retail category management

Supply chain

Personal effectiveness

Communication

Influencing and negotiation

Innovation

Response to change

Responsibility

Self-development

Working with people

Coaching and counselling

Cooperation and teambuilding

Creating and inspiring commitment

Delegation

First Data Resources

Third-party credit- and debit-card processing, 2,500 employees. Format: each competency is defined for up to five levels of performance and, for assessment purposes, six performance ratings. Each level has its own definition, and three sets of behavioural indicators arranged under: "competency not achieved; competency achieved; and competency exceeded". The framework is constantly under revision.

Example definition: Dealing with problems

This competency covers both the ability to identify problems and the contribution to solving them. Contributing competencies will include creative, conceptual and analytical thinking, innovation, drive for achievement and decision-making.

Conceptual thinking relates to being able to see the "big picture". It includes seeing patterns and connections between situations which are not at first obvious. It requires elements of forward-thinking and strategic planning. It links to analytical thinking, innovation and initiative.

Analytical thinking is the ability to break problems down into their component parts, and analyse them logically to reach conclusions.

Decision-making relates to the ability to make timely and considered decisions and stick to them.

Level 5 *[highest]*:

Here, you understand how your work and the work of others contributes to corporate objectives and you are able to identify significant improvement opportunities. You can create detailed problem analysis, cost-benefit cases and action plans to solve problems or make significant improvements. In addition, they can take corrective action on improvement projects which involves working outside the original parameters of your group.

Employees may display some of the following examples of behaviour:

Competency not achieved:

Displays only insular knowledge of own job or department;

Impact/influence on significant improvement opportunities is negligible;

Problem/cost-benefit analysis is confined to basic skill level only;

Involvement of outside influences will visibly weaken determination or quality of input;

Easily sidetracked/focused by issues that arise outside of original brief;

Fails to make difficult and unpopular decisions;

[. . .]

Competency achieved:

Displays a sound comprehension of how their role is linked to corporate objectives;

Investigates and produces ideas for significant improvement;

Analysis of problem is detailed with cost-benefit figures and action plans fully and methodically documented;

Displays determination to complete an improvement where outside influences are evident;

Associated problems, identified via analysis, are effectively managed with minimal impact to the original issue/solution;

Encourages problem-solving;

[. . .]

Competency exceeded:

Proactive solution gives corporate benefits that add value beyond solving the problem;

Documentation is to a standard suitable for executive use;

Strives for continuous improvement to enhance products and/or work processes, and actively promotes process improvement;

Makes difficult decisions confidently;

Identifies problems, situations and solutions not obvious to others;

Copes with difficult, reactive situations under extreme pressure, deadlines, etc;

[. . .]

Freeserve

Internet service provider and portal, 300 employees. Format: the company's competencies are currently under development. The company plans to introduce a single set of behavioural competencies, supplemented by technical competences for different groups of staff.

Draft core competencies

Communication

Creative/innovative

Customer focus

Internet-savvy

Leadership

Results-orientation

Teamworking

Risk management

Freeserve-savvy

Hanover Housing Association

Housing association, 750 employees. Format: core framework with additional competencies for specific groups of staff. Internally-developed technical competences, behavioural competencies and emotional intelligence-type competencies are in use. Each non-technical competency has a definition and is assessed at one of five levels of performance: below; almost meets; meets; just above; and above.

Core competencies

Attention to detail

Communication

Decision-making

Delivery

Initiative

Organisation and work planning

Technical competence

Business awareness

Parkside Health NHS Trust

Healthcare, 2,100 employees. Format: sets of behavioural and emotional intelligence-type competencies for specific staff groups. The framework for managers has 10 competencies, each weighted to reflect its importance for first-line, middle and senior managers. There are also sets of technical competencies, both internally developed and those based on National Vocational Qualifications, for specific roles and staff groups.

Management competencies

Behaving ethically

Providing leadership and strategic vision

Team development

Individual appraisal and development

Communicating effectively

Influencing others

Managing information

Creative and critical thinking, and decision-making

Focusing on results through quality

Personal development

Westminster City Council

Local authority, 5,700 employees. Format: single menu of competencies used by whole workforce – normally, around four of the competencies are jointly agreed as relevant to the demands of a particular job. Each competency is split into three levels: Directs (top two or three tiers); Manages (middle and junior management levels); and Delivers (front line). Each level has between three and 10 performance elements.

Competencies

Planning and organisation

Speedy and effective decision-making

Tenacity and initiative

Organisational culture and job knowledge

Using a strategic approach

Marketing and promotional skills

Communication and personal impact

Using information effectively

Practical implementation skills

Focus on customer needs

Management skills

Business acumen

Motivation

Contract-management and monitoring skills

References

Boutet, Marjolaine, Milsom, John and Mercer, Colin (2000), "Revising management competencies: ensuring cross-cultural validity – Rothmans International", *Competency & Emotional Intelligence Quarterly*, vol. 7 no.2, pp.12–16, 25–26, Winter 1999/00.

Methods of designing frameworks

Miller, Linda, Rankin, Neil and Neathey, Fiona (2001), *Competency frameworks in UK organisations*, Chartered Institute of Personnel and Development.

Rankin, Neil (2000), "Performance through people: the seventh annual competency survey", *Competency & Emotional Intelligence Benchmarking 1999/00*, pp. 2–13.

Rankin, Neil (2001), "Raising performance through people: the eighth competency survey", *Competency & Emotional Intelligence Benchmarking 2000/01*, pp.2–23.

Warner, John (2001a), "Reflecting company culture in competency design at BNFL", *Competency & Emotional Intelligence Quarterly*, vol. 8 no.4, pp.37–43, Summer.

Warner, John (2001b), "Piloting the introduction of competencies", *Competency & Emotional Intelligence Quarterly*, forthcoming.

Learning points

- Competencies are definitions of expected performance. They can cover what is done at work (tasks, actions, technical skills), how it is performed (soft skills, behavioural competencies, inputs), or both.

- "What" types of competencies are usually more specific and detailed, are often related to a particular job or groups of jobs. Lists of them are usually kept separate from the list(s) of "how" types of competencies, and often take the form of a list per type of job.

- "How" types of competencies are usually broader ranging. Lists tend to be shorter, and often cover a wider range of jobs, roles, etc.

- A project leader is required to manage the process of designing and implementing competencies. Current practice favours using a project team with external advisers providing expert help. They should begin by identifying the business benefit, and must win support from key individuals, line managers and other end-users. These and other considerations are summarised in Checklist 1.

- Overruns in the time and resources required to develop the framework lead to demotivation among employees and managers. Frameworks can also be easily over-engineered. Most employers find that they should have given more attention to involvement, communication, training, and to the introduction of competencies in general, and less to the design phase.

- Group meetings are commonly used to develop competency frameworks. Most employers also use one-to-one interviews; they may be restricted to the most important stakeholders and influential individuals. Repertory grids, the critical incident technique and behavioural event interviews are three further methods that are often used. Some form of benchmarking is almost universally practised.

- Four in 10 employers use a pilot programme before they introduce competencies across the whole organisation. A pilot programme has several advantages, although it will extend what is often already an unacceptably lengthy period before the full roll-out.

- It is good practice to check competencies for unfair discrimination, but few users do so. Measures to reduce bias include ensuring that representative samples are used when developing competencies, providing training to managers in bias-free assessment, and monitoring assessments they make.

- Many employers favour flexible competency frameworks. Some retain a single list, but include additional competencies linked to responsibility or status levels. Alternatively, some use a single list, but attach responsibility or seniority levels to each competency. In a further variation, some employers create a single list, but use it as a menu. Others prefer to produce a series of frameworks for specific groups.

- The median number of competencies in use by employers is 10, within a range of three to 26. There is no discernible trend towards reducing the numbers of competencies. Most of the top competency names are of the behavioural and, particularly, the interpersonal type (to which the term "emotional intelligence" is now being applied).

- Problems with competency frameworks are widely reported by users; and have three prime causes: poor project management; faulty design; and/or insufficient buy-in. The cause of reported problems needs to be established; see Checklist 2.

Chapter 2

Key issues

Introduction

This chapter develops in detail some of the themes covered in chapter 1. There, we provided an overview across all the themes connected with the successful development and application of competencies, from the way that the design process should be conducted, and the formats that the competency framework can take, to validation, piloting and problem-solving when difficulties occur.

In chapter 2, two authorities on employers' experience of using competencies, George Boak and Professor Adrian Furnham, provide a stronger focus on the principal strategic issues that deserve early consideration when a new or updated competency framework is being planned. George Boak's work with employers over the years has led him to distil the key characteristics of competency frameworks that determine their success or failure into three themes: accuracy; acceptability; and accessibility. He explains what these involve and how they can be addressed. Adrian Furnham, who has worked with many organisations as an expert adviser, here concentrates on the findings from an in-depth research project that he conducted for the Careers Research Forum. The results provide an invaluable assessment of the prime pitfalls, success factors and potential benefits involved in the application of competencies.

Characteristics of effective competency frameworks

George Boak

Competency frameworks have the potential to provide invaluable guidance for all who are involved in self-development, recruitment, training, appraisal, promotion and succession planning. The models can help us to shape the culture of an organisation, particularly by linking individual behaviours to the corporate mission. Competencies also enable greater flexibility in working practices, and support systems of more equitable pay and remuneration. However, not all competency models achieve this potential. Some lie abandoned or forgotten on shelves and in drawers. Others operate in only one sphere of corporate life – often the training sphere – or exercise only broad, ineffectual guidance on behaviour. From my observations, the difference between more-effective and less-effective models appears to lie in their relationship to three key characteristics:

- accuracy;

- acceptability; and

- accessibility.

Where a model fails to meet any one of these criteria, it will fall short of its full potential. I have found it helpful to be explicit about these characteristics when a model is being developed, and to test for them at each stage of the process.

Accuracy

An accurate model expresses the actual capabilities required for effective performance. It will not omit any competencies that are required for effective performance, and will not include any competencies that are superfluous. The descriptions of the competencies should be sufficiently specific and clear that they can be used to guide individuals' behaviours, and for training and development, recruitment, appraisal, and the range of other uses to which the model will be put.

It should go without saying that a competency model should be accurate – except that accuracy is not always easy to achieve. For example, it is usually reasonably easy to establish an accurate picture of the competencies that are required now, in the present, by using behavioural interviews, focus groups and questionnaires; but for many employers, this is of relatively limited value. They need models that describe the competencies required to manage tomorrow's challenges, not those of the past or the present. This entails a degree of informed speculation – which may prove to be incorrect – about expected challenges and appropriate competencies.

Although accurate, specific descriptions of competency behaviours are desirable, the descriptions should not be so specific that the first small change to procedures or processes renders them obsolete – a balance must be sought between the specific and the general (Thompson, Stuart and Lindsay, 1996). For the sake of stability, a model should be reasonably durable – frequent changes to a model tend to confuse the users and lead to more difficulty in gaining acceptance of the second, third and fourth drafts. The model should be sufficiently flexible to accommodate marginal changes – although any radical alteration to a job role is likely to mean that the competency descriptions should be revised, just as over time a progressive series of marginal changes will lead to a need for revision. Given the current pace of change, it is unlikely that an organisation can comfortably forecast challenges more than five years into the future, and it is therefore realistic to consider a five-year maximum lifespan for a competency model.

If time presents a problem for accuracy, so too does diversity: can a general model of competency be accurate for each individual job? To some extent, every job is different – and perhaps merits an individual competency model to express the abilities truly required for effective performance. However, for the sake of stability and unity, it is often more acceptable to design a competency model that applies to a wide population. There are a number of examples of sophisticated models that contain descriptions of a core competency at work at different levels of responsibility within an organisation. This tension, between the specific individual job and the desire for a common language of competency, can be resolved by promoting the viewpoint that some competencies in the model are likely to be more relevant than others to each individual (Boyatzis, 1982), and for the systems for using the competencies to include discussion and negotiation with each person about particularly relevant competency areas for their job.

Not all competency models strive for accuracy. Some organisations devise inspirational models – setting out those competencies they wish to encourage, linked to the core values they wish to promote. Some organisations adopt all or parts of generic models developed elsewhere. There are usually some cost-saving advantages in following these approaches, but they can run greater risks with regard to accuracy and realism than if the company develops and tests its own competencies. Unrealistic models can be overly rational – the failing of many of the textbook descriptions of management over the years; and even practitioners' theories about what leads to success may not reflect reality (Yeung, 1996; Argyris, 1990; Klemp and McClelland, 1986). Where models begin at any point other than the actual behaviours of effective individuals, then there should be a thorough reality-testing of the proposed competencies with the user group to ensure they are reasonably close to accuracy and that they will be accepted.

Acceptability

To be effective, a model should be accepted as accurate and helpful by the people who will use it – those whose required competencies it describes, and others, including line managers and relevant personnel and training specialists. From my experience, the acceptability of a new model is usually based on:

- how far it accords with the experiences of users;

- the degree of "face validity" (the apparent legitimacy to the layperson) of the methodology that has been used to develop the model; and

- the degree to which it is in harmony with other priorities affecting the user – including task priorities, other initiatives, and other skills/competency models that apply to the user.

Acceptability is partly achieved through consultation, whereby a more accurate (and, therefore, more acceptable) picture of the required competencies is established; opportunities are created for those consulted to engage with ideas about competency and with early drafts of the model. A methodology that will often win the respect of users will be based on examination of best practice, consultation, the selective and appropriate use of lessons learned from elsewhere, and consideration of the unique (or special) factors in the current situation.

It is crucial when developing a competency model to investigate the other priorities, initiatives and models that may affect the acceptability of the model, and to consider how they can be managed. These can include task priorities, traditional ways of working, overt and covert values, published policy documents, human resource policies and procedures, and other models of skills and competencies. There may be some inevitable conflicts between these factors and the new model – one of the reasons for developing a new model is often to *change* some existing behaviours and values. It may also be possible, with a little thought, to avoid some unnecessary conflicts, to achieve some valuable harmonies, and to align the model with the aims of key groups within the organisation. This is part of the broader political process that applies to any new initiative (for a useful view of these issues see Mansfield and Mitchell, 1996, chapter 14). Specific to behavioural competency models is the room for manoeuvre in the design process. The shape of the competency model will often have considerable influence on its acceptability.

Shaping the model

A behavioural competency model is a collection of the skilful behaviours demonstrated by effective performers. The first McBer generic model, for example, contained 65 behaviours (Boyatzis, 1982); the original Management Charter Initiative (MCI) personal competence model for senior managers contained 31 (Management Charter Initiative,1993). The behaviours are usually clustered under headings – called competencies, abilities or skills – that provide a structure for the model. These are the "headlines" of the model, which command immediate attention.

A function of the clustering is to make the model more accessible, and therefore more acceptable. It is easier at first sight to grasp the eight MCI senior manager competencies, for instance, than the 31 separate behaviours. The clustering can be justified by the existence of common themes between behaviours, which may indicate underlying characteristics, qualities or capabilities (Klemp, 1980). In some models, the behaviours are clustered using factor analysis, in others the clustering is a matter of logic or convenience in which design decisions about the acceptability and accessibility of the model can play a part.

It may be desirable to use the headlines of the competency model to signal certain valued attributes, while some of the other characteristics of an effective performer may not be identified as headline competencies, but instead are represented by behaviours in many or all of the competencies. For example, the attributes of Self-confidence and Proactivity may naturally overlap, or underpin, other capabilities. At the same time, they may not, by themselves, be particularly valuable characteristics: a self-confident or proactive individual with no other competencies is a danger to themselves and others. Creativity is another example of a competency that may often be better distributed throughout a model, in the contexts of, for example: Achieving results, Customer focus, or Strategic thinking.

We can see this as a hidden matrix that underlies a competency model. It is often unnecessary for the users of the model to see this matrix – it is usually easier and more convenient for them to focus at first on the headline structure, and to absorb the underlying competencies as they use the model. Just as an architect must have a more technical understanding of the design of a house than the people who will live in it, however, it is useful to be aware of this hidden matrix when designing a model, and to be able to discuss it with and explain it to the project's stakeholders.

There may be some acceptability conflicts between the different stakeholders in the model. For example, senior management may wish to promote values through the model that are not recognised as current practice by other users – participative leadership styles, for example. Unless senior management is prepared to follow through, and take action to support behaviour that is expressed in the competencies – especially where the model departs from current reality – the model's credibility will be at risk.

On the other hand, where models are embedded into the core processes of an organisation and senior management expect the competencies to be used, they rapidly become accepted at all levels. Some of these issues are illustrated in the case study in box 2.1.

2.1. Competency models and harmony: an example

In a project to develop a competency framework for a national operating company of a multinational oil corporation, there were a number of factors and initiatives to consider. New policy statements about the broad direction and the values of the company had recently been issued from corporate level; there were policies at national level agreed with the Government, including a policy relating to the promotion of citizens of the country; a local policy statement on the use of human resources was less than 12 months old; there were also two other competency frameworks to consider – one old and one (in the area of appraisal) relatively new.

After exploring each of these initiatives, it was possible to place our new competency model within or alongside some of them. We used language that complemented the new policy statements, and we showed how the use of the model would help to implement them. By

---

careful use of the headlines, we were able to represent our model as the natural successor to the old one, and as an extension of the model used in appraisal.

The initial aim was to produce a model only for the most senior level of management in the company, although it was envisaged that a second model would be developed for the next level of managers and professionals, and then a third for the up-and-coming group of younger high-fliers, some of whom who would be at senior level in 10 to 15 years. In the long run, it was important to provide continuity through an integrated model of leadership and management at these levels and, as the project progressed, its aim expanded to produce linked models for all three levels – there were also natural economies in following this approach.

Accessibility

An accessible model is relatively easy for intended users to understand, and to apply the descriptions of competency. In pursuit of accessibility, a balance must be struck regarding the size and clarity of the model: large and detailed models are often difficult to use but, at the other extreme, a small model may contain descriptions that are too vague and broad to be of value. The complexity of the language and of the layout is another area where the model must strike a balance between being comprehensive – but perhaps difficult to apply – and being easy to understand at first glance but of limited use for detailed practical application. Tensions can arise during the design phase between achieving accuracy and ensuring accessibility.

I worked for several years with the original McBer generic model, which I used as part of a programme for helping senior managers to develop. Based on thorough and well-documented research, the McBer model had a high degree of face acceptability, but the language in which it was written was often difficult for users to interpret. The language, layout and accessibility of the occupational standards in the UK that underpin National and Scottish Vocational Qualifications (including the management standards originally developed by the Management Charter Initiative) have come in for similar criticism (Beaumont, 1996). The 1997 revisions to the layout and language of the Management Standards (MCI, 1997) attempted to overcome the problem in ways that seemed to be at least partially successful (Adams, 1997a; Adams, 1997b; Channell, 1997).

The inclusion of grades of ability within a model can often help users by adding the perspective of comparison to the descriptions. This is a notable feature of the later McBer models, as described in Spencer and Spencer (1993), and of most of the employer-specific models used for performance review (Matthewman, 1997).

Accessibility is also partly to do with how the models are introduced to the people who will have to put them into practice. Users can benefit considerably from exercises and specially-designed materials to help them achieve familiarity with the competencies. These can include introducing users to an outline (or the headlines) of the model, creating self-test questionnaires based on the model, and running exercises that encourage users to place the competency behaviours firmly in the context of their own working situation.

Careful thought about the aims of using the model is usually rewarded. It may not be necessary for users to be able to understand all of a model. In one hospital trust in the United Kingdom's National Health Service, for example, the board of directors planned to introduce a performance review system based on the management standards. The original idea was to use the standards in all their detail, including performance criteria and range statements – but the board was unwilling to provide more than a very short introduction to the standards for each user. The amended plan was to use only brief summaries of the standards to help managers identify the key competence areas for their job, and this was much more effective. Sometimes, more detail can mean less effect. In other cases, where behavioural models are used for skills assessment, questionnaires that are based on the headlines of the model have indicated where the user should look further at the detail of the competency, in order to improve their performance.

The accessibility of a competency model can be improved over the time it is in use. The original briefing papers, exercises and questionnaires can be modified or extended in the light of experience. Users develop and share their understanding of the competencies; practical interpretations evolve for any inadvertently-cryptic areas of the model. With continuing use and experience, feedback may indicate where the model itself might be revised (perhaps in the light of changing circumstances) to make it more accurate. And the review process can begin.

Conclusion

Effective competency models are accurate, acceptable and accessible: sometimes these characteristics complement each other, but sometimes there are tensions and conflict. It is useful to be explicit about these characteristics when you are developing a model, to explore what each implies in the context of your project, and to benchmark against each one separately to ensure that the competencies you are defining will bring positive benefits to your organisation.

Issues and pitfalls in using managerial competencies

Professor Adrian Furnham

It is almost 30 years since McClelland (1973) began to popularise the concept of competence, and nearly two decades since Boyatzis's book *The competent manager* was published (1982). The concept has spread like wildfire in human resource management circles, and employers have increasingly felt the need to develop a set of a personal competencies for their own managers. Despite the popularity of the concept, various researchers, consultants and writers began to note that employers still had problems devising, initiating and maintaining their competency frameworks (Strebler, Robinson and Heron, 1997). The Careers Research Forum (CRF) sponsored research conducted by myself into the current situation (Furnham, 2000). The CRF is a UK-based forum of some 50 major employers in both public and private sectors and initiates research into career, development and management topics on a regular basis.

The competency research strategy first involved a review of the salient literature. Then, various groups of people were interviewed, either by using a structured face-to-face or telephone interview format, or by asking them to complete a brief open-ended questionnaire. Finally, consultations were held with four groups of people active in this field: academic writers and researchers; management consultants and trainers; HR directors and managers; and line managers in various companies who are "required" to use the framework that was supposedly devised for their benefit.

This project set out to answer some of the "big" and "unresolved" questions around managerial competency frameworks, including the benefits of introducing and using competencies for managers, and the extent to which organisations are satisfied with the outcomes. The research also investigated the problems that have been encountered and the lessons that have been learned. Other issues included the extent to which the use of competencies has been evaluated, and the respective roles and responsibilities of human resources/personnel specialists, line managers and external consultants in designing and implementing the frameworks. The 10 issues that arose from the research are discussed in turn below.

Ten key issues

1. Should we use the term "competency"?

While this may be a relatively minor point, it remains for some non-personnel specialist an important and contentious issue. Because the whole competency movement has moved on since the 1990s, the "competency" term is not as widely used as it was. To a large extent, the earlier that organisations involved in the research had introduced their framework, the more likely they have been to stick with the language and concept. Some are quite happy with this situation; others have sought to change it.

Those who have chosen not to use the term have done so for various reasons. To many people, "competency" sounds mediocre. Further, not having a competency or not being competent implies incompetence, which is a serious issue in business. Others have preferred to use their own term, such as *high performance behaviours*, *management practices*, or *standards*, with which they can identify. They argue that these labels are better understood by line managers, and have the individual stamp of their company. They're genuinely unique to them.

More recently, companies seem to have become interested in "selecting potential". In essence, this means the organisations are future- rather than past-oriented, and they want a language to reflect this. Somehow "competency" does not fit well, and they are seeking clearer synonyms. This issue of language is important in communicating ideas to line managers. For some organisations, it may be wiser to quietly drop the term in favour of something more easily understood and containing less "historical baggage".

2. How many competencies do we need?

Whatever research methods they use, most organisations end up with a framework typically having between eight and 15 competencies, though some organisations may have as many as 30 general or core competencies (each with a number of behavioural indices). One lesson that many companies report is that a list of 10 or 15 competencies is probably too long. It becomes unwieldy for the managers, and adds much to the bureaucratic burden. However, others that are tied into industry standards find that they can cope quite adequately with as many as 20 supposedly unique competencies.

If there is a pattern for organisations in the number of competencies on their general list, it is curvilinear. At first, competencies increase in number to be comprehensive and all-inclusive, but then they are reduced in number because they simply become unwieldy. Later on in the process, it is quite common for there to be two lists: general competencies and job-specific competencies. Personnel specialists feel most comfortable with the former type of list, and line managers with the latter.

Most organisations start with two approaches: (general) competencies and (specific) behaviours. Thus, one may have 10 competencies with four to five behaviours or criteria for each. This yields a 50-item assessment form. If one has 20 competencies and each, in turn, has six behaviours/criteria/levels, the list expands to 120 items. It soon becomes apparent that the search for comprehensiveness leads to a very unwieldy assessment form, and a frighteningly bureaucratic exercise for the line manager. There is always a trade off between comprehensiveness (with its downside of bureaucracy) and the best, most parsimonious, level of description. The systems that work best are short, simple and comprehensible, rather than comprehensive. This is, and has been, an important issue in explaining why frameworks have failed: even those practitioners in personnel management complain about the time taken to complete documentation and the perceived lack of benefit from the exercise.

3. How is the competency framework derived?

There are a number of issues here: should one do the research in-house or use consultants? Is the initial research essential to the buy-in process? How important is it to do research across all sections or departments of the organisation? How long should this phase last? Is any one methodology more helpful than another to generate a useful, and unique, framework?

The CRF research has tended to show the following. It is unwise to rely entirely on consultants for the work involved in developing competencies, as they tend to provide lists they have used before and are comfortable with; and it is particularly unwise to use more than one consultancy at the same time, because they will tend to compete and over-engineer solutions. Having a small, bright, dedicated and multifunctional working party for early research works well. Where the team responsible for introducing competencies has done extensive pilot work across the organisation, the introduction has tended to be more successful. Line managers like to be consulted – often individually rather than in focus groups and meetings – and taken seriously. Failure to listen to specialist groups, particularly in engineering/finance, has often led to later problems.

Many organisations attribute their problems with the competency approach to the time taken to generate the framework, from deciding to go down that route to producing agreed and finalised documentation. It seems usual for it to take two to three years between announcing the initiative and the documentation appearing. Expectations have often been badly managed, and this has often led to cynicism and scepticism. As noted above, there are many ways to generate a list or framework of competencies. However, this does not seem a very contentious issue. The critical issue lies in timing and managing expectations about when the framework will be finished and how it will help line managers, in particular, and the organisation in general. Communicating clearly about purpose and progress right from the beginning can solve many of the problems.

4. When and how to use consultants

To a large extent, this depends on the consultants used, the relationship between personnel specialists and the particular consultants involved, and the general practice of using consultants within the organisation. Consultants can be used at various stages, typically:

a. conducting early research as part of designing the framework;

b. launching the project;

c.   providing training associated with the framework;

d.   auditing the process; and

e.   redesigning and updating the project.

Naturally, consultants have different specialities and approaches, and hence are used differently. The most common uses are in research and training; organisations have tended to be happier with the latter rather than the former. Outside trainers are often valued for their skill and impartiality. Furthermore, even some of the biggest organisations appear to have "outsourced" the training department. Some line managers resent consultants, and it can become an issue in the initial stages of the project. Without doubt, the nature of the final competency framework is more a function of the consultants used (if so) than the uniqueness of the organisation itself.

5. Should the framework apply to the whole organisation?

Most organisations start with the explicit aim of trying to devise a framework that is generally applicable across all departments, sections and regions for those at or above a specific level of seniority. Thus, for instance, part-time or support staff are not initially included and may never be so. A universal framework such as this is thought to be important to ensure that a common language is used within organisations, and that the managers and personnel specialists at all levels use and understand the same terms.

After a period of time, however, it is quite common for organisations to start to distinguish between general and specialist competencies. This occurs after technical specialists complain that they cannot work with the framework; it might meet the managerial business needs of the organisation but not the clear and specific requirements of technical specialists. This situation then presents the organisation with a dilemma. What often occurs is that the number of specialist competencies grows, while the general competencies are reduced in number or fall into disuse. The overall effect is ultimately for each department to have its own competency framework, thus significantly diminishing the whole point of the exercise. Again, this is an issue of balance. Allowing specialists to have a small number of three to four competencies to add to a short but manageable list of six to eight general competencies works well. This is the "compromise position" in which many organisations find themselves.

By contrast, those that resist introducing specific competencies often have the use of the whole framework threatened.

6. Who should champion the project?

The issue of finding an organisational champion or organisational support is not unique to the problem of introducing competency frameworks. However, the issue seems more crucial when considering the design, introduction and maintenance of projects that lie within the field of personnel management. Where competency frameworks have failed, research has frequently noted two related developments: the loss of the champion, and/or the withering of board-level support.

The fact that the introduction of competency frameworks is expensive, time-consuming and dependent on extensive consultation means not only that the project has to be well managed, but also that it is seen to have an attractive, credible and very energetic champion. This person may not be a personnel specialist and could equally – and perhaps more effectively – be a chief executive or director. But their presence is essential. Many organisations report "running out of steam" once a champion has left, moved on, or had his/her attention drawn elsewhere.

Just as importantly, if the board does not endorse the introduction of the framework, the competency project seems doomed to failure. The visible signs of the board's support include going on training courses, attending early research meetings and being seen to use the system. This support is needed not only at the initial phase but right through the process.

Perhaps the single most common source of failure lies in the fact that support for the introduction of the framework was either never really there in the first place or was not sustained over the long and difficult period of getting it embedded in the organisation. The introduction of any personnel management initiative is often met with both resistance and apathy by the rest of the organisation. It takes a very particular individual or set of individuals to drive the process until it is accepted and established.

7. How often and why do frameworks need updating and revising?

There are three phases to the successful implementation of all frameworks:

- *phase one:* planning/creating;
- *phase two:* implementing/launching; and
- *phase three:* maintaining.

Typically, the money and energy are exhausted in the first phase, which takes longer and proves more difficult than anticipated. While there is, of necessity, money and energy left for the launch and the training support of the competency framework, this can easily evaporate in the really important phase – maintaining the system and ensuring that it is used in the organisation.

The tangible product of the competency framework system is often a manual that describes all features of it. People talk of "the bible"; "the black book"; "that bloody manual". It typically appears two to three years after the idea of having a competency framework is first mooted. Many manuals are expensively and impressively produced, and proudly distributed to all line managers. The cost and effort are significant, and many represent years of work. Typically, there is a call to change and revise the system a few years after launch. This is a normal and healthy reaction. However, it is not easy to reproduce or adapt the manual. There is also the natural resistance of those who have spent considerable time on the manual; therefore, it is rare to see frameworks as thoroughly revised and updated as they should be. There appears to be a negative relationship between the amount of work done in the initial "manualisation" and the desire to change the system.

Nearly all personnel specialists and line managers acknowledge the need for constant revising and updating. However, this appears never to be done with the same thoroughness as the first attempt. Indeed, the prospect of changing the system and documentation significantly seems difficult and threatening, so it is never done properly. And this, in due course, leads to the situation where there are calls for the abandonment of the whole framework. The more that flexibility and the expectation of revision is built in from the first phase, the more likely the competency framework is to endure. Those that "came in early" (1990–96) probably have more difficulty than those that got in later and witnessed others having problems with changing their competency frameworks.

It seems to be the case that, like all systems, there needs to be a balance between continuity and change. Competency frameworks clearly need revisiting every two to three years to ensure they are still relevant. Resistance to updating is a common source of failure. Many users report that when frameworks were introduced they were concerned with the current, rather than the future, needs of the organisation.

8. For what processes should the framework be used?

One of the initial attractions of the competency framework idea was that it would help integrate a variety of people-management functions – specifically: recruitment and selection; development and training; and performance appraisal. The idea was that the system would generate both the concepts and the databank of performance criteria for each of those systems. Different employers began at different points – some started investigating the idea of introducing competencies because they had problems with retention, others with development and still others with appraisal. The research seems to suggest that personal development programmes represent the most successful use of competencies.

Most employers use frameworks for training, then selection and fewer for appraisal. The latter nearly always has serious problems associated with it. Most line managers need to be introduced to the language of competency by first applying it to themselves and understanding their own behaviour. The language of general management competence helps managers focus on what they should be doing and also provides company-wide consistency around these issues.

9. What training is required?

There are three types of training that need to be provided to support all competency frameworks:

• The individualisation of work plans. Many organisations find that their frameworks need to have two parts to them – one consisting of competencies that apply to everyone at their level,

and those that apply to them only (generic versus personal).
The latter may be called *key objectives, key result areas, key
practices*, etc – whatever the label, they all require personal
specifications. Individuals need training in writing their own
work plan, particularly in specifying success criteria. While it is
not difficult to list competencies and behaviours, individuals
frequently find it problematic coming up with measurable
criteria to evaluate each competency. There needs to be training
and facilitation around this issue.

• Progress/interim reviews. Most managers are poor at, and
  fundamentally neglect, giving staff feedback on their
  performance. This is not in the context of an end-of-year
  appraisal, but an interim discussion about progress on specific
  competencies. They need to be taught how to structure and
  conduct these sessions so that they feel confident in giving both
  positive and negative feedback to their staff.

• Rater training. Where individuals' competencies are assessed
  and given performance ratings by line managers, it is most
  important that they know the pitfalls of rating and do not fall
  into one of the many traps that seriously under-value the
  numeric (or even verbal) feedback generated. Rater training
  courses are about the measurement and assessment of
  competencies to ensure that measurement is accurate and
  reliable.

All three of the above training issues are particularly appropriate
where competency frameworks drive the appraisal process and
especially where the latter has an element of performance-related pay.

10. What are the problems of linking competencies to pay?

This is an enormously complex and sensitive issue and explains why
so few competence frameworks drive performance-related pay
systems. The issue revolves predominantly around the reliability of
the ratings of competence; who rates (boss, peer, subordinate); the
comparability of ratings across raters (the soft versus the tough boss);
and the size of the pay reward relative to base rate of pay. Certainly,
the evidence suggests that the introduction of competency
frameworks other than through developmental issues raises the
expectations that performance/competence will be rewarded (possibly
by pay). While the use of competency frameworks in appraisal is
sold on the ability to improve consistency and equality, the opposite

is often the case. Both managers and staff are deeply sceptical, even cynical, about all appraisal systems. Introducing a competency framework that supposedly cures all the problems of appraisal and performance-related pay is expecting too much.

Some surprising omissions

Discussions for the research project with line managers and personnel directors proved most interesting. However, what was *not* said, or alluded to, was perhaps as interesting and important as what was actually expressed. Six themes of direct interest to the aims of the research were little discussed, even after prompting. They are as follows.

Succession management and personnel planning

Though it is perfectly easy to see how useful competencies are for succession planning, they tend not to be used exclusively to drive the process. It seems as if the competency framework "informs" those responsible for these functions, but does not constrain or limit them to this method. Part of the problem appears to be that the organisations' frameworks do not take specialist competencies sufficiently into account. Other reasons include not having a succession management strategy; but, perhaps more importantly, the problem lies in the fact that so few companies have good databases on the current competencies of staff.

Filling critical jobs

It is always interesting to show how useful a system/framework is in solving particular problems, such as filling critical jobs. Inevitably, these tend to be either highly specialist jobs or very senior middle-management jobs. Ironically, most companies' frameworks seem especially unsuited for filling either type of vacancy, particularly the former. Again, the language of competencies has helped to clarify discussions when such posts have been filled but seems not to drive the process.

Predict future competencies

Some organisations became aware that frameworks were either too static or too backward-looking to be useful. Hence, some focused on the issue of employees' potential and the competencies that seemed to predict it. This was not the same as attempting to predict how the competency might need to change to respond to new and different situations. Thus, for instance, very few organisations have attempted to conduct future-oriented strategic planning and link the anticipated future needs and structure of the company to future frameworks. As an example of this lack of planning, there seemed little evidence that any one competency would become more or less important over time – let alone any indication of which competencies that would disappear altogether and which others that would emerge over time.

Competencies and leadership

Everyone who was interviewed for the research project agreed that the successful introduction of their competency frameworks depended heavily on them being championed by high-profile organisational leaders, preferably the chief executive and the members of the board. However, few interviewees talked about the leadership style found in the organisation (such as it being authoritarian or democratic) and how this style itself may have helped or hindered the whole process of introducing a framework. It is no doubt the case that leadership styles differ in different parts of an organisation. This may have accounted for the reason why a competency-framework approach could be embedded so easily and quickly in some parts but resisted so much in others.

Further, it was never clear for many individuals whether leadership (as opposed to management) was one of many competencies, constituted a "supra-competence", or represented the sum of all (or most) of the competencies put together. The competency movement has in some senses usurped the concept of leadership. There was, for instance, no talk of the different competencies required for transactional versus transformational leaders.

Corporate culture

In the 1990s, there was a great deal of interest in the concept of corporate culture and many attempts were made to provide ways of assessing or categorising it. It was argued that corporate culture had a very powerful and often "subliminal effect" on organisations that influenced all aspects of the business, such as structure, systems and processes. Thus, one could use various corporate culture models to predict which organisations would embrace and which resist the introduction of competency frameworks. The idea of corporate culture was, however, hardly ever mentioned to describe organisational processes or considered when attempting to explain why they succeeded or failed.

The link between the business plan and the competencies

While the textbooks all point to the essential idea that competencies must be derived from, and driven by, the business plan, this appeared to be more rhetoric than reality. When an organisation's competency framework was being planned, there seemed to be concern with the linkage, but, after that, the idea seemed to have been dropped. It is obviously very difficult to translate business/strategic plan ideas and concepts to the language of competency. The former is about strategy and process and the latter about people. Not only is the linkage difficult, but business plans can change radically – not only from year to year but also over the course of a single year. Thus, even if the link was well-established in the first place, it would have to be reforged at least on an annual basis. Seeing that it took some companies two to three years to bring about their frameworks, the constant updating that would have been required to keep up with the changing business plan seemed to slip.

The idea that the competency framework was clearly linked to the business plan was rarely mentioned by interviewees. The poor correlation between the all-important and ever-changing business plan and the static competency framework often proved a significant problem. The two were rarely in harmony and integrated . . . despite the fact that "theory" suggested they should be.

Benefits

What competencies have undoubtedly brought about are four clear benefits:

1. Language: At best, competencies have provided a common, shared, rich and descriptive language to describe people and performance. At worst, they have introduced jargon and psychobabble, and imposed specific meanings on everyday words that have not been properly understood.

2. Measurement: Competencies have helped to realise the idea that performance needs to be measured in order to be managed, and that measurement can improve feedback. This has led to the recognition of the importance of good human resource databases to improve decision-making. It has also made people aware of the problems of measurement, and has helped replace attitudes like "What is important isn't measurable, and what is measurable isn't important" with "What is important must be measured".

3. Consistency: Nearly always, the idea has been borne out in practice that the competency approach can lead to improved consistency across the whole organisation in the way in which people are managed (in terms of their selection, development and appraisal). Personnel management processes and personnel professionals were consistent, up-to-date and sophisticated, but with consistency often came bureaucracy and rigidity.

4. Development: Competencies certainly helped organisations to focus on the need for development, and also helped identify ways of going about it. They also often helped trainers develop courses and measures like 360-degree feedback forms.

Keys to success

The characteristics of the successful introduction of competency frameworks seem to be:

Simple: They should be parsimonious, not over-complex, and more understandable than fully comprehensive frameworks.

Salient: They must be relevant to line managers, staff, senior managers, and the business objectives and plan.

Supported: They have to be fully supported in terms of staff and money, but, most importantly, morally championed consistently from the top.

Flexible: It must be recognised that all systems – competencies included – are temporary and need updating regularly, based on changing circumstances.

Rewarding: The application of the competency system must be rewarding, particularly for line managers and staff. The former need to see it helps the process of good management and the latter need feedback, qualifications and other rewards.

Developmental: The system needs to be initially linked to developmental opportunities for senior managers.

Communicated: The aims, deadlines and benefits of the competency project need to be spelt out clearly, regularly and simply . . . and best not oversold.

Adaptable: The system must allow for certain individual departments to add specific or technical competencies; it should have both unique and shared competencies.

References

Adams, Katherine (1997a), "Testing the limits of language", *Competency & Emotional Intelligence Quarterly*, vol. 4 no.2, Winter 1996/97.

Adams, Katherine (1997b), "The MCI's 'plain English' standards of competence and the new demands of management", *Competency & Emotional Intelligence Quarterly*, vol. 4 no.4, Summer.

Argyris, Chris (1990), *Overcoming organizational defences*, Allyn and Bacon.

Beaumont, Gordon (1996), *Review of 100 NVQs and SVQs: a report submitted to the Department for Education and Employment*, Beaumont.

Boyatzis, Richard E (1982), *The competent manager: a model for effective performance*, McBer and Co/Wiley.

Channell, Joanna (1997), "How to implement plain language in standards of competence", *Competency & Emotional Intelligence Quarterly*, vol. 5 no.1, Autumn.

Furnham, A (2000), *Management competency frameworks*, London, Careers Research Forum.

Klemp, George O Jr (1980), *The assessment of occupational competence, report to the National Institute of Education, Washington USA*, cited in Boyatzis, 1982.

Klemp, George O Jr and McClelland, David C (1986), "Executive competence: what characterises intelligent functioning among senior managers?" in *Practical intelligence: nature and origins of competence in the everyday world*, Sternberg, R J and Wagner, R K eds, Cambridge University Press.

McClelland, D (1973), "Testing for competency rather than 'intelligence' ", *American Psychologist*, vol. 28, pp.1–14.

Management Charter Initiative (1993), *The senior management standards*, The National Forum for Management Education and Development.

Management Charter Initiative (1997), *The management standards*, The National Forum for Management Education and Development.

Mansfield, Bob and Mitchell, Lindsay (1996), *Towards a competent workforce*, Gower.

Matthewman, Jim (1997), "Making competency pay work", *Competency & Emotional Intelligence Quarterly*, vol. 5 no.1, Autumn.

Spencer, Lyle M Jr and Spencer, Signe M (1993), *Competence at work: models for superior performance*, Wiley.

Strebler, M, Robinson, D and Heron, P (1997), *Getting the best out of your competencies*, Brighton, Institute for Employment Studies.

Thompson, J E, Stuart, Roger, and Lindsay, Philip R (1996), "The competence of top team members: a framework for successful performance", *Journal of Managerial Psychology*, vol. 11 no.3.

Yeung, Arthur K (1996), "Competencies for HR Professionals: an interview with Richard E. Boyatzis", *Human Resource Management*, vol. 35 no.1.

Learning points

Characteristics of effective frameworks

- Effective competency frameworks address three factors: accuracy; acceptability; and accessibility.

- Accuracy: an accurate framework expresses the actual capabilities required for effective performance; it omits no essential ones, and excludes peripheral or superfluous ones. The descriptions of the competencies should be sufficiently specific and clear that they can be used in practice; however, they should not be so specific that subsequent revision and updating is impeded.

- Acceptability: to be effective, a framework should be accepted as accurate and helpful by the people who will use it. Acceptance is usually based on: how far the framework accords with their experiences; the apparent legitimacy of the design methodology; and the degree to which the framework is in harmony with other priorities affecting the user.

- A balance must be struck regarding the size and clarity of the framework: large and detailed models are often difficult to use but, at the other extreme, a small model may contain descriptions that are too vague and broad to be of value.

- The accessibility of a framework can be improved over time.

Key issues and pitfalls

- Employers should describe their frameworks as "competencies" only if relevant to them and line managers.

- Many employers find that more than nine competencies is too many. The assessment processes that work best are short, simple and comprehensible, rather than comprehensive.

- When designing the framework, it is unwise to rely entirely on consultants. A small, bright, dedicated and multifunctional working party for early research works well. The introduction has tended to be more successful where it has done extensive pilot work across the organisation.

- Many organisations attribute their problems with competencies to the long time taken to generate the framework. The critical issue lies in timing and managing expectations about when the framework will be finished and how it will help line managers and the organisation. Communicating clearly about purpose and progress right from the beginning can solve many of the problems.

- Allowing specialists to have a small number of three to four competencies to add to a short but manageable list of six to eight general competencies works well. Employers that resist introducing specific competencies often have the use of the whole framework threatened.

- The issues of finding a champion and gaining senior-level support are crucial.

- There are three phases to the successful implementation of all frameworks: phase one: planning/creating; phase two: implementing/launching; and phase three: maintaining. The vital phase of maintaining the system and ensuring it is used must not suffer from neglect, as it often does.

- The development of an expensive and complex competency manual often discourages subsequent updating. In addition, framework design is often based on current, rather than future, organisational needs. There needs to be a balance between continuity and change. Competency frameworks need revisiting every two to three years to ensure they are still relevant. Resistance to updating is a common source of failure.

- There are three types of training that need to be provided to support all competency frameworks: (1) helping individuals agree their own objectives and competency-based success criteria; (2) training line managers to give staff feedback on their performance on a continuous basis; and (3) training assessors where competencies are given performance ratings.

- Competencies are insufficiently linked to business plans. There needs to be greater integration, and frameworks need to be more flexible and updated more frequently.

- Competencies have undoubtedly brought about four clear benefits: (i) competencies have provided a common, shared, rich and descriptive language to describe people and performance; (ii) competencies have helped to realise the idea that performance needs to be measured in order to be managed, and that measurement can improve feedback; (iii) the competency approach leads to improved consistency across the whole organisation in the way in which people are managed; (iv) competencies help focus on the need for development, and also identify ways of going about it.

- Keys to success: the characteristics of the successful introduction of competency frameworks are: (a) frameworks should be not over-complex; (b) they must be relevant to managers, staff and the business objectives; (c) they have to be fully supported in terms of staff and money, and championed consistently from the top; (d) competency frameworks should be flexible to facilitate regular updating; (e) the application of the competency system must be psychologically rewarding; (f) the system needs to be initially linked to developmental opportunities for senior managers; (g) the aims, deadlines and benefits of the competency project need to be spelt out clearly, regularly and simply; and (h) the system must allow for some departments to add specific or technical competencies.

Chapter 3

Technical issues

Introduction

This chapter builds on the themes developed in chapters 1 and 2. So far, we have looked at the basic factors involved in designing, introducing and updating competency frameworks. Chapter 1 provided an overview of these issues, while chapter 2 focused in depth on the strategic issues linked to the successful implementation of a competency approach. Here, we turn to technical matters. Katherine Adams explains the workings of three of the best methods of identifying and defining competencies. She then explores the different types of competencies, and traces back these differences to their American and British origins.

Three key methods

Katherine Adams

Of the many methods now available to identify competencies that will genuinely make a difference to the organisation, some have a greater claim to rigour than others. Among the most popular of the more scientific methods are the critical incident technique, behavioural event interviews and the repertory grid. Below, the basic details of each method are explained, and their advantages and disadvantages. This information should help to give readers an appreciation of what each method involves, and assist them in planning the resources required to develop or revise a competency framework. However, the actual application of these techniques may require training and/or expert guidance.

The critical incident technique, behavioural event interviews and the repertory grid have come to prominence in the field of competency design by varied routes. Of the three methods, only behavioural event interviews were specifically designed to be used in competency analysis, and they are really a specialised version of the earlier critical incident technique, whose origins lie in the study of individuals'

thoughts and motivations. The repertory grid, too, has come a long
way since its beginnings in the field of clinical psychology.

Though there are some marked differences between the techniques,
there are also similarities in the way they are used in competency
research. All three tend to be used as a way of identifying the
behavioural competencies required in particular job roles, often with
a focus on the behaviour of superior, as opposed to average or
inferior, performers. Though they can all be adapted for use in focus
groups and even form the basis for questionnaires, their main mode
of use tends to be in one-to-one interviews. Developing practice
seems to be further blurring the distinctions between the methods,
with practitioners importing ideas and good practice from one
technique into another. Many reputable consultants would stress the
need to use each of these methods in conjunction with one or both
of the others, as well as with other techniques such as expert panels
and benchmarking against other organisations' competencies.

The critical incident technique

The critical incident technique was devised by psychologist J C
Flanagan as a way of finding out about people's motivation and
behaviour (Flanagan, 1954). It is based on the principle that
identifying and discussing a few "critical incidents" in someone's life
will provide an accurate basis for predicting his or her behaviour in
similar situations. The critical incident technique was readily adopted
by occupational psychologists as a way of analysing people's
behaviour at work, in particular as an element in job analysis. It
offered a way of getting beyond what people said about their motives
and skills to discover their actual behaviour in the job, in critical
incidents from which they had derived some kind of learning.
Examples of such incidents might be a confrontation with a
colleague or subordinate, or a sudden, unforeseen event to which the
individual had to respond.

In job analysis, the critical incident technique is typically used to
gather information about superior and average (and sometimes
inferior) performers in a particular role, usually by asking the job
incumbents themselves about critical incidents they have faced. A
variant is to ask a manager about critical incidents faced by his or
her subordinates. The aim is to gather detailed information about
the behaviour of those facing the critical incidents, which can be
analysed once all the discussions are complete. The link with

competency research is clear: asking about the toughest, most important parts of people's jobs is seen as a good way of uncovering the most important competencies required.

The technique in practice

In a typical critical incident technique interview, the interviewer will start by explaining what a critical incident is and ask the interviewee to identify one that he or she has faced at work. The interviewee then briefly describes the incident and, if it looks promising, is asked to go into more detail. Much of the skill of the technique lies in the interviewer's ability to probe the interviewee for useful information, using an approach that might develop as follows:

- What was the situation?

- Who was involved?

- What were your objectives/what were you supposed to do?

- What did you actually do?

- What did you achieve/what was the outcome? and

- What were the least/most effective behaviours in the situation?

3.1. Hints on using critical incidents

- Ask for a positive critical incident first;

- If the interviewee describes a very complex incident, ask for the most important or memorable aspect of it;

- When gathering information on critical incidents, a good rule of thumb is that you have obtained sufficient detail if you could recreate the incident on video without having to invent much of it;

- Use "Who", "What" and "Why" questions to probe for facts; use "Why" with care, as it may elicit theoretical rather than factual responses; phrase questions in the past tense, not the present, future or conditional tenses;

- Look for patterns: ask questions that will verify inferences you are beginning to draw about the interviewee's patterns of behaviour;

- Understand that the interview may be an emotional experience for the interviewee; you may need to stop probing and simply listen respectfully for a while; and

- Immediately the interview is finished, write a summary and, if possible, a full account; write everything in the first person and use the interviewee's own words as much as possible.

Sources: McClelland, David C (1976), *Guide to behavioural event interviewing*, McBer, 1976; and Spencer, Lyle M Jr and Spencer, Signe (1993), *Competence at work: models for superior performance*, Wiley, 1993.

Once one incident has been thoroughly discussed, the process is repeated with several more. According to an occupational psychologist at Pearn Kandola, a human resources consultancy: "You can usually generate 30 to 40 observable behaviours in a one-and-a-half to two-hour interview. I like to do quite a lot of interviews: you're looking for corroboration, for consistent kinds of behaviour in different people."

The interviews are carefully recorded – perhaps using a voice recorder, followed by transcription into text – and then analysed. When the critical incident technique is used for job analysis, a consultant at Development Dimensions International (DDI) said that: "The focus is on behaviours that lead to success on the job: you need to demonstrate a direct link between behaviours and the activities performed." He stresses, that, for employers, "the critical incident technique is just one aspect of a thorough job analysis. Other aspects include reviewing previous job analysis documentation and job descriptions, direct observation of people at work and interviews with job experts to get at job activities as well as behaviours." DDI groups all the data gathered from these sources into "dimensions": the job activities and the behaviours required for successful performance in these activities. This information is then sent back to the client, so that the dimensions can be rated and ranked by importance, and the amount of the job covered by the dimensions can be rated.

For employers that want to ensure the rigour of their competency model, the final step will involve some form of validation. Pearn Kandola said that: "We produce questionnaires based on all the competencies and behaviours identified and send them to a sample of the population [the people doing the jobs concerned]. Individuals are asked to rate the relevance of the competencies to the job, to rate themselves against the competencies, and to ask a colleague to rate them, too. The results are then subjected to statistical and qualitative analysis."

Advantages and disadvantages

The critical incident technique offers an "open-ended" method of probing behaviour rather than forcing choices, thus helping to minimise interviewer bias, and sometimes throws up surprising results. Compared with such techniques as brainstorming, which ask people to think about abstract concepts like "effectiveness" and which may encourage people to give the responses they think are wanted, the critical incident technique lays great emphasis on real, concrete events, generated by the interviewees themselves. By focusing on the aspects of a job that are critical to success, proponents of the critical incident technique claim that it gives immediate access to the most important competencies. The technique has the advantage of being generally very interesting for both interviewer and interviewee, and of producing a lot of information quickly. The resultant behavioural descriptions also tend to be fairly down to earth and reflect the actual language used by people in the organisation.

As for the disadvantages, it is sometimes argued that by focusing only on *critical* incidents, the technique overlooks the vast majority of the work that individuals carry out, because this is mundane. The critical incident technique also relies heavily on the skill of the interviewer and, even with careful handling, may only result in rather rough-and-ready data. Finally, anyone using the critical incident technique needs to be aware of the potentially embarrassing nature of critical incidents, to emphasise the confidentiality of the interview, and to exercise care and sensitivity.

Behavioural event interviews

Behavioural event interviews were developed (McClelland and Dailey, 1972) as a variant of the critical incident technique by the man who many regard as the founding father of the competencies movement, David McClelland. Advocates of the behavioural event interview often explain the difference between behavioural event interviews and the critical incident technique in terms of people versus jobs. For instance, "where Flanagan was interested in identifying the task elements of jobs, McClelland was interested in the characteristics of the people who did a job well" (Spencer, McClelland and Spencer, 1994).

However, as we have seen, the critical incident technique can be used to focus on behaviours as well as on job activities. The difference is perhaps mainly one of emphasis, with behavioural event interviews stressing the "people" aspect more than the critical incident technique does. Certainly, one of McClelland's innovations was to introduce into the interview more questions about the individual's thoughts, feelings and motivation (known as probes based on the "thematic apperception test") in addition to the critical incident technique's emphasis on actions and results.

In addition, McClelland built around the behavioural event interview technique an entire methodology for identifying competencies, known as the "job competence assessment" method. The key features of this method are that it compares superior with average (and sometimes inferior) performers, that it uses a coding system to help analyse the results of the behavioural event interviews, and that it pays considerable attention to validating the resulting competency model. The method involves five distinct phases:

1. Deciding the criterion for superior performers in a particular role (such as productivity, total sales, supervisors' ratings – ideally, this should be as objective as possible);

2. Identifying a number of superior and average performers on the basis of the previously-agreed criterion (the "criterion sample");

3. Gathering information about their behaviour, thoughts, feelings and motivation, by means of behavioural event interviews and other methods (for example, expert panels, surveys, an expert system database, or observation);

4. "Coding" and "thematically analysing" the behavioural event interview and other data for the presence and frequency of behaviours, and clustering these under competency definitions to produce a competency model; and

5. Checking both the "criterion" and "predictive" validity of the model.

The interviews in practice

In essence, a behavioural event interview is carried out in the same way as an interview based on the critical incident technique. However, the need to collect detailed information about motivation means that the interviews may take longer: Chris Dyson of the Hay Group said that: "Our interviews typically last three to three-and-a-half hours." Unlike critical incident technique interviews, behavioural event interviews are always used to ask a job incumbent about his or her own job. McClelland's advice (McClelland, 1976) is to ask the interviewee to describe in detail the five or six most important recent situations that he or she has experienced in the job: two or three high points or major successes, and two or three low points or key failures. He also recommends an extra step: asking the interviewee to describe what he or she thinks it takes for someone to do the job effectively. The point of this is not to get generalisations, but to identify further critical incidents that shed light on some of the organisation's "folklore" values.

To minimise bias, it is important that behavioural event interviews should be conducted "blind": that is, the interviewer should not know whether the interviewee is classed as a superior, average or below-average performer. Another important point is not to restrict the interviewee's choice of subjects (avoiding, for example, a leading question such as: "Tell me about a critical incident in which you had to deal with a people problem"). Advocates of the behavioural event interview method say that an interviewee's choice of incident may in itself be highly indicative, with different types of performer focusing on markedly different aspects of their work.

McClelland's technique stresses the importance of audio taping and then transcribing each behavioural event interview in full. When writing up the interview, the interviewer should also note details like the interviewee's job responsibilities, draw out themes in the interview, and describe his or her impressions, opinions and tentative conclusions. These may draw on the interviewee's conversational style; words and phrases that he or she uses repeatedly; his or her appearance; and anything that seems to be missing or out of place compared with the other people interviewed. The analysis of behavioural event interview data involves two steps:

- coding the interview transcripts for recognisable behaviours that fall under previously-defined competencies in a competency "codebook" or "dictionary"; and

- using "thematic analysis" to identify new behaviours or combinations of behaviour, and to bring these together in related groups, or clusters, that are given new competency headings.

To carry out the analysis, researchers read the transcripts and underline each concrete behaviour that was mentioned by the interviewee. Any behaviours matching up to those in the competency dictionary are coded in the margin. Behaviours are coded for the relevant competency each time they occur, to provide data on frequency. To ensure rigour, each transcript is usually analysed independently by at least two different people. Only then is it revealed which transcripts come from interviews with superior and which from those with average performers (or, for that matter, which come from those with below-average appraisal ratings). The analysts then meet as a team to discuss and document their findings regarding both criterion samples: the frequency of recognised behaviours that can be linked to competencies in the dictionary, and the frequency of new behaviours that are tentatively clustered into new putative competencies.

Two McBer researchers, Lyle and Signe Spencer, have suggested that thematic analysis is "the most difficult and creative part of the competency analysis process" (Spencer and Spencer, 1993). They say that: "The real task of the analysts' competency-definition meeting is to argue out and agree on the best words or labels to describe each competency cluster." The result of these discussions is a customised competency model for the particular role being researched. Typically, this will indicate both the competencies required for superior performance, and the "threshold" competencies required by anyone doing the job. According to the Spencers, "efficient competency models list the five to nine most important competencies" required for superior performance. A model should define each competency by reference to types of behaviour, and provide one or more real examples of the behaviour drawn from the behavioural event interview data. In recent times, competency models have also tended to scale each competency in terms of higher and lower "levels", each linked to particular kinds of behaviour.

Validating the data

As this account makes clear, the conduct and analysis of behavioural event interviews (as, indeed, of critical incident technique interviews) relies to a great extent on the skill of the interviewers and analysts, and subjectivity and bias clearly pose a major threat. In an attempt to minimise the problem, the job competence assessment method incorporates a number of validation steps.

The first of these involves attempting to ensure a degree of "inter-rater reliability". Using the competency model derived from the steps described above, two or more analysts independently code a new sample of behavioural event interview transcripts, then meet to reconcile their codings and refine the model in the light of this discussion. These steps can be repeated until a satisfactory level of reliability (established by statistical analysis) is achieved. Proponents of the method claim (Boyatzis, 1982) that inter-rater reliability of as much as .8 to .9 can be achieved (where 1.0 = total reliability).

After this, two further kinds of validation can be carried out. First, a check can be made that the competencies correctly identify known superior versus average performers (or superior versus below-average) by using the model to score transcripts of behavioural event interviews from another criterion sample or by developing psychometric and other tests to measure people in a criterion sample against the competencies in the model. And, second, the competencies can be investigated to see whether they correctly predict superior and average (or below-average) performance. Here, the competencies are used as a basis for selection or training, and participants can be tracked to see if they perform better (or worse) in the future than they did in the past.

Advantages and disadvantages

Chris Dyson of the Hay Group said: "If we conduct behavioural event interviews with a sample of 40 or so people, the resulting model can usually predict superior performers with a certainty of over 80%." To achieve such results, however, requires rigorous training of interviewers and analysts. Chris Dyson said: "We train our people for five days; then they need to do a number of interviews before they're accredited. And we review their performance periodically to make sure they're conforming to good practice and applying our rigorous protocol."

Apart from the time and effort involved in training and monitoring those involved in applying behavioural event interviews, the other main disadvantage is the cost of conducting, transcribing, coding and analysing the interviews. This second point means that they are not a realistic option for research into many jobs. Though behavioural event interviews are usually associated with research into management competencies, Chris Dyson said: "We recommend behavioural event interviews for those jobs which are considered critical to the success of the organisation, not necessarily just the most senior roles. If you've got 2,000 people doing a job and there's a 20% improvement in performance to be had, then the return on investment will clearly be worth it."

One of the big advantages of the behavioural event interview method is the sheer volume of information it generates. Advocates say it compares very favourably with other methods in terms of generating useful competency models: "In general, [expert] panels get about 50% accuracy when compared with behavioural event interview data, and tend to omit some of the unique competencies needed for a role" (Boulter, Dalziel and Hill, 1996).

BEIs versus CITs

What about the pros and cons of behavioural event interviews compared with the critical incident technique? One of the main differences is the way behavioural event interviews emphasise issues like motivation, thoughts and feelings. Though the critical incident technique may be used to probe for motivation, behavioural event interviews may produce more of the information needed to identify competencies like "achievement motivation" or logical ways of thinking or solving problems.

On the other hand, there are those who see behavioural event interviews' emphasis on people as a disadvantage. Pearn Kandola said: "If the only focus is on the person, there's a good chance of institutionalising prejudices about 'good performers'. People tend to talk about the things they like doing – which may not be the behaviours that are really relevant. The advantage of the critical incident technique is that it ties down behaviour to activities in the job itself."

In general, though, it is hard to draw hard and fast lines between the two techniques, as practitioners increasingly adopt ideas from one technique into another. For instance, the extensive recording and transcription of interviews, sometimes claimed as an advantage of behavioural event interviews, is something that can readily be adopted by users of the critical incident technique. Nor may the issue of coding be a decisive factor. Though one of Hay/McBer's selling points is its vast generic competencies dictionary derived from thousands of behavioural event interview-based studies, some critical incident technique practitioners offer similar resources. Development Dimensions International said: "Using the critical incident technique needn't mean starting with a clean slate. We have a databank of job activities and associated behaviours derived from our extensive experience of job analysis, and these can be used for preliminary analysis of new critical incident technique studies, though some tailoring is usually necessary."

The repertory grid

As mentioned previously, the issue of minimising interviewer bias is an extremely important one for practitioners of both the critical incident technique and behavioural event interviews. It is also a vital issue for the third technique considered here – the repertory grid.

Devised by George Kelly, a clinical psychologist, the repertory grid technique was specifically designed to overcome the problem of observer bias and put the interviewee's perspective first, without the need for the interviewer to add his or her own interpretation. Kelly's "personal construct theory" (Kelly, 1955) argued that individuals build up a system of hypotheses or "constructs", through which they interpret the world about them. Kelly invented the repertory grid technique as a way of getting people to exhibit these construct systems. Though first used exclusively in clinical psychology, Kelly's ideas were later adopted in market research and human resource management, especially for training needs analysis, job analysis, teambuilding, counselling and competency research.

How to elicit constructs

In essence, the technique aims to draw out people's views and judgments by means of a series of comparisons. The first step is to establish the things (or "elements") that are to be compared. In a competency study, the elements will probably be individuals, though they could be activities, events, or even putative competencies previously identified by other research methods. Typically, though, the interviewee might be asked to bring to the interview the names of between six and 12 work colleagues, perhaps his or her subordinates, to include good, average and poor performers. The name of each element is written on a small card, and the process of "construct elicitation" begins.

The interviewee is asked to choose any three cards at random, and then asked: "Can you tell me a way in which two of these people are like each other, and different from the third, in terms of the way they work?". This question will vary according to the type of elements selected. For instance, if the elements are activities involved in the interviewee's own work, the question might be couched in terms of "the demands they make on your skills". Questions such as these are designed to elicit a two-ended (or "bi-polar") construct. For example, where the elements are the interviewee's subordinates, the interviewee might answer: "Well, x and y are very confident with clients, but z is more nervous". The construct in this case would be "confident with clients – nervous", in other words, the beginnings of a competency description. The interviewer should note it down before asking for more constructs for the three elements being considered.

Once all the constructs for that particular triad (group of three elements) have been exhausted and noted down, the interviewee is asked to pick another three cards at random, and the process continues until all the possible triads have been covered, or until the interviewer senses that no further constructs are forthcoming (for example, because the interviewee begins to repeat him or herself). Pearn Kandola said: "In a two-hour interview, we might expect to collect between 12 and 18 constructs."

3.2. Hints on using the repertory grid

- Choose elements that are as specific and precise as possible (such as real people); avoid abstract nouns such as "my ideal subordinate";

- Do not mix types of element, such as people with activities;

- Do not have elements that are sub-sets of other elements (for example, making presentations generally, and making presentations to the managing director);

- Be sure to ask for both poles of the construct;

- Use compare-and-contrast techniques;

- Keep your interventions to a minimum: the interviewee may need some periods of silence to reflect on the choices that he or she is being asked to make;

- Ask the interviewee to express a preference for one pole of the construct in general, not among the elements that gave rise to that construct; and

- It may be helpful to elicit just a few constructs, "ladder" them, and put them into the grid, before returning to elicit more constructs.

Source: Stewart, Valerie, Stewart, Andrew and Fonda, Nickie (1981), *Business applications of repertory grid*, McGraw-Hill.

"Laddering"

The process of construct elicitation is the heart of the repertory grid method. However, to gather worthwhile data, it is advisable to use an extra step known as "laddering", designed to probe the thinking behind the constructs. The interviewer reads out the list of constructs in turn, and asks the interviewee for his or her preference for one pole over another. For instance, the question might be: "Who do you see as most effective: nervous people or those who are confident with clients?" When the interviewee has responded, the interviewer probes for more detail, using "Why" questions. This process will generally elicit more, "higher-level" constructs, until the interviewee cannot explain him or herself any further, perhaps resorting to formulations like: "Well, I suppose that's just how I am", or "That's what's important to me". Chris Dyson of the Hay Group, which occasionally uses repertory grids in addition to behavioural event interviews as a source of extra data, said: "We have a theory that you have to go through seven levels of 'Why' before you reach people's core constructs."

The process is called "laddering" because the "Why" questions take the discussion "up the ladder" of higher-order constructs. Once the interviewee's core constructs have been reached, so that he or she cannot explain them in terms of any further constructs, the process reverses. Now the interviewer guides the discussion back "down" the ladder, often using "How" questions, to find out more about the new constructs that have been elicited; for example: "Can you tell me some more about how people who are confident and those who are nervous approach their work?".

In competency analysis, these questions should aim to identify in detail the very specific behaviours used by individuals or involved in activities, for example by asking: "Can you tell me what the confident ones do that makes them different from the nervous ones?". This will enable the analysts to fill out the behavioural detail of the competency labels (constructs) when it comes to drawing up a model.

Analysing the results

The results of these interviews can be analysed in a number of different ways, depending on the ultimate aim of the research. For some purposes, it will be enough to conduct the interviews up to the point described so far – that is, eliciting constructs (competencies), asking for the preferred pole, and laddering for behaviours – without the need to go as far as drawing up repertory grids. These data can then be subjected to a similar kind of analysis to that used for behavioural event interviews. At the simplest level, this may just mean a frequency count: counting up how often particular competencies are mentioned by all those interviewed. However, since people rarely use the same words to describe their constructs, this technique may have limited appeal.

Probably more useful is content analysis, which involves sorting the competencies under a number of categories before doing a frequency count. As with behavioural event interview analysis, having several people independently involved in this process will improve its rigour. The data generated should, however, be treated with care. Pearn Kandola said: "We would never use repertory grids on their own. They are good at generating competency labels such as 'this person is a better planner than that one', and you can use laddering to generate observable behaviour statements. But there usually won't be enough of these statements to make a complete competency model. We pool the statements with others derived from techniques like critical incident technique, so that we're looking at hundreds of statements overall, and cluster them, looking for corroboration between interviewees."

Alternatively, the data generated from repertory grid interviews can be used as a first step. Following content analysis, the information can be used as the basis for further competency research – perhaps, as the starting point for a questionnaire survey of a larger population of employees.

The grid

Although it is possible to generate useful competency data without drawing up actual repertory grids, this is the next step for those seeking an extra level of analysis. The interviewer asks the interviewee to rate each of the elements discussed in terms of each of the constructs that have been elicited – for example, to rate individuals against competencies. Each construct/competency can be used as a simple Yes/No scale or, if finer judgments and eventual computer analysis are required, turned into a scale with five or more points. The ratings are noted down in the form of a grid, with the elements/individuals as the columns and the constructs/competencies as rows.

During this process, which may involve some discussion, new constructs may emerge, existing constructs may be redefined, and new elements may even be offered. The purpose of this step is to test how convenient each construct is: not every element may be rated on every construct, and constructs with narrow applicability can be discarded or redefined. It also allows one to see in detail how the interviewee uses his or her constructs. Other options are also open at this stage. For instance, if the interviews are couched in terms of people's effectiveness at work, interviewees can be asked to rank the constructs/competencies in order of importance according to this criterion.

Once drawn up, repertory grids lend themselves to all kinds of sophisticated analysis of the interrelationships between constructs (or, indeed, elements) within a particular interviewee's grid. For example, visual focusing offers a way of comparing the ratings given to each construct with those given to every other construct in a particular grid. This allows the analyst to work out which constructs (for example, which competencies) the interviewee sees as similar, and which as dissimilar. Still more sophisticated techniques like cluster analysis and principal-component analysis take these kinds of correlations further, with analysis usually based on the use of computer programmes.

Other kinds of analysis are also possible for those wanting more detail about a particular individual's system of constructs. For instance, if the interviewees have been asked to rank the constructs/competencies in order of importance for someone's effectiveness at work, they can also be asked to rate the individual elements according to this criterion (that is, to identify the superior, average and inferior performers). These two rankings can then be cross-checked with the grid data (where each individual is rated against each competency) to indicate whether the competencies that the interviewees consider most important are really being used to discriminate between good and poor performers.

Advantages and disadvantages

One of the main advantages claimed for the repertory grid technique is that it allows researchers to draw out from individuals the values that lie behind their judgments of people or events. Like the critical incident technique and behavioural event interviews, the emphasis is on real people or tangible activities. But the process can often be an eye-opener for the interviewee too, making explicit some values that were previously unformulated. From this point of view, the repertory grid may be more powerful than simply asking people to straightforwardly describe critical incidents.

Certainly, this means that a competency model that uses repertory grid data is likely to have high "face validity", a high level of acceptance on its apparent merits. Unfortunately, "one problem with the pen pictures of effective performance generated by this technique is that they all have high face validity until you see another one. Any description of effective performance looks appealing" (Stewart, Stewart and Fonda, 1981) (a criticism that might, with some justice, be levelled against any of the techniques considered here). However, adherents do claim a high degree of accuracy for the technique: "We find that PQs [performance questionnaires] designed on the 'workshop' principle have somewhere between a 12% and a 20% yield of items discriminating between effective and ineffective performers, while PQs designed from repertory grid interviews have a yield of between 67% and 85%" (Stewart and Stewart, 1977).

As for the disadvantages, like the critical incident technique and behavioural event interviews, the repertory grid technique tends to be time-consuming to conduct, analyse, interpret and discuss, and it demands specialised training and expertise. Similarly, it also requires interviewees who are analytical and articulate, so it is not appropriate for all jobs.

Pearn Kandola said that: "The problem with using the repertory grid to ask people about the individuals they manage is that they often don't have full access to the range of behaviours these individuals use at work. So you need other sources of data, such as critical incident technique interviews with jobholders, to balance out the weaknesses." On the other hand, using the repertory grid to interview job experts (such as incumbents, their managers, and personnel specialists) about job tasks or job demands: "Means asking more complex questions: the information is yet further removed from reality because you're asking people to take a view on the importance of a characteristic in performing an activity. However, the research experience of McBer is that experts typically only get 50% of the differentiating competencies, and usually miss the unique ones."

A final word

Users of the techniques and much of the literature on them warn against the use of any single method in isolation to identify competencies. To ensure rigour, a number of different methods should generally be used in combination. And, a number of validation steps should also be carried out to test the resulting competency model. Finally, any competency research should involve wider consideration of the organisation's environment, aims and future plans. Only thus can researchers ensure that the competencies are acceptable to their target group and – perhaps most importantly of all – that they are not just "historical", but relevant to the way the organisation sees itself developing in the future.

Competency or *competence*: the different schools of thought

Katherine Adams

The current popularity of competency is due largely to the pioneering work carried out by an American consultancy firm over 30 years ago. That groundwork continues to support a proliferation of competency developments in the USA, the UK and worldwide, and the very word "competency" owes much of its currency to it.

Ironically, though, the concept bears little resemblance to the notion of "competence" as it is promoted through the UK's National Vocational Qualifications system.

Although the origins of competency-based education and training can be traced back as far as the 1920s, the modern competency movement can really be said to have started in the late 1960s and early 1970s. The prime mover at that time was David McClelland, a Harvard psychology professor who founded a consultancy called McBer. In a ground-breaking paper (McClelland, 1973), he argued that traditional academic examinations did not predict job performance or success in life, and were also often biased against minorities, women and others. He said that researchers should be looking for ways to identify other variables – "competencies" – that could predict success and which were unbiased, or at least less biased.

In the early 1970s, consultants at McBer began to try out ways of identifying these competencies. One of the first projects was conducted for the US State Department and its aim was to identify the characteristics of successful diplomats. McBer's researchers took a criterion sample – that is, a sample of the most effective performers as measured by a specific criterion. They devised a technique called behavioural event interviewing, based on the earlier critical incident method (both tools are described in the previous section). Interviewees are asked to think of several important on-the-job situations in which things turned out well or badly and then to describe these in exhaustive narrative detail. For the State Department project, both successful and unsuccessful diplomats were interviewed and the resulting transcripts analysed to identify the characteristics – competencies – that differentiated the two samples. This competency model was then validated using new samples of diplomats and new tests to measure individuals' competencies.

Over the next decade or so, McClelland and the consultants at McBer carried out a number of similar studies, many of them with managers. In 1981, the American Management Association commissioned another McBer consultant, Richard Boyatzis, to examine whether a generic model of managerial competency could be derived from these different models.

Competency defined

Boyatzis re-analysed studies of more than 2,000 people in 41 management jobs in 12 organisations. Each model was based on the job competence assessment method developed by McClelland. Importantly, Boyatzis set down an explicit definition of the notion of "competency" that had underpinned the McBer work. A competency, he said, was "an underlying characteristic of an individual which is causally related to effective or superior performance in a job" (Boyatzis, 1982). Competencies can be motives, traits, skills, aspects of one's self-image or social role, or a body of knowledge which one uses.

Reflecting McClelland's earlier concerns, Boyatzis placed the concept of competency firmly in the context of effective performance: "effective performance is the attainment of specific *results* (outcomes) through specific *actions* while maintaining policies, procedures and conditions of the organisational environment" (emphasis added). And a person's *competencies* allow him or her to perform these actions. A competency is an ability: "A person's set of competencies reflect his or her capability. They are describing what he or she *can* do, not necessarily what he or she does, nor does all the time, regardless of the situation and setting" (emphasis added).

Having defined competencies as "those characteristics that differentiate superior performance from average and poor performance", Boyatzis had to deal with the question of how to define those characteristics that are essential to performing a job, but do not lead to superior performance. One example he gives of such a characteristic is "speaking the native language of one's subordinates" and his solution was to define these as threshold competencies. Although motives, traits, self-image and social role, skills and knowledge all count as competencies, Boyatzis says that they form a kind of hierarchy. Each competency may exist in an individual at various levels: motives and traits are the unconscious level; self-image and social role are the conscious level, and skills are the behavioural level. Knowledge, he says, has a pervasive effect on all the other competencies.

A generic model

Boyatzis analysed the various studies and picked out those characteristics that distinguished effective performance in a job but were not unique to a specific product or service. This resulted in a list of 21 putative generic management competencies, of which 19 were eventually included in the generic model (see box 3.3). Of these, 12 are defined as competencies and seven as threshold competencies.

3.3. Boyatzis's model of management competency

Richard Boyatzis identified 19 generic management competencies, arranged in five clusters:

Cluster	Competencies
1. Goal- and action-management	Efficiency-orientation, proactivity, diagnostic use of concepts, concern with impact
2. Leadership	Self-confidence, use of oral presentations, conceptualisation, logical thought*
3. Human resource management	Use of socialised power, managing group process, positive regard*, accurate self-assessment*
4. Directing subordinates	Use of unilateral power*, developing others*, spontaneity*
5. Focus on others	Perceptual objectivity, self-control, stamina and adaptability

* Threshold competencies.

The final competency in the model is "specialised knowledge" (a threshold competency), which forms a category on its own.

The competencies in the model were "clustered" at the skills level to produce groups of similar competencies. Boyatzis cautioned that it was far more serious if a manager lacked one or more of the competencies within a cluster than if he or she lacked an entire cluster. He also stressed that the resulting model was an "integrated" one: "You cannot understand a manager's competence by looking at one of his or her competencies or even at one of his or her competency clusters out of context of his or her other competencies."

Finally, Boyatzis tested the predictive effect of his generic model to see how well it could differentiate between superior, average and poor managers. Overall, the results were enough for Boyatzis to claim that this was a genuine generic model of managerial competencies: the competencies correctly classified 51% of managers as compared to a random prediction that would have correctly classified only 33%.

However, Boyatzis did warn that this was just a preliminary attempt to determine what such a generic model should include, and that further research was needed. The predictive validity of the model only proved that these competencies represent about half of those that are required for effective management. He argued that "about a third of the variance in performance of a manager can probably be accounted for by these generic management competencies, about a third of the variance can probably be accounted for by job- and organisation-specific management competencies, and the remaining third of the variance is probably due to situational factors."

Competencies dictionary and database

The degree of success achieved by Boyatzis encouraged other researchers at McBer to undertake further work on generic competencies. In 1989, Lyle and Signe Spencer began to analyse all the competency studies completed by McBer to date. These covered not just managers but also entrepreneurs, and technical and professional, sales and "human service" workers from a wide range of organisations. Over 20 years, more than 100 different researchers had produced a total of 286 models, two-thirds of them American, the rest drawn from studies carried out in 20 other countries or multinationally. Each model was generally organised into between three and six clusters of competencies, with roughly two to five competencies per cluster. Each competency had a narrative description plus three to six behavioural indicators – that is, specific behavioural examples of ways of demonstrating the competency in the job. Each competency was also often illustrated with a typical example drawn from the interviews with superior performers.

The Spencers compared all the models and translated the findings into a common language (Spencer and Spencer, 1993). Next, the behavioural indicators were analysed to identify the lowest common denominator or smallest unit of observation directly comparable across all the models. Then they listed all the behavioural indicators mentioned in any of the models. Around 760 different types of behaviour were identified. Of these, 360 indicators defining 21 competencies were found to account for 80% to 98% of behaviours reported in each model, and these were compiled into a preliminary dictionary of behavioural indicators. The remaining 400 indicators described rarely-observed competencies and were not included in the dictionary.

The Spencers' next task was to code all the competency models for all the behavioural indicators in the dictionary; most models were found to contain 50 to 150 indicators. Using the behavioural event interview data, each model was entered into a competencies database. This database has several uses. Where there are several studies of one job, researchers can query the database to produce generic competency models. Database queries can also test similarities among different levels of a job family, different types of jobs, or job studies from different environments. Interesting cross-cultural conclusions have been drawn: for example, the Spencers say that competencies for superior performance in similar jobs are found to be essentially the same everywhere in the world.

NVQs: the great divide

The work of McClelland and the McBer consultancy has spawned an enormous industry. Firms in the USA, the UK and worldwide have used the methodology to develop their own competency models and apply them to the whole range of human resource management processes. However, though McClelland is credited with popularising the notion of competency, not everyone who uses the concept now would recognise his ideas. Indeed, a good deal of confusion has grown up around the term precisely because people use it in very different ways.

McClelland's radical departure was that whereas traditional job analysis looked at elements of the *job*, competency assessment looks at the *people* who do the job well, and defines the job in terms of their characteristics. As we have seen, McClelland also stressed the importance of superior performers: competencies are defined as precisely those characteristics that produce effective performance. A third distinguishing feature of competency, according to this conception, is that it is an underlying characteristic that causes someone's actions.

But although McClelland's approach has been very influential, it has been largely ignored by the publicly-funded competence movement

in the United Kingdom. The occupational standards programme
funded, and sponsored, by the British Government may not have
such a long history as the McBer approach, but it has had a
significant impact – mainly through National Vocational
Qualifications (NVQs), which are based on these standards.

Where McClelland focused on people, the standards/NVQ approach
stresses the job. McClelland's person-oriented behavioural event
interviewing identifies characteristics of successful performers; in the
UK, job-oriented functional analysis has been used to identify the
roles and tasks of an occupation.

Secondly, where McClelland's approach is concerned with the
behaviour of *superior* performers, occupational standards/NVQs in
the UK are made up of elements of competence with performance
criteria indicating *minimum* competence levels. This is the result of a
historical concern with establishing minimum standards for the
purposes of certification and licensing. One example is the
now-discarded "chartered manager" idea originally espoused by the
Management Charter Initiative.

Finally, rather than seeing competency as a characteristic that *causes*
certain actions, the standards/NVQ approach construes it as
"something which a person who works in a given occupational area
should be able to do. It is a description of an action, behaviour or
outcome which the person should be able to demonstrate" (Training
Agency, 1988) (emphasis added).

MCI – bridging the gap?

Perhaps the nearest that the approach sponsored by the UK
Government has come to the McClelland model is in the work
carried out by the Management Charter Initiative (MCI). Although
the occupational standards originally developed by the MCI follow
the official standards/NVQ approach, the MCI also produced a
parallel "personal competence model". This was developed by using
person-oriented techniques, such as critical incidents and repertory
grids, to identify the behavioural competencies that distinguish
superior performers. What is more, the resulting "personal
effectiveness competencies" bear a good deal of resemblance to
Boyatzis' own competency model (Evans and Kerrison, 1994; Evans,
1995). However, it is unclear exactly what relationship is supposed to
exist between the personal effectiveness competencies and those that

make up the occupational standards and are actually assessed for the purposes of National Vocational Qualifications.

The work of the MCI has perhaps achieved as great a prominence within the world of employment in the UK as have NVQs in general – sufficiently so for many managers to believe that "MCI" or "management standards" are separate entities, rather than being one aspect of an overarching state qualifications system. It is all the more ironic, therefore, that this, as one of the most successful aspects of the NVQ approach, was closed down in 2000 by the British Government with no firm idea of what body would replace it, nor any publicity about its actions (Wustemann, 2001).

All in all, though, the differences between the approach pioneered by McClelland and that promoted by the British government could scarcely be greater. Even the terminology is different, with US writers referring to *"competency"* (plural: *"competencies"*) and much UK literature talking about *"competence"* (plural: *"competences"*). Many practitioners have complained about the confusion that this divergence of approach engenders.

Which is better?

In the past, there was considerable debate about the relative merits of the two approaches: the US competencies versus the UK's competences. McClelland's emphasis on superior performance may well strike a chord with business people, who see the introduction of "minimum standards" as beside the point. Some have argued (Holmes and Joyce, 1993) that Boyatzis's distinction between actions and the competencies that produce them is vital if competency is to have any genuine predictive power. Others have pointed out (Elkin, 1991) that McClelland's system leads to a manageable list of competencies, as opposed to the weighty burden of units and elements making up UK standards of competence and NVQs.

On the other hand, there has been a good deal of criticism of the McBer approach, with commentators arguing, for instance, that:

- Boyatzis's definition of a competency is so broad that it can cover almost anything, without getting to the heart of what is common to motives, traits, skills, and so on (Woodruffe, 1991);

- the distinction between competencies and threshold competencies is unclear: in fact, the difference between the two is simply a matter of degree (ibid); and

- because the kind of models produced by McBer are historic (that is, being based on what has been associated with successful performance in the past), they are less suitable for organisations operating in times of rapid change (Iles, 1993).

Others have questioned the value of generic competencies as opposed to specific ones that have the advantage of reflecting particular organisational cultures and language, and which are clearly relevant to those who are expected to use them.

In practice, it seems that many organisations mix and match aspects of the two approaches to meet their own needs. While such pragmatism may be attractive, there are dangers. For instance, consultant Charles Woodruffe has pointed out that an organisation putting together both McClelland-style person-related competencies and NVQ-style job-related competences cannot satisfactorily assess people, because any particular behaviour may be evidence of competencies of both types. "Those making the assessment [can] become confused and double-mark any given behaviour," he says (Woodruffe, 1991).

More recently, occupational psychologist and business adviser Karen Moloney said that the "profusion of competency models emerging [. . .] confuse two totally different concepts: personality characteristics like 'openness' and activities like 'managing a budget' " (Moloney, 2000). Miller, Rankin and Neathey (2001) comment that: "Such lack of differentiation lays this approach open to problems with assessment and, hence, with use and management of the [assessment] system, as well as leading to concerns regarding equal opportunity issues."

Neil Rankin adds: Experts such as Karen Moloney rightly point to the dangers of mindlessly developing competency frameworks that are internally contradictory, or contain competencies that are incapable of fair and consistent assessment. However, from a user's standpoint, much of the debate about *competency* versus *competence*, and the dogmatic insistence on separate spellings and usage, serves to obscure rather than enlighten.

A better approach, I would argue, is to establish the basic principles that are intended to govern the development, use and updating of a competency framework – and stick to them. Foremost among these, I believe, are a commitment to the involvement of employees and managers in the design, implementation and use of the competencies; observance of equal opportunities values; and having a goal of using competencies to realise a real improvement in business performance.

References

Boulter, Nick, Dalziel, Murray and Hill, Jackie eds (1996), *People and competencies: the route to competitive advantage*, second edition, Hay/McBer and Kogan Page.

Boyatzis, Richard E (1982), *The competent manager: a model for effective performance*, McBer and Co/Wiley.

Elkin, Graham (1991), "Competency-based HRD", *Training and Development*, pp.14–18, March.

Evans, Lesley (1995), "The relevance of behavioural skills to national competitiveness", *Competency & Emotional Intelligence Quarterly*, vol. 2 no.3, pp.32–37, Winter 1994/95.

Evans, Lesley and Kerrison, Sue (1994), "MCI personal competence model: uses and implementation", *Research and Development* series, report no.24, Employment Department Learning Methods Branch, October.

Flanagan, J C (1954), "The critical incident technique", *Psychological Bulletin*, vol. 51, pp.327–358.

Holmes, Len and Joyce, Paul (1993),"Rescuing the useful concept of managerial competence: from outcomes back to process", *Personnel Review*, vol. 22, no.6, pp.37–52.

Iles, Paul A (1993), "Achieving strategic coherence in HRD through competence-based management and organization development", *Personnel Review*, vol. 22, no.6, pp.63–80.

Kelly, G A (1955), *The psychology of personal constructs*, Norton.

McClelland, David C (1973), "Testing for competence rather than intelligence", *American Psychologist*, vol. 28.

McClelland, David C (1976), *Guide to behavioural event interviewing*, McBer, 1976.

McClelland, David C and Dailey, C (1972), *Improving officer selection for the foreign service*, McBer and Co.

Miller, Linda, Rankin, Neil and Neathey, Fiona (2001), *Competency frameworks in UK organisations*, Chartered Institute of Personnel and Development.

Moloney, Karen (2000), "Who we are and what we do: thoughts on personality and competence", *Competency & Emotional Intelligence Quarterly*, vol. 7 no.2, pp.36–40, Winter 1999/2000.

Spencer, Lyle M Jr, McClelland, David C and Spencer, Signe M (1994), *Competency assessment methods: history and state of the art*, Hay/McBer Research Press.

Spencer, Lyle M Jr and Spencer, Signe M (1993), *Competence at work: models for superior performance*, Wiley.

Stewart, Valerie and Stewart, Andrew (1977), *Practical performance appraisal: designing, installing and maintaining performance appraisal systems*, Gower.

Stewart, Valerie, Stewart, Andrew and Fonda, Nickie (1981), *Business applications of repertory grid*, McGraw-Hill.

Training Agency (1988), "The definition of competences and performance criteria", guidance note 3 in *The development of assessable standards for national certification* series.

Woodruffe, Charles (1991), "Competent by any other name", *Personnel Management*, pp.30–33, September.

Wustemann, Louis (2001), "Bye bye MCI (and METO too)", *Competency & Emotional Intelligence Quarterly*, vol. 8 no.3, pp.34–35, Spring.

Learning points

Key research methods

- Among the most popular of the more scientific methods of developing behavioural competencies are the critical incident technique, behavioural event interviews and the repertory grid.

- The critical incident technique usually involves asking the job incumbents themselves (or their managers) about critical incidents they have faced. The aim is to gather detailed information about the behaviour of those facing the critical incidents, which can be analysed once all the discussions are complete. After an introduction by the interviewer, the interviewee then briefly describes an incident and, if it looks promising, is asked to go into more detail, with the interviewer skilfully probing and exploring the description. The process is repeated with several more incidents. The interviews are carefully recorded.

- The technique is based on real events provided by interviewees, focusing on critical incidents to highlight key competencies linked to success. The descriptions of the competencies tend to be in the actual language used within the organisation.

- Behavioural event interviews are a variant of the critical incident technique, and give more emphasis to individuals performing jobs than the job itself. In general, a behavioural event interview is carried out in the same way as an interview based on the critical incident technique. However, the need to collect detailed information about individuals' motivation means that the interviews may take longer.

- The technique is claimed to have high levels of accuracy and consistency. However, the interviews are expensive to conduct, transcribe, code and analyse.

- The repertory grid technique aims to draw out people's views and judgments by means of a series of comparisons. The results of these interviews can be analysed in a number of different ways, including drawing up a grid of ratings given by the interviewee.

- The advantages of the technique include its emphasis on real people and events, and uncovering important values. Competencies based on repertory grids are likely to have a high acceptance, and are claimed to be highly accurate. However, the technique is time-consuming to conduct, analyse, interpret and discuss.

Two approaches

- There are two different approaches to competencies, based on US and UK developments with variations in spellings.

- The US approach was pioneered in the late 1960s and early 1970s by David McClelland. Richard Boyatzis set down an explicit definition of the notion of "competency": "An underlying characteristic of an individual which is causally related to effective or superior performance in a job". Competencies can be motives, traits, skills, aspects of one's self-image or social role, or a body of knowledge which one uses.

- Boyatzis placed the concept of competency firmly in the context of effective performance: "effective performance is the attainment of specific results (outcomes) through specific actions while maintaining policies, procedures and conditions of the organisational environment". And a person's competencies allow him or her to perform these actions. A competency is an ability: "A person's set of competencies reflect his or her capability. They are describing what he or she can do, not necessarily what he or she does, nor does all the time, regardless of the situation and setting". Employers in the USA, the UK and worldwide have used the methodology to develop their own competency models.

- McClelland's approach has been largely ignored by the publicly-funded competence movement in the UK. The occupational standards programme funded, and sponsored, by the British Government has had a significant impact – mainly through National Vocational Qualifications (NVQs), which are based on these standards.

- Differences: Where McClelland's approach focuses on people, the standards/NVQ approach stresses the job. Where McClelland's approach is concerned with the behaviour of *superior* performers, occupational standards/NVQs in the UK are made up of elements of competence with performance criteria indicating *minimum* competence levels. Finally, rather than seeing competency as a characteristic that *causes* certain actions, the standards/NVQ approach construes it as "a description of an action, behaviour or *outcome* which the person should be able to demonstrate".

Chapter 4

Making the business case

Introduction

This chapter continues the process of exploring in more detail the themes covered in chapter 1. Among the points that we made there was the desirability of making a demonstrable business case for the introduction and application of competencies. This, we noted, represented the "Holy Grail" of the personnel profession. Here, Stephen Martin and Lionel Laroche draw on their own experience of making such a business case and give a worked example of how competencies' contribution can be measured. Its details will naturally vary from organisation to organisation, and from time to time, but, as they say, "the ability to make a rational case in financial terms represents a powerful 'new' weapon in the armoury of any ambitious personnel management function."

Demonstrating the bottom-line impact of HR: a case study

Stephen Martin and Lionel Laroche

One of the great frustrations for those who work in human resource management is an inability to make an economic case for an investment in it in the terms that make the most impression on those who hold the purse-strings – by showing the impact on the bottom line. Yet the basic methodology for making effective return-on-investment (ROI) calculations to value the impact of personnel management initiatives has been around for some time. Why have personnel practitioners – seemingly themselves convinced of the business justification for investing in personnel management programmes – shied away from using the same kind of analysis that other functions habitually use?

One possible explanation is personnel and training specialists' fear even to make the case in the face of the continuing scepticism of many line managers that investments in human resources contribute appreciably to the financial success of the organisation. Another likely cause is that the personnel profession is not interested in getting involved in such prosaic pounds-and-pence debates; they are content to leave such grubby financial matters to others while they involve themselves in the loftier questions of human development, ethics and diversity. Or is the reason, dare we suggest, that the personnel profession is populated with the innumerate, and the thought of analysing costs and benefits and coming to a mathematical conclusion is just beyond the ken of most of us?

Our view is that the answer lies in a more basic realm, though in a way it is a conclusion that is no less unkind to our profession. It is simply that few personnel managers are aware of the research and the processes that permit rational ROI assessments to be made in the world of personnel management. And, because so few are aware, the method does not get used. Whatever the explanation, it is a serious and missed opportunity. If there is a credibility gap affecting the personnel management function, this is one way to bridge it. It is also an issue that has a huge impact on human performance at work. If we believe that the implementation of best-practice personnel management processes in development, training, performance management, compensation, recruitment and selection and the rest are critical to the performance of organisations, then their absence is a serious restriction on individuals who want to develop and perform at work. Clearly, the ability of the personnel profession to make the case and to win resources in competition with other worthy causes is critical to the perception of the function, and to the credibility of its claims to make a demonstrable difference to human and organisational performance.

The business scenario

The following case study is drawn from a real proposal, offered to the New York-based executive committee of an international financial services organisation. The task was to persuade financially-sophisticated people who were sceptical of the contribution of personnel initiatives that making a significant investment in a major programme of competency analysis and applications in recruitment, development and performance management was worth it to an organisation in a shrinking market sector and facing tough times well into the foreseeable future – just the sort of challenge the average personnel practitioner would relish.

The business scenario was not untypical of those that personnel specialists have to face in many market sectors. The company had grown over a number of years from a standing start into a major player in its sector. It had a strong customer base, and enjoyed effective relationships built on a strong technical foundation for its products. But, as with many such organisations, it faced an uncertain future as its main market had matured and was probably already beyond saturation point. Technical developments in other arenas were now threatening the very rationale on which the company's original product range was built.

The executive committee – prompted by a recent board-level recruit to the corporate services portfolio – was realising that it was ill-equipped to manage through a period of ever-quickening change, and was in danger of failing to match the technical skills, agility, creativity and drive for achievement that some of its own corporate customers were able to demonstrate. For some members, including the chief executive, the need for a drive towards improving the capability of their people was becoming clear. Many, however, remained unconvinced – beyond allowing a modest increase in the technical training budget. The money could be spent on many other things. So how to make the case, and in terms that would win over the sceptics?

The proposition

The proposition was to build and implement competency models – initially for the senior level itself, and later as a broader pilot – across the sales and marketing function. The focus for implementation would be on recruitment and selection, development and succession planning. The rationale for using competencies to underpin these and the other applications to come later was to present an effective model for the capabilities and behaviours that would enable the business to grow and develop in line with its newly defined business strategy.

The organisation had ambition; it was not content to be the biggest player in a shrinking market, through to an inevitable point of oblivion somewhere on a not-too-distant horizon. Clearly, more of the same would not provide a springboard for change. Developing and using exemplar-focused competencies that reflected the strategic needs of the organisation and the development needs of individuals was seen as an effective way to kick-start the change process. The basic information on which the board presentation was constructed was as follows:

The sales and marketing team:

- The function was globally dispersed, with major concentrations in three regional locations. It totalled some 100 staff.

- Salaries varied across regions, but a reasonable average was US$90k plus 50% variable bonus payable for "on-target" performance, generating typical total compensation of around US$135k.

- Staff turnover for the group was around the 20% mark, although actual levels varied between regions.

The senior management team:

- Included the chief executive officer and the team reporting directly to this level, plus selected members of their direct-report teams. In all, the target group numbered 20 individuals.

- All of the senior team was located in either the UK or USA, although many of the group had international responsibilities.

- Succession to the senior group, and development of the senior group itself, were the key management issues identified by the chief executive officer and board members.

The challenge was to show, in financial terms, how an investment in competency analysis and applications could be justified. The organisation was familiar with cost-benefit analysis as a process for assessing prospective and competing technical projects; why should this potential investment be treated any differently? It was a good question, and the answer was that there was no reason why it should be treated differently, other than the traditional reticence of personnel specialists towards using such a methodology.

Cost-benefit analysis

Sales and marketing recruitment

"Elementary laws of statistics predict that the output of a group of workers would form a normal, bell-shaped distribution" (Smith, Gregg and Andrews, 1989). Where research has been conducted, the empirical evidence is that employees' productivity does indeed form a normal bell-shaped distribution curve, the vast majority of whom have been recruited, selected and trained using "traditional" methods. It was a reasonable assumption that this "rule of thumb" applied to the organisation concerned. So, in the case of the 100 or so people working within the sales and marketing teams, there would most likely be a normal distribution of performance. That is, a small proportion of staff would be performing at superior levels, most would be performing around the middle at an acceptable level of performance, and another small group would be at or below the margins of acceptability.

From this, the next reasonable assumption was that the continued use of existing methods of recruitment, training and development would ensure the maintenance of the normal performance distribution curve. With a reported 20% labour turnover rate within the sales and marketing group, there was a high cost associated with maintaining average performance. But the target was to raise performance towards superior levels.

"Superior" performance is defined statistically by researchers as one standard deviation above average performance – roughly the level achieved by the top 10% of staff in a given work situation (Spencer and Spencer, 1993). By identifying the competencies that differentiate superior performance from average performance (that is, those used by the top 10%, and that predict superior performance), the selection and training processes could be refocused to recruit people who possess these competencies or who are capable of developing them quickly. Again, the conclusion of extensive research is that for sales jobs, one standard deviation above the mean is worth 48% to 120% of output (Hunter, Schmidt and Judiesch,1990). For this organisation, the calculation of the cost/benefit for the competencies project for sales and marketing was as follows:

a)   Given an existing labour turnover rate of 20%, there will be 20 new recruits within one year (current staff level of 100).

b) Two of these new recruits are likely to be "superior" performers, based on using existing processes of recruitment (top 10%).

c) The opportunity is then to recruit the remaining 18 people at a superior level, rather than at average or below.

d) Using current actual salary + bonus levels (typically US$135k) as the basis of the calculation*, the following benefit in terms of improved performance would be derived, if the selection process worked perfectly:

$18 \times (\$135k \times 0.48) = \$1,166k.$

e) But it will not work perfectly. So the number has to be discounted by a "degree of imperfection". Research (Boyle, 1988) indicates that the "criterion validity correlation" related to the use of behavioural interviewing as a method of staff selection is 0.48 to 0.61. The middle of this range is 0.545, which we shall use as the "discount" factor. So the calculation continues:

$18 \times (\$135k \times 0.48) = \$1,166k \times 0.545 = \$635k.$

f) So, by using competency-based behavioural interviewing techniques as the basis for selection in sales and marketing, at least as effectively as most other organisations that use it, the company could expect to derive $635k in additional value within one year of implementation – given current levels of labour turnover and total compensation, and the opportunity in the market to achieve it.

g) The basic cost of the competency project for sales and marketing was $130k; these numbers generate a one-year gross ROI of 488%.

This calculation is based on a turnover rate of 20%. More effective recruitment, it is reasonable to assume, would have a positive impact on this relatively high rate, although there may be a range of factors producing the high attrition rate. While less turnover would have a negative impact on the net value of the competency intervention in subsequent years, there would be positive financial impact through reduced recruitment and other costs. These savings are not included here.

Another factor not taken into account in the calculation is the learning curve that the new recruits will have to go through to get up to speed in their new job. Again, while this may be a factor that "discounts" the net value derived from the competency-based recruitment, it is reasonable to assume that more competent recruits will learn and contribute more quickly than the average performers likely to have been recruited through existing methods. Either case is very difficult to quantify; the working assumption is that these two effects discount each other out.

It can also be reasonably argued that not all the benefits will be achieved in the first year, and that at least a two-year realisation is more likely. If performance is ramped up over a two-year period, 25% of the benefits would be generated in the first year, 75% in the second and the full 100% in the third, all other things remaining equal. But all these benefits would in theory be cumulative since there would be the opportunity to replace average and poor performers with top performers – to the point where everyone is a top performer.

Again, it is very difficult to make plausible assumptions about these effects over time. And in the final analysis, even if the numbers in the original calculation exaggerate the impact by a factor of 100% (that is, the calculated value is twice the actual value), it still makes a compelling case.

Cost-benefit analysis

Sales and marketing training

For the other 80 staff in the sales and marketing team who were not new recruits in year one, the issue became one of identifying the impact that competency-based training and development would have on performance. (Other applications, such as performance management and compensation, would also have a positive impact, but are not included in this analysis.) As with the earlier example, the value of moving the whole sales population to "superior performance" is research based. A general and reliable rule of thumb has been developed from extensive analysis that values "one standard deviation" as equivalent to 40% of the compensation paid to that group (cited in Smith, Gregg and Andrews, 1989). In addition, as with recruitment, the implementation of competency-based training would not be perfect. Creditable research indicates that the average effect of competency-based technical and sales training is a positive shift of the performance curve by 0.67 of one standard deviation (Falcone, Edwards and Day, 1986).

Using the same basic process as earlier, the potential impact of implementing competency-based technical and sales training across the whole group (excluding new recruits) was calculated as follows:

80 staff @ average total compensation of US$135k = $10.80m paybill

Value of one standard deviation: $10.8m × 0.4 = $4.32m

"Imperfection discount" factor: $4.32m × 0.67 = $2.89m

So, by successfully applying competency-based technical and sales training and development to the whole group, the company could reasonably expect a positive financial impact to the value of $2.89m within one year of implementation. Even by allowing for a relatively large budget of say $750k to cover the additional costs of training needs analysis, planning and delivery across the group, this still represented a healthy 385% ROI (the actual cost of the project had been accounted for in the earlier calculation). Of course, some of the same timescale and negative discount arguments referred to above could also be made here, counterbalanced by other factors that may produce a positive impact but are also not taken into account. Given that, in many organisations, the minimum required one-year ROI for capital projects is typically in the range of 20% to 40%, such arguments become somewhat academic.

Cost-benefit analysis

The senior management group

Research in the field indicates that there is generally wider variance in performance in senior jobs, due to their greater spans of control and discretion, the longer timescales over which they operate, and the greater degree of complexity involved. This is consistent with the much higher variable compensation usually offered at the senior levels in organisations. It follows that the potential impact of improved performance at this level on the overall performance of the organisation is much greater than at middle and junior levels. However, to avoid the danger of exaggeration, it was prudent to continue to use the "40% rule" for the cost/benefit calculation in respect of the senior group.

Making some assumptions about total compensation at the senior
level, the calculation for the company was as follows:

20 staff at estimated average total compensation of
US$150k: 20 × $150k = $3.0m paybill

Value of one standard deviation: $3.0m x 0.4 = $1.2m

"Imperfection discount" factor: $1.2m x 0.67 = $804k

Against the project cost of $80k, and adding an estimated additional
training and development cost of $250k, this generates a gross ROI
of 243% on successful implementation.

Conclusion

For this organisation, which was making difficult and expensive
investment decisions, evaluating competing proposals and allocating
scarce resources in the real world, with real money, this methodology
proved helpful and, ultimately, convincing. While the procedure
outlined here may not be perfect – and, indeed, we have highlighted
some of the inadequacies of the calculations – it represents a major
step forward in terms of making the case for investment in personnel
management-related programmes. We do of course accept, and
indeed habitually make, the case for serious consideration of
non-financial benefits derived from such projects. But it is difficult
to deny that the ability to make a rational case in financial terms
represents a powerful "new" weapon in the armoury of any
ambitious personnel management function.

Note: * Salary is used rather than "output" because, without
extensive research, it is very difficult in most jobs to establish a
reliable value for the output directly derived from a particular job –
with the notable exception of sales jobs.

References

Boyle, Sean (1988), "Can behavioural interviews produce results?", *Guidance &
Assessment Review*, vol. 4 no.1, February, pp.4–6.

Falcone, A, Edwards, J and Day, R (1986), "Meta-analysis of personnel training
techniques for three populations", presentation to the Academy of Management,
Chicago.

Hunter, J, Schmidt F and Judiesch, M (1990), "Individual differences in output variability as a function of job complexity", *Journal of Applied Psychology*, vol. 75, pp.28–42.

Smith, M, Gregg, M and Andrews, D (1989), *Selection and assessment: a new appraisal*, Pitman.

Spencer, Lyle M and Spencer, Signe M eds. (1993), *Competence at work: models for superior performance*, Wiley.

Learning points

- The methodology for return-on-investment (ROI) calculations to value the impact of personnel management initiatives can be used to produce the same type of financial analysis that is habitually used in other functions within organisations. Failure to use ROI justifications reduces the credibility of personnel specialists and human resource initiatives.

- ROI calculations lend themselves to some forms of competency initiative. The case study here is based on a real-life example, where competencies would form the basis for recruitment, training and succession planning. The rationale for using competencies was to enable the business to grow and develop in line with its newly defined business strategy.

- For competency-based sales and marketing recruitment, the one-year gross ROI was 488%. For their competency-based training, the one-year ROI was 385%. For senior management development within sales and marketing, the one-year ROI was 243%.

- The non-financial benefits of using competencies merit serious consideration, but the ability to make a rational case in financial terms represents a powerful "new" weapon in the armoury of the personnel management function.

Chapter 5

The law

Paul Epstein

Barrister, Cloisters chambers, Temple, London

Equal Pay

Introduction

Sources of the law

This section of the handbook is primarily concerned with the law relating to gender disparity and sex discrimination in pay. The law in this area is unfortunately somewhat complex. The primary piece of legislation is the Equal Pay Act 1970 ("EPA 1970"). It is also governed by the Sex Discrimination Act 1975 ("SDA 1975"). Equal pay is significantly influenced by European legislation. It is governed by Article 141 of the EU Treaty (formerly Article 119) and the Equal Treatment Directive 75/17/EC ("ETD"). Since gender disparity in pay usually occurs where a woman is paid less than a man, references below are to the position of women's pay.

The domestic law of the UK relating to pensions is contained in a mirror scheme to the EPA 1970, and is provided by the Pensions Act 1995 ("PA 1995") and the Occupational Pension Schemes (Equal Treatment) Regulations 1995 SI 1995/3183. Section 62 of PA 1995 provides that "an occupational pension scheme which does not contain an equal treatment rule shall be treated as including one". It further provides that an equal treatment rule has the effect that where a woman is employed on like work with a man, on work rated as equivalent, or on work of equal value, any rule that relates to the terms on which she becomes a member of a pension scheme – or how members of the scheme are treated – is modified so as to be not less favourable than the comparable man's rule. Among other things, the 1995 Regulations make detailed provision for the remedies available to a woman who succeeds on a claim for breach of the equal treatment rule before a court or tribunal.

Although probably of little importance in the field of equal pay, it is worth noting that the SDA 1975 outlaws discrimination on the ground of marital status. Therefore, a married person of either sex who has been discriminated against in relation to pay or contractual terms and conditions may in theory bring a claim under the SDA 1975.

Similarly, where a person is treated less favourably in relation to contractual or non-contractual pay or other terms and conditions on racial grounds, there is no reason why that person may not bring a claim under the Race Relations Act 1976 ("RRA 1976").

Equal Pay Act 1970

In broad terms (discussed in further detail below), the EPA 1970 provides that a woman who unjustifiably has less favourable contractual terms than a man with whom she compares herself is entitled to receive the same contractual terms that he does. In such a case, the EPA 1970 operates by inserting into the woman's contract what is described as an "equality clause". This equality clause has the effect that the woman's contract includes the same contractual terms and conditions as the comparator man's contract. Although the word "pay" is included in the title of the statute, the right to an equality clause conferred on a woman by Section 1 is not limited to "pay"; instead, the EPA 1970 is applicable where a woman has less favourable contractual terms than a man. However, since the EPA 1970 is concerned with contract, non-contractual pay is not covered by it (see further below).

The EPA 1970 is concerned with cases where a woman carries out like work to that of a man, work rated as equivalent to that of a man, or work of equal value to that of a man. Each of these three concepts is discussed in more detail below. The right conferred on a woman by the EPA 1970 means, among other things, that a woman is entitled to equal pay where she and a man are doing the same work for unequal pay. The right also applies where they are performing different jobs, but where the work that they perform is of equal value. This is of particular importance where there is job segregation, that is, where certain jobs are predominantly carried out by women, and other jobs are predominantly carried out by men.

European legislation

Article 141 of the EU Treaty may also be relied on by a woman claiming equal pay. This Article is one of the pieces of European legislation that is described as being of direct effect, that is, it confers rights on a woman against a private employer as well as against a public one. Article 141 seeks to ensure that "the principle of equal pay for male and female workers for equal work or work of equal value is applied", and that there is "equal pay without discrimination based on sex". The advantage to a woman relying on Article 141 is that the definition of "pay" is broader than the right conferred by the EPA 1970.

The ETD was adopted on 10 February 1975. Its purpose is to amplify and clarify the protection offered to women who do not receive equal pay. Article 1 of the ETD states that "the principle of equal pay for men and women outlined in Article [141] of the Treaty, hereinafter called 'principle of equal pay', means, for the same work or to work for which equal value is attributed, the elimination of all discrimination on grounds of sex with regard to all aspects and conditions of remuneration".

An EU Directive, such as the ETD, may only in principle have vertical effect, as opposed to horizontal effect. Vertical effect means that, if certain conditions are satisfied, a Directive may be relied on by an individual as conferring rights against a public employer, but not against a private employer. Where those conditions exist, a Directive is said to have vertical direct effect. The Court of Appeal in the case of *Preston and Others v Wolverhampton Healthcare NHS Trust and Others* [1997] IRLR 233 (in a case which has subsequently been to the House of Lords on two occasions, and then to the European Court of Justice ("ECJ")) held that the ETD does not have direct effect. However, whether it does or does not have direct effect, a woman may rely on the EDT as a guide to the meaning and effect of Article 141.

The European legislation should be read in the light of the decisions of the ECJ. The ECJ is the Court of the EU to which questions may be referred by national courts on the meanings of Article 141 and the ETD.

Relationship between domestic and European legislation

Section 1 of the EPA 1970 is concerned with the ' "terms' (whether concerned with pay or not) of a contract under which a woman is employed ('the woman's contract').)" Therefore, the EPA 1970 on its face appears to be concerned with the terms under which a woman *is* employed and not to what happens *after* she ceases to be employed. However, Article 141 has been held to apply to post-termination employee benefits (see the section on pay below).

Where the issue is possible sex discrimination in relation to a non-contractual benefit, such as a discretionary non-contractual bonus, a woman may bring a complaint under the SDA 1975, rather than under the EPA 1970.

Equally, where a woman complains that she is receiving unfavourable terms and conditions of a contract based on her sex, but is unable to identify a male comparator, a claim may be brought under the SDA 1975, rather than the EPA 1970. The reason is that the EPA 1970 requires a comparator man to be identified.

Equal Opportunities Commission and its Code of Practice

The Equal Opportunities Commission ("EOC"), was established under the SDA 1975 to work towards the elimination of discrimination, to promote equality of opportunity between men and women generally, and to keep under review the working of the EPA 1970. The EOC issued a Code of Practice on equal pay which was brought into force on 26 March 1997. By Section 56A(10) of the SDA 1975, a failure on the part of any person to observe any provision of the Code of Practice does not of itself render him or her liable to proceedings, but the Code of Practice, and any breach of it, is admissible in evidence in proceedings under the EPA 1970 and the SDA 1975. In large measure, the Code of Practice is directed towards encouraging employers to review pay systems for sex bias, and providing a framework for doing this. On 22 January 2001, the Equal Pay Task Force, set up by the EOC, provided a report called "Just Pay" indicating that very few employers had carried out a review of pay systems for sex bias.

Checklist 3. Fact-finding about competencies and the law

It is vital that competencies are carefully designed and introduced to ensure equality of opportunity. However, their day-to-day application may introduce, or magnify, unfair discrimination, and this can only be detected through effective monitoring practices. This checklist highlights some of the areas where problems might occur, and further investigation undertaken. The text of chapter 5 provides more details, particularly about differences in treatment allowed under the law.

- Where competency-related pay is used:

    1. Do men and women receive equal reward, in terms of pay, bonuses and employee benefits, in cases where their jobs are the same, rated as equivalent or of equal value?

    2. Do married versus unmarried people receive equal reward?

    3. Do members of different ethnic groups receive equal reward?

    4. Where only part of the workforce is covered by competency-related pay, do those not covered by it receive equal reward, as in (1) above? (eg part-timers versus full-timers; grades where women predominate versus grades where men predominate).

- Where competencies are used as part of the decisions about who is recruited, who is promoted, who receives training and development, who is dismissed, made redundant, and so on:

    5. Do these decisions operate so that men and women receive equal terms and conditions, and equal treatment?

    6. Similarly, do married versus unmarried people receive equal terms and conditions, and equal treatment?

    7. Similarly, do members of different ethnic groups receive equal terms and conditions, and equal treatment?

- Where competencies are used as part of the grading system or job-evaluation system:

    8. What types of competencies are used in the system: technical (ie job-related/hard) and/or behavioural (ie personal/soft)? If the latter solely are used, how are they to be defended as "analytical" and/or "objective"?

    9. Can the scheme be defended as having been applied fairly and consistently?

- The weight attached to competencies:

    10. How important are competencies in making any of the personnel decisions covered by 1–7 above? Currently, under sex discrimination law, even competencies that are

merely "taken into account" are covered. However, on or before July 2003, such decisions will be covered by race discrimination law as well.

- Individuals with disabilities:

    11. Does the use of competencies in reward, recruitment or any other personnel decision operate so that individuals with disabilities receive less favourable treatment?

    12. Have "reasonable adjustments" been made to personnel processes involved in these decisions? The types of competencies, their definitions and assessment may be covered by this legal requirement, as well as access to premises, etc.

- Age:

    The UK's legal protection against discrimination must be extended to cover age by December 2006:

    13. Will personnel decisions that take competencies "into account" show evidence of age discrimination?

Relationship between competencies and equal pay

There can be a complex relationship between, on the one hand, the use of competencies to assist in recruitment and retention of staff and in awards of pay and benefits, and, on the other hand, the law relating to equal pay. Equal pay legislation is concerned with whether a woman is being treated less favourably than a man in the same employment in relation to their jobs; it therefore focuses on the work being carried out. For example, in an equal value case, it focuses on the work of the woman and the man "in terms of the demands made on her (for instance under such headings as effort, skill and decision)" (Section 1(2)(c) of the EPA 1970). Accordingly, the legislation is not concerned with behavioural or emotional intelligence-type competencies; instead it focuses on technical/functional competences of the job-related kind.

What is "pay"?

For the sake of convenience, reference is made in this chapter to "pay" as a shorthand for the rights conferred by domestic and European legislation. Pay is not merely wages or salary. Potentially, it can cover a large part or all of the remuneration packages offered by employers, such as bonuses, overtime, performance-related pay, pensions, health insurance, cars and training. Some specific examples are referred to below.

It is important to appreciate that when a woman complains of not receiving equal pay, she is entitled to look at each individual component of her remuneration package, and compare it with a comparable part of the comparator man's package. This means that the comparison exercise being carried out is not an evaluation of the packages of the woman and the man as a whole. This was decided by *Jämställdhetsombudsmannen v Örebro Läns Landsting* [2000] IRLR 421 ECJ. In that case, a woman received a lower salary than her comparator man, although she received an inconvenient-hours supplement that he did not. The ECJ decided that that supplement was not to be taken into account when deciding whether or not there was equal pay.

Article 141 is not limited to contractual pay; it is defined to mean "the ordinary basic or minimum wage or salary and any other consideration, whether in cash or in kind, which the worker receives directly or indirectly, in respect of his employment, from his employer".

In *Garland v British Rail Engineering Limited* [1982] IRLR 111 [1982] ECR 359, the ECJ held that Article 141 applied to a non-financial benefit offered after retirement, such as a travel concession.

In *Lewen v Denda* [2000] IRLR 67, the ECJ held that a Christmas bonus comes within the meaning of "pay", even if it is paid voluntarily by the employer, and even if it is paid mainly or exclusively as an incentive for future work or loyalty to the business, or both.

In the leading case of *Barber v Guardian Royal Exchange Assurance Group* [1990] IRLR 240, [1990] ICR 616, the ECJ held that (i) the benefits paid by an employer to a worker in connection with his or her compulsory redundancy are within the scope of Article 141, whether they are paid under a contract of employment, by virtue of legislative provisions, or on a voluntary basis, and (ii) a pension paid under a contracted-out private occupational scheme falls within the scope of Article 141.

The law

Pay under Article 141 was held by the ECJ in *R v Secretary of State for Employment ex parte Seymour-Smith and Perez* [1999] IRLR 253, [1999] ICR 447, to include compensation for unfair dismissal, in the course of a challenge to the validity of what was then the two-year qualifying period in the UK for claims for unfair dismissal.

Equal treatment for men and women in same employment

Under Section 1 of the EPA 1970, a woman may bring a claim for equal pay where she is employed on like work with a man, on work rated as equivalent with that of a man, or on work of equal value to that of a man, *in the same employment.* Section 1(6) goes on to define that as follows: "Men shall be treated as in the same employment with a woman if they are men employed by her employer or any associated employer at the same establishment or at establishments in Great Britain which include that one and at which common terms and conditions of employment are observed, either generally or for employees of the relevant classes." Section 1(6)(c) provides that "two employers are to be treated as associated if one is a company of which the other (directly or indirectly) has control, or if both are companies of which a third person (directly or indirectly) has control."

An important question is when a woman may compare her pay with that of a man in an organisation where work has been subcontracted, there are franchises or joint ventureships, or where employment-agency staff are used. This question is likely to gain in importance in a climate of contracting out and/or job segregation between the sexes.

In *Lawrence v Regent Office Care Ltd* [2000] IRLR 608, the applicant women were carrying out catering duties, having been transferred to a private company, following a contracting out by a local authority. In that case, they sought to compare the terms of their employment with men still employed by the local authority. The Court of Appeal referred to the ECJ two questions, namely (i) whether Article 141 was directly applicable, so as to permit the women to compare their pay with that of men employed by the local authority performing work of equal value to that done by them; and (ii) whether an applicant who seeks to place reliance on the direct effect of Article 141 may do so only if the current employer is in a position where it is able to explain why the employer of the chosen comparator pays its employees as it does. It is therefore hoped that the ECJ will resolve these questions.

In the more straightforward comparisons under Section 1(6), that concern common terms and conditions of employment, (i) does not require that a comparator must be employed at the same establishment as the woman; (ii) however, there must be a comparison between the establishment at which the woman is employed and at which the comparator man is employed, and common terms and conditions must be observed generally at the establishment or establishments, or for employees of the relevant classes to which the woman and the man belong.

Employed/self-employed

The protection conferred by the EPA 1970 applies to a woman "employed" by the employer. Section 1(6) provides that " 'employed' means employed under a contract of service or of apprenticeship or a contract personally to execute any work or labour". Therefore, it provides protection to a person who is an employee. One issue that arises is whether or not it confers protection on a person employed under a contract for services. The answer is that where that person is employed under "a contract personally to execute any work or labour", the EPA 1970 applies. In other words, it may well apply to a self-employed person, depending on the terms of her contract. It will exclude those who are retained by an employer to provide services, where those services are not required to be provided personally by any one or more individuals.

"Like work"

The definition of "like work" is found in Section 1(4) of the EPA 1970. It provides that "a woman is to be regarded as employed on like work with men if, but only if, her work and theirs is of the same or a broadly similar nature, and the differences (if any) between the things she does and the things they do are not of practical importance in relation to terms and conditions of employment; and, accordingly, in comparing her work with theirs, regard shall be had to the frequency or otherwise with which any such differences occur in practice as well as to the nature and extent of the differences".

Consideration by an employment tribunal ("ET") of like work is a two-stage process (see the leading case of *Capper Pass Ltd v Lawton* [1976] IRLR 366, [1977] ICR 83, EAT). At the first stage, the ET has to make a broad judgment, whether the work is "like work". The ET should not undertake too minute or pedantic an examination, and should not be constrained to find that work is not like work merely because of insubstantial differences. In order to be like work, the work need not be of the same nature, it need only be broadly similar. There is therefore a general consideration of the type of work involved and the skill and knowledge required to do it. At the second stage, if the work is of a broadly similar nature, it is then necessary to go on to consider the detail, and enquire whether the differences between the work being compared are of "practical importance in relation to terms and conditions of employment". Once it is determined that work is of a broadly similar nature, it should be regarded as being like work unless the differences are plainly of a kind that the ET in its experience would expect to find reflected in the terms and conditions of employment. Trivial differences, or differences not likely in the real world to be reflected in terms and conditions of employment, ought to be disregarded.

So far as differences of practical importance are concerned, the comparison required by Section 1(4) of the EPA 1970 is to be made not between the contractual obligations of the man on the one hand and the woman on the other, but between the things that each actually does and the frequency with which they are done – see *E Coomes (Holdings) Ltd v Shields* [1978] IRLR 263 CA, [1978] ICR 1159.

According to *Electrolux Ltd v Hutchinson* [1976] IRLR 410 EAT, [1977] ICR 252, for differences in contractual obligations to amount to differences of practical importance, it must be shown that the different duties are done to some significant extent. Another way of looking at the matter is to ask whether differences in the things done by a man and those done by a woman (which, since this is stage two of the analysis, are not sufficient to make the work not of the same or a broadly similar nature), are such as to put the two employments into different categories or grades in an evaluation study.

Although they are of perhaps limited use in illustrating points of principle, the cases nevertheless show the view taken by ETs of whether differences amount to differences of practical importance. For example, in *British Leyland (UK) Limited v Powell* [1978] IRLR

57, EAT, Mrs Powell was employed as a van driver in the company's catering section. She claimed equal pay with another driver, Mr Heath, who was also employed in the catering section. The only difference in their duties was that occasionally Mr Heath was required to drive on public roads, while all Mrs Powell's driving was on the factory premises. The EAT upheld the ET decision that this was not a difference of practical importance. In *Dugdale v Kraft Foods Limited* [1976] IRLR 204 (reversed on other grounds [1977] 1 AER 454, EAT [1977] ICR 48), the female applicants were employed in the company's quality-control department on different jobs and on different rates of pay to their male comparators. The company claimed that this was unequal work, since the men had to work different hours, including night shifts and Sunday overtime, the men lifted heavier weights, and had to test samples of bulk mixes. The ET held that these were not differences of practical importance. However, in *Thomas and others v National Coal Board* [1987] IRLR 451, the EAT upheld an ET decision that there was a difference of practical importance between female canteen assistants working on days, and a male canteen attendant working on nights, since nights involved extra and different duties for the male canteen attendant.

Work rated as equivalent

The definition of work rated as equivalent is contained in Section 1(5) of the EPA 1970: "A woman is to be regarded as employed on work rated as equivalent with that of any men if, but only if, her job and their job have been given an equal value, in terms of the demand made on a worker under various headings (for instance effort, skill, decision), on a study undertaken with a view to evaluating in those terms the jobs to be done by all or any of the employees in an undertaking or group of undertakings, or would have been given an equal value but for the evaluation being made on a system setting different values for men and women on the same demand under any heading."

Accordingly, for a job evaluation study ("JES") to satisfy the requirements of Section 1(5) EPA 1970, it must relate to the job of the woman and the man comparator, and the demands made on them under various headings. This is very different to considering the worker according to his or her behavioural or emotional-intelligence competencies. Instead, it focuses on functional competences.

One question that arises is the type of JES that is necessary to satisfy the requirements of Section 1(5). It is immediately apparent that the section itself does not dictate the way in which the JES should be constructed or carried out. The main types of JES are referred to by the EAT in *Eaton Limited v Nuttall* [1977] IRLR 71, [1977] ICR 272. Reference ought to be made to the appendix to that decision by readers requiring full details. However, the main approaches to job evaluation are job ranking, paired comparisons, job classification, points assessment and factor comparison.

A commonly used system is points assessment. In a points assessment JES, each job and its comparator job or jobs are analysed under separate headings for the demands made on the jobholder, for example in relation to effort, skill or decision. Each heading has a maximum number of points available to it. The appropriate number of points are then allocated to each job under each heading. Sometimes, this method weights the factors by allocating the points, and then using a multiplier for each relevant heading, so to increase the importance of that heading in the overall points assessment. When the points for each job have been totalled, a "banding" decision is often made, according to which jobs within a band of a certain number of points are allocated to the same grade, for example, 100 to 110 would be allocated to Grade 1, 111 to 120 Grade 2, and so on.

Where there is a valid JES, and that JES rates the jobs as equivalent or does not rate the jobs as equivalent, the JES will normally be taken as conclusive by the ET. What then are the grounds on which a JES may be attacked? The first ground is that the JES is not an "analytical" study. Although this word does not appear in the statute, the Court of Appeal ("CA") in *Bromley v H & J Quick Limited* [1988] IRLR 249, [1988] ICR 623 held that the use of the word "analytical" is not a gloss on the statutory provisions; it indicates conveniently the general nature of what is required, namely that the jobs of each worker covered by the study must have been valued in terms of the demand made on the worker under various headings. It held that it is not enough that benchmark jobs had been evaluated on a factor-demand basis as required by Section 1(5) if the jobs of the applicants and their comparators were not.

Second, a JES may be successfully attacked if it is not objectively constructed or applied. For example, a JES may be constructed so as to include headings or extra headings in relation to demands traditionally associated with male jobs, and have fewer headings, or exclude headings altogether, in relation to demands made in traditionally female jobs. Therefore, by way of illustration, if a female nurse were to be comparing herself to a male janitor employed in the same establishment, an unobjective JES might exclude factor headings for demands such as sensitivity, and relationships with non-colleagues. Nevertheless, where jobs on an objective view make different demands, for example where a job makes physical demands of a man, it is appropriate for that heading to be included in the JES, see *Rummler v Dato-Druck GmbH* [1987] IRLR 32, ECJ, [1987] ICR 774. In addition, even where a JES is objectively constructed, the result of the JES may not be valid where those applying the JES wrongly allocate marks as between the woman and her comparator(s). This presents a further ground on which a JES may be attacked.

Sometimes, an employer has carried out an exercise with a JES but not implemented it. It may for example not have altered the grading or pay structure, which it should have done if it were to follow the results of the JES. May a woman whose work has been rated as equivalent with that of a man, who is on more favourable terms and conditions, rely on that JES for the purposes of a claim under Section 1(2)(b)(i) EPA 1970? This is not an easy question since that sub-paragraph refers to "any term of the woman's contract *determined by the rating of the work*", but a JES does not determine the terms of a woman's contract, it is the employer that makes the determination. There are two difficult and apparently irreconcilable decisions on this point. The leading case is *O'Brien v Sim-Chem Limited* [1980] IRLR 373, HL, [1980] ICR 573. The House of Lords ("HL") wrestled with the meaning of these words. Ultimately, the leading judge said of the words "this beats me", and the HL held that where a JES exercise has been carried out in cooperation with the employer's recognised trade unions, it is a valid JES for the purposes of the EPA 1970. By contrast, the EAT in *Arnold v Beecham Group Limited* [1982] IRLR 307, [1982] ICR 774 held that although a JES may bind an employer before an employer has implemented it, nevertheless it is not a JES for the purposes of the Act if the employer has not accepted its validity. On the facts of that case, the EAT held that the employer and the trade unions had accepted the JES as valid, and therefore it bound the employer.

It follows that the view of the EAT was that before there is a valid JES the parties must have accepted it as a study. This begs the question of the position where an employer carries out a JES without the agreement of the employees or unions. The case of *Dibro Limited v Hore* [1990] IRLR 129, EAT, [1990] ICR 370 shows that such a JES may be valid for the purposes of the EPA 1970.

Work of equal value

The third way a woman may bring an equal pay claim is to show that she is performing work of equal value. This is an alternative to claims of like work or work rated as equivalent. It may not be brought as an additional claim. The reason is that Section 1(2)(c) EPA 1970 provides that there may be an equal value claim "where a woman is employed on work which, *not being work in relation to which paragraph (a) or (b) above applies* [i.e. like work, or work rated as equivalent], is, in terms of the demands made on her, for instance under such headings as effort, skill and decision, of equal value to that of a man in the same employment".

Accordingly, the way in which a woman may successfully present a claim under this part of the legislation is by showing the work that she carries out is of equal value to that of a man, having regard to the demands made on her by her work and those made on her comparator by his work. In order to do this, a JES will be required, which commonly will be on a points assessment, as described above.

Nevertheless, the current procedure for bringing an equal value claim is perplexing in the extreme. There are special ET rules of procedure that apply to equal value claims, known as the "complementary rules of procedure". Typically, and unfortunately for both employees and employers, a case may take many years before completion. As the Equal Pay Task Force said in *Just pay*, in relation to equal pay generally, "bringing cases takes too long, requires too many hearings and is too expensive" (paragraph 4.8). In March 2001, Sir Andrew Leggatt reported on his review of tribunals, including ETs. The Government published this on 16 August 2001 and has issued a consultation paper on the report. It is to be expected that there will be changes to the procedure for equal pay claims. At the time of going to press, the most recent amendments to equal-pay-claims procedures are contained in the Employment Tribunals (Constitution and Rules of Procedure) Regulations 2001 SI 2001 No.1171, which came into force on 16 July 2001 (although originally anticipated to come into force on 18 April 2001). The amendments to the Equal Value ET Rules are contained largely in Schedule 3.

The first step for an ET concerned with a claim involving equal value is, except in cases where it is satisfied that there are no reasonable grounds for determining the question in the affirmative, to determine whether to require an expert to prepare a report on the claim (Rule 10A(i)). This means that, at the first stage, the employer has an opportunity to mount an attack using a "no-reasonable-grounds" defence, and seek to have the matter struck out.

If there is no such attack, or if such an attack is unsuccessful, the ET may then go on to require an independent expert to prepare a report. That report will compare the reference job against the comparator job or jobs. Depending on the number of comparisons that are required to be made, it may be a lengthy process. There are detailed ET rules concerned with the way in which the expert is required to prepare the report, and the supervisory control that the ET has over him or her.

Where an ET has required an independent expert to prepare a report, and such a report has been prepared, there will then be a hearing to determine the question of equal value. At that hearing, any party may make an application for the independent expert to attend for cross-examination on the contents of the report and any other relevant matters. There is limited scope for cross-examining the expert on matters of fact, see Rules 11(2C), (2D) and 10A(19). There is a similar limitation on the ability of the parties to call their own non-expert witnesses on questions of fact.

At any time after the ET has received the report of the expert, any party may, on giving reasonable notice to the ET and any other parties, call one expert witness. That witness may be cross-examined by any other party.

There are various reasons why an ET may not refer an equal value claim to an independent expert. One is where, at a preliminary stage, it holds that there are no reasonable grounds for concluding that an equal value claim would be made out (see above). The second is where the employer runs a defence that there is in existence a JES that has rated the jobs of the woman and her comparator(s) as not being equivalent. The reason is that Section 2A(ii) EPA 1970 provides that "there shall be taken . . . to be no reasonable grounds for determining that the work of a woman is of equal value as mentioned in Section 1(2)(c) above if (a) that work and the work of the man in question have been given different values on a study such as is mentioned in Section 1(5) above; and (b) there are no reasonable grounds for determining that the evaluation contained in the study was . . . made on a system which discriminates on grounds of sex". It follows that an applicant may resist that defence by attempting to demonstrate that the JES was not a valid JES, being one that discriminated in its construction or application; alternatively, that the JES was not accepted as valid by the employer. A further reason is that an employer may persuade the ET that even if the jobs were to be found to be of equal value, there is such a good genuine material factor defence (see below), that it would be inappropriate to appoint an independent expert to prepare a report. The ET has discretion whether or not to allow such an application.

If no independent expert's report is ordered by the ET, and if the claim is not dismissed on the basis of no reasonable grounds, the ET will go on to consider the merits of the claim at a hearing on the basis of the evidence before it, including any expert evidence adduced on behalf of the parties.

Genuine material factor defence

There is a defence to an equal pay claim provided by Section 1(3) EPA 1970, that states that "an equality clause shall not operate in relation to a variation between the woman's contract and the man's contract if the employer proves that a variation is genuinely due to a material factor which is not the difference of sex and that factor – (a) in the case of an equality clause falling within sub-section (2)(a) or (b) above, must be a material difference between the woman's case and the man's; and (b) in the case of an equality clause falling within sub-section (2)(c) above, may be such a material difference". This is commonly known as the genuine material factor defence.

Nevertheless, there has been recent uncertainty about the precise circumstances in which the employer is required to prove a genuine material factor defence. Will the employer be required to make out such a defence to defeat a claim where a woman shows that, for whatever reason, there is an unequal pay, or only in a case where a woman shows that the unequal pay is tainted by discrimination on the grounds of sex? The HL has decided that it is the latter. In *Glasgow City Council v Marshall* [2000] IRLR 272, the applicants, seven women and one man, brought equal pay claims comparing their work to that of teachers of the opposite sex. The employers argued that the difference in pay was due to the different collective bargaining structures. They also referred to statistics showing the breakdown of sex by relevant employees and relied on the absence of sex discrimination. The applicants did not challenge the absence of sex discrimination. The ET accepted that there was no sex discrimination but held that the employers had failed to establish a Section 1(3) defence. The HL held that the ET had erred, and that there was no requirement for an employer to demonstrate a good and sufficient reason for the variation within Section 1(3) where the absence of sex discrimination had been demonstrated. The scheme of the EPA 1970 is that a rebuttal presumption of sex discrimination arises once gender-based comparisons show that a woman, doing like work or work rated as equivalent or work of equal value to that of a man, is being paid or treated less favourably than the man. The variation is presumed to be due to the difference of sex; the burden passes to the employer to show that the explanation for the variation is not tainted by discrimination on grounds of sex. In that latter case, the employer must show that the proffered explanation or reason is genuine and not a sham or pretence; that the less favourable treatment has been caused by this reason; that the reason is not the difference in sex; and, finally, that the difference is a significant and relevant difference between the woman's case and the man's case.

There are numerous illustrations of reasons that may amount to a genuine material factor defence. They include market forces: *Rainey v Greater Glasgow Health Board Eastern District* [1987] IRLR 26, HL [1987] ICR 129; financial constraints: *Benveniste v University of Southampton* [1989] IRLR 122, CA; the difficulty of attracting night workers: *Kerr v Lister & Co Ltd* [1977] IRLR 259, EAT; the woman and the comparator(s) being on a different salary scale: *Waddington v Leicester Council for Voluntary Services* [1977] IRLR 32, EAT (though see further below if any such salary scale is itself tainted by discrimination); grade or salary protection: *Snoxell and Davies v Vauxhall Motors Ltd* [1978] 1 QB 11, EAT (though the defence failed in that case), *Farthing v MOD* [1980] IRLR 402, CA; administrative convenience: *Barry v Midland Bank plc* [1998] IRLR 138, CA; location: *Navy, Army and Air Force Institutes v Varley* [1976] IRLR 408, EAT, and hours of work (though there cannot be discrimination against part-time workers, see below): *Leverton v Clwyd County Council* [1989] IRLR 28, HL.

Although the range of matters that may be considered as genuine material factor defences is wide, if the defence is to succeed the factors must themselves not be tainted by discrimination on the grounds of sex. Thus, there will be an examination of how the underlying reason for the different treatment itself came about. Therefore, although an agreement made in a collective bargain may amount to a Section 1(3) defence, it will not do so where the collective agreement itself is tainted on grounds of sex. In *Barber v NCR (Manufacturing) Ltd* [1993] IRLR 95, EAT, it was held that the collective agreement, on which the different treatment was based, did not justify a finding that that difference was genuinely due to a material factor other than sex. Similar consideration will apply in relation to market forces, financial constraints, salary scales, or any of the other reasons that may be accepted in principle as genuine material factor defences.

Remedies

A woman who succeeds in a claim for equal pay may obtain a declaration as to the terms of her contract, and an award of arrears of remuneration or damages. Although Section 2(5) EPA provides that a woman may only bring a claim for arrears of remuneration or damages for a period no earlier than two years before the date on which the proceedings were begun, the ECJ in *Preston* [2000] IRLR 506 held that the two-year backdating limitation was contrary to community law. When the House of Lords reconsidered the case, it decided that the part-time employees seeking access to the occupational pension scheme could bring claims backdated to the beginning of their employment or 8 April 1976, whichever was the later [2001] IRLR 237.

Discrimination

Introduction

Discrimination on the grounds of race, sex, marital status and disability is in general unlawful. Race discrimination is outlawed by the Race Relations Act 1976 ("RRA 1976"). Sex discrimination and discrimination on the grounds of marital status are outlawed by the SDA 1975. Unlawful disability discrimination is outlawed by the Disability Discrimination Act 1995 ("DDA").

In general terms, the employment anti-discrimination provisions in the RRA 1976 and SDA 1975 follow an identical approach. (an important recent difference is that amendments have been made to the SDA 1975 as a result of certain European legislation; see further details below). It has also been held in a number of cases that the RRA 1976 and the SDA 1975 should be interpreted as part of the same legislative provisions outlawing race and sex discrimination. This means that cases interpreting provisions in one Act are authority on the interpretation of the same provisions in the other Act. However, the DDA is not part of the same legislative framework, and its provisions are not to be construed identically with those of the RRA 1976 or the SDA 1975.

Race discrimination

As regards existing employees, it is unlawful for an employer to discriminate on racial grounds against an employee:

- in respect of the employee's terms of employment;

- in the way in which the employer affords him or her access to opportunities for promotion, or to any other benefits, facilities or services, or by refusing or deliberately omitting to afford him access to them;

- by dismissing him or her; or

- by subjecting him or her to any other detriment.

(see RRA 1976 section 4(2)).

As regards candidates for employment, it is unlawful for an employer to discriminate against another person:

- in the arrangements that it makes for the purpose of determining who should be offered that employment; or

- in the terms on which it offers an individual that employment; or

- by refusing or deliberately omitting to offer him or her that employment.

(see RRA 1976, section 4(1)).

What is discrimination?

There are two principal kinds of discrimination: direct and indirect.

Meaning of direct discrimination

This occurs where an employer on racial grounds treats an employee less favourably than it treats or would treat others. Therefore, if, for example, an existing employee is the subject of racist taunts on the grounds of his or her race, that is direct discrimination. Similarly, if an instruction is given that people of a particular ethnic group are to receive less favourable terms and conditions, again that is direct race discrimination.

Meaning of indirect discrimination

The technical definition of indirect discrimination is contained in Section 1(1)(b), which provides that there is indirect discrimination where an employer applies to an individual "a requirement or condition which he applies or would apply equally to persons not of the same racial group as that other but – (i) which is such that the proportion of persons of the same racial group as that other who can comply with it is considerably smaller than the proportions not of that racial group who can comply with it; and (ii) which he cannot show to be justifiable irrespective of the colour, race, nationality or ethnic or national origins of the person to whom it is applied; and (iii) which is to the detriment of that other because he cannot comply with it".

Accordingly, there is unlawful indirect race discrimination where the following elements are present:

- a requirement or condition;

- the proportion of people from one racial group who can comply with that requirement or condition is "considerably smaller" than a comparator individual or group;

- that requirement is not justifiable; and

- the person complaining of race discrimination cannot comply with the requirement.

In other words, indirect race discrimination may occur where an employer applies an apparently neutral term to employees, but which is such that it has a disproportionately adverse impact on one or more individuals of a particular racial group.

An example will help to explain the operation of the concept of indirect discrimination. An employer may impose on its workforce, as a term of employment, that employees attain a certain level of educational qualification. That will be a requirement or condition of continued employment with the employer. It may be that the requirement or condition in question has a significant adverse impact on certain racial groups, because they do not possess that qualification. If the numbers who can comply with that requirement are considerably smaller than the comparators, it will then be for the employer to show that the requirement is justifiable. The employer will need to do that by relying on objective factors. If it is unable to do so, this will amount to unlawful indirect discrimination.

Meaning of "racial grounds"

The "racial grounds" on which an employer must not discriminate are "colour, race, nationality or ethnic or national origins". Similarly, the "racial group" in relation to indirect discrimination is a group of persons defined by reference to colour, race, nationality or ethnic or national origins.

Requirement or condition

It is important to note that indirect discrimination will only take place where a "requirement or condition" has been applied to the employee concerned. A requirement or condition is a "must", "something which has to be complied with": see the Court of Appeal's judgment in *Perera v Civil Service Commission* [1983] IRLR 166. In other words, if it is still possible under an employer's procedures for an employee to achieve promotion, for example, despite lacking a particular specified quality, the specified quality will not be a requirement or condition. (Note that, from 12 October 2001, in order for a claim of indirect *sex* discrimination to succeed, it is not necessary to demonstrate that a requirement or condition has been applied; instead, it will only be necessary to show that there has been the application of a provision, criterion or practice.)

Therefore, factors that are merely "taken into account" in relation to selection for employment or promotion will not be requirements or conditions. Such factors taken into account might include, for example, an ability to communicate in English, intellectual capacity and potential, maturity, commonsense and an ability to get on with people: see the *Perera* case.

In order to ensure that competencies do not constitute indirect discrimination, it is desirable that an employer's procedures make clear that the competencies are merely factors that will be "taken into account" in assessing employees and do not represent factors that the employee must have in order to obtain employment, for example. Nevertheless, caution must be exercised here, since, following the introduction of the changed conditions for indirect sex discrimination, these same factors, even if not a must-have – and, therefore unlikely to allow a complaint of indirect race discrimination to succeed – may nevertheless amount to a provision, criterion or practice that may enable a complaint of indirect sex discrimination to be upheld.

Significant adverse impact

To use the words in the legislation, there may be indirect race discrimination where a "considerably smaller" proportion of individuals of a particular racial group can comply with the requirement or condition than the comparator individual or group. This in itself raises two significant questions. The first is who are the people who ought to be considered when deciding whether or not the application of the requirement or condition has the objectionable consequences? Commonly, this is referred to as the "pool". In other words, this is the pool of people who are considered for the purposes of determining the effect of the requirement or condition. The second question is what is meant by a "considerably smaller" proportion, and what figures ought to be analysed to decide this?

It has been said in legal rulings that the pool ought to be decided by looking at the most appropriate group of individuals to whom the alleged requirement or condition applies. Therefore, to take an illustration, if a 24-hour three-week rotating shift pattern were to be applied to all those working on production in a particular factory, the requirement or condition of continued employment is to work the shift pattern; the pool of individuals to whom that requirement or condition is applied could be considered as those individuals currently employed by the employer on that production.

However, the choice of pool is often a highly contentious matter between a complainant and a respondent. The reason is that the choice of pool will often significantly affect the analysis of the impact of the requirement or condition. For example, a complainant might legitimately wish to argue that it is artificial merely to look at those employees currently employed by the employer, since it is a self-selecting group who have an atypically high ability to comply with the shift pattern, and excludes those who either were unsuccessful in job applications, or failed to apply. In that case, a complainant might contend that the appropriate pool for consideration of the requirement or condition is a national pool, and seek to rely on national statistics collected or analysed by the Office for National Statistics, or other research bodies.

The most recent word in the Court of Appeal on the choice of pool is *Allonby v Accrington and Rossendale College* [2001] IRLR 364, which holds that the identification of the pool is a matter of logic rather than of discretion or fact-finding, and, once the requirement or condition has been defined, there is likely to be only one pool that serves to test its effect.

What then is the meaning of a "considerably smaller" proportion of people of one racial group who can comply with the requirement or condition? The first approach to establishing this is always to identify the individuals within the reference group, and determine what percentage of them, if any, can comply with the requirement or condition. This percentage must then be compared with the percentage of those in the comparison group who can comply with the requirement or condition. However, mere comparison of statistics may not be the only approach taken by an ET. The reason is that a small pool may sometimes be thought to be too small to be statistically valid. Therefore, according to the CA in *London Underground Limited v Edwards (No.2)* [1998] IRLR 364, an area of flexibility is applicable to whether a particular percentage is to be regarded as substantially smaller in any given case. According to the CA, an ET is entitled to use its general knowledge and expertise to look outside the pool for a comparison and take into account national figures. Similarly, where there is a small number of a particular racial group employed as compared with the comparator group, an ET is entitled to infer that it is unattractive work to the complainant's racial group.

In each case, it is a question of fact for an ET whether the percentage of those who can comply is considerably smaller. In *Edwards No.2*, the CA upheld the ET's finding that there was a considerably smaller difference where 100% of male train operators could comply with a requirement or condition as compared with 95.2% of women, namely a difference of 4.8 percentage points. By contrast, there are suggestions in *R v Secretary of State for Trade and Industry ex parte UNISON* [1996] IRLR 438, HC that 4% would not be considerably smaller. Percentages have also been considered by the ECJ in *R v Secretary of State for Employment ex parte Seymour-Smith and Perez* [1999] IRLR 253. That was a case where the state had to justify a disparate impact. (There is a difference between the position of a state justifying an adverse impact as compared with a private employer). The ECJ indicated that although disparate impact is a question of fact for national courts, it thought it unlikely to exist where 77.4% of men fulfilled the condition as opposed to 68.9% of women, namely a difference of 8.5 percentage points. However, the ECJ held that a considerably smaller percentage may be revealed either by a sufficiently large difference in one year, or "if the statistical evidence revealed a lesser but persistent and relatively constant disparity over a long period" (para. 61). Therefore, complainants will typically seek to use statistics going back a period of years.

Justifiability

Where there is a requirement or condition that has a significant adverse impact on a particular racial group, that will not amount to unlawful race discrimination unless that requirement or condition is not justifiable. It is for the employer to demonstrate justifiability. The CA in *Hampson v Department of Education and Science* [1989] IRLR 69, [1989] ICR 179 held that justifiability "requires an objective balance between the discriminatory effect of the condition and the reasonable needs of the party who applies the condition". In order for an employer to justify a requirement or condition, it must demonstrate that the requirement or condition satisfies a legitimate aim, is necessary for achieving that aim, and is proportionate. It is not necessary that the employer has considered the question of justifiability at the time of imposing the requirement or condition. It is therefore possible for an employer, that has given no thought to the matter at the time, to succeed on a justifiability defence at an ET by showing at the ET that there are justifiable grounds for its imposition. Nevertheless, it is good practice, and will be easier to succeed in a justifiability defence, if the employer has at the time of imposition of the requirement or condition addressed why it is needed, what the impact on the workers will be, and whether other measures could achieve that aim.

Can comply

The final element of a complaint of unlawful indirect race discrimination is whether or not a complainant can comply with the requirement or condition. This means whether or not he or she can comply in practice. Where an employee complains to an employer that he or she cannot comply with a requirement or condition, it is sensible for the employer to explore with the employee the reasons why the employee says that that is the case. An ET will examine as a question of fact whether or not the employee can comply. This is different from whether the employee wishes to comply, and is also different from whether it is physically possible for the employee to comply.

New Directive on equal treatment

The Council of Ministers of the European Union has passed a new Directive on implementing the principle of equal treatment between persons irrespective of racial or ethnic origin (Directive 2000/43/EC). Broadly, the provisions of this new Directive cover ground similar to that covered by the RRA 1976. The Directive provides for member states of the EU to enact legislation combating both direct and indirect discrimination based on racial or ethnic origin (but not nationality).

However, it should be noted that the definition of indirect discrimination in the new Directive is broader than that currently contained in the RRA 1976. The new definition will cover an apparently neutral "provision, criterion or practice" that would put persons of a racial or ethnic origin at a particular disadvantage (Article 2.2(b)). Clearly, this will catch more situations than the more restrictive formula of "requirement or condition" under the existing legislation. As stated above, "requirement or condition" only covers competencies that *must* be complied with so that non-compliance with the competency is an absolute bar – for example, in qualifying for promotion. "Provision, criterion or practice" will catch competencies that are merely "taken into account" in assessing an employee, rather than being requirements, if they would put persons of a racial or ethnic origin at a particular disadvantage.

Nevertheless, under the Directive, indirect discrimination will not be taken to have occurred where a provision, criterion or practice is

145

objectively justified by a "legitimate aim" and the means of achieving that aim are "appropriate and necessary".

The EU member states, including the UK, must enact legislation implementing the Directive in national law by 19 July 2003, at the latest.

Race Relations (Amendment) Act 2000

Among other things, the Race Relations (Amendment) Act, which came into force in early 2001, outlaws discrimination by any public authority in carrying out any of its functions, imposes a positive racial equality duty on all public authorities, and extends the RRA 1976 to government appointments outside the employment field. The specific details are outside the scope of this work.

Sex discrimination

As regards *existing* employees, it is unlawful for an employer to discriminate on grounds of sex against an employee:

- in the terms of the employment that it affords the employee;

- in the way in which the employer affords him or her access to opportunities for promotion, or to any other benefits, facilities or services, or by refusing or deliberately omitting to afford him or her access to them;

- by dismissing the employee; or

- by subjecting him or her to any other detriment.

(see SDA 1975, section 6(2)).

As regards *candidates* for employment, it is unlawful for an employer to discriminate on grounds of sex against another person:

- in the arrangements it makes for the purpose of determining who should be offered that employment;

- in the terms on which it offers the person that employment; or

- by refusing or deliberately omitting to offer him or her that employment.

(see SDA 1975, section 6(1)).

With effect from 12 October 2001, the SDA 1975 has been amended by regulations, known as the Sex Discrimination (Indirect Discrimination and Burden of Proof) Regulations 2001 SI 2001 No. 2660. In relation to discrimination in employment, these amend Section 1(2) of the SDA 1975 so as to change the definition of indirect discrimination. That sub-section now provides that a person discriminates against a woman if "he applies to her a provision, criterion or practice which he applies or would apply equally to a man, but – (i) which is such that it would be to the detriment of a considerably larger proportion of women than of men, and (ii) which he cannot show to be justifiable irrespective of the sex of the person to whom it is applied, and (iii) which is to her detriment."

The Regulations have also, as their name suggests, changed the burden of proof, so that there is now a burden on an employer to prove that sex discrimination has not occurred. The Regulations do this by inserting a new Section 63A(ii) which provides that "where, on the hearing of the complaint, the complainant proves facts from which the tribunal could, apart from this section, conclude in the absence of an adequate explanation that the respondent [that is, the employer] – (a) has committed an act of discrimination against the complainant which is unlawful . . . the tribunal shall uphold the complaint unless the respondent proves that he did not commit, or, as the case may be, is not to be treated as having committed, that act."

As with race discrimination, there are two ways in which a complainant may succeed in a complaint of sex discrimination. The first is where there has been direct discrimination, and the second is where there has been unjustifiable indirect discrimination. In order to succeed in a complaint of indirect sex discrimination, it must be demonstrated that there has been the application of a provision, criterion or practice, that a considerably smaller proportion of women can comply than men, that the provision, criterion or practice is unjustifiable, and that the complainant cannot comply with the provision, criterion or practice.

Provision, criterion or practice

The new section 1(2)(b)of the SDA 1975 means that the trigger for determining whether or not there is an adverse impact on one sex is no longer whether or not the employer imposes a requirement and/or a condition. The new test is "provision, criterion or practice".

This includes a requirement or condition (see the new definition inserted into the SDA 1975), but is wider. This works to the advantage of a person seeking to prove discrimination, since the provision about which complaint is made must no longer be a must-have. Therefore, it may in principle offend against the Act even if not applied in all cases.

The relevance to those involved in recruitment, retention or promotion of employees is that henceforth a competency that is merely desirable as opposed to being essential may qualify as a "provision, criterion or practice". It will no longer be possible to escape the protection of the anti-discrimination legislation by naming a competency as desirable rather than essential. This in turn shifts the focus on to the justifiability of the provision, criterion or practice.

Burden of proof

Before the coming into force of the burden of proof regulations, the burden of proof in a sex discrimination claim was on the complainant, to prove that she had unlawfully been discriminated against. However, in practice, under the provisions of the legislation, once a prima facie case of sex discrimination had been made out by the individual, the evidential burden of proof was on the employer to show that the reason for the treatment of the employee was not tainted by discrimination on grounds of sex. Therefore, if, for example there was one male applicant for a post, and 10 female applicants, and the male applicant was successful, when each of the 11 candidates had apparently the same or similar qualifications and experience for the post, on a complaint by one or more of the female applicants, it was effectively for the employer to prove why the male applicant was successful.

Marital discrimination

By Section 3 of the SDA 1975, there is protection for married people against discrimination in employment. The protection is identical to the protection offered against discrimination on the grounds of sex. Therefore, an individual may succeed in a claim for marital discrimination if he or she has been directly or indirectly discriminated against.

It is, however, important to note that the comparison for the purposes of a claim of marital status discrimination is between married people of one sex who can comply as compared to unmarried people of the same sex, that is between married and unmarried women, or between married and unmarried men.

An example will help to show how an individual could bring a claim for indirect marital discrimination. An employer may employ a large number of women. Those women may be employed on changing shift patterns. Equally, it may be that because of the particular constituency of the workforce it is overwhelmingly married women who have children and childcare responsibilities, and that unmarried women do not. In such a case it may well be that the married women are significantly less able to comply with any requirement or condition as to the shift pattern. It would then be for the employer to show that it was justifiable to apply the shift patterns to married as well as unmarried women.

This means that a sensible precaution for those involved in recruitment and retention is to compile and review statistics on the marital status of applicants and employees, both male and female.

Disability discrimination

Discrimination against disabled people is currently governed by the Disability Discrimination Act 1995 ("the DDA"). There is also a Code of Practice for the elimination of discrimination in relation to disability, and Guidance on matters to be taken into account in determining whether a person has a disability. Both of these latter documents are important and must be looked at together with the DDA. ETs will pay particular attention to them in deciding DDA claims.

The Court of Appeal has noted that it may be "positively misleading" to approach the DDA with assumptions and concepts from the SDA 1975 and RRA 1976 (see *Clark v TDG Ltd t/a Novacold* [1999] IRLR 318 CA, per Mummery LJ). Unlike the earlier discrimination Acts, (i) the DDA does not draw the distinction between direct and indirect discrimination on specified grounds; (ii) it provides a defence of justification to less favourable treatment that would constitute direct discrimination and be without such a defence under the earlier Acts; and (iii) it does not replicate the express requirement of the SDA 1975 (s.5(3)) and the RRA

1976 (s.3(4)) that, when a comparison of the cases of persons of different sex or persons of different racial groups falls to be made, the comparison must be such that the relevant circumstances in the one case are the same, or not materially different, in the other. In other words, there is no need for a comparator (actual or hypothetical) under the DDA. Consequently, the terms "discriminate" and "discrimination" are not used in the DDA in the same sense as in the SDA 1975 and RRA 1976.

The DDA deals with disability discrimination in respect of both existing employees and the recruitment of new employees.

As regards *existing* employees who are disabled, it is unlawful for an employer to discriminate against a disabled person whom it employs:

- in the terms of employment that it affords the employee;

- in the opportunities that it affords him or her for promotion, a transfer, training or receiving any other benefit;

- by refusing to afford him or her, or deliberately not affording him or her, any such opportunity; or

- by dismissing the employee, or subjecting him or her to any other detriment

(section 4(2), DDA).

As regards *recruitment*, it is unlawful for an employer to discriminate against a disabled person:

- in the arrangements that it makes for the purpose of determining to whom it should offer employment;

- in the terms on which it offers that person employment; or

- by refusing to offer, or deliberately not offering, him or her employment

(section 4(1), DDA).

An employer discriminates against a disabled person if (i) it treats the person less favourably than it treats or would treat other persons; and (ii) it does so for a reason that relates to the disabled person's disability; and (iii) it cannot show that the treatment in question is justified (section 5(1)). There is, therefore, a "justification" defence (in contrast to the SDA 1975 and the RRA 1976, under which direct discrimination on grounds of sex or race can never be shown to be justified). Treatment will only be justified, however, if the reason for it is both material to the circumstances of the particular case and substantial.

The leading case on the meaning of "material" and "substantial" is *Jones v Post Office* [2001] IRLR 384, CA. In essence, the CA held that where an employer has reasonably approached the question of whether the reason for the treatment is material and substantial, it is not for the ET to substitute its view on that question. In particular, the ET is not permitted to make up its mind on justification on the basis of its own appraisal of medical evidence, or to conclude that the reason is not material or substantial because the medical opinion on the basis of which the employer's decision was made is thought to be inferior to a different medical opinion expressed to the ET. Arden LJ held that the word "material" means that "there must be a reasonably strong connection between the employer's reason and the circumstances of the individual case" (paragraph 37), and the word "substantial" means that "the reason which the employer adopted as his grounds for discrimination must carry real weight and, thus, be of substance. However, the word "substantial" does not mean that the employer must necessarily have reached the best conclusion that could be reached in the light of all known medical science."

Disability

A disabled person, for the purposes of the Act, is someone who has a physical or mental impairment that has a substantial and long-term adverse effect on his or her ability to carry out normal day-to-day activities (Section 1). It is essential to look at the detailed provisions of the DDA and at the Guidance in order to determine whether there is a disability. The types of disability that qualify for protection are numerous and varied.

Reasons for treatment

The requirement that, to constitute discrimination, the less favourable treatment must be "for a reason which relates to the disabled person's disability" does not require that the employer was motivated to discriminate against the disabled person because of his or her disability. There merely needs to be a causal connection. Therefore, it may be discrimination where a disabled person performs poorly as a result of his or her disabilities and has been treated less favourably as a result of his poor performance. Further details are in the Code of Practice.

Relationship with competencies

How does the above apply to the use of competencies? By way of example, an employer's use of competencies to assess candidates for employment will form part of the "arrangements" that the employer makes for determining who should be offered employment (see above). If the use of these competencies is such that the employer treats a disabled person less favourably than other candidates (for example because of the disabled person's poor performance) and the employer does this for a reason that relates to disability (the poor performance) that would constitute unlawful discrimination under the DDA if the employer cannot show that the treatment in question is justified.

The duty to make reasonable adjustments

In addition to the above forms of discrimination, there is a duty on an employer to make reasonable adjustments in its arrangements (and the physical features of its premises) where they would place a disabled person at a substantial disadvantage in comparison with non-disabled persons (Section 6). The employer must take such steps as are reasonable to prevent the arrangements (or features) from placing the disabled person at a substantial disadvantage. Specifically, the DDA gives as an example of the steps that an employer might have to take in "modifying procedures for testing or assessment".

An employer discriminates against a disabled person if it fails to comply with the duty to make reasonable adjustments and it cannot show that the failure to comply with that duty is justified (Section 5(2)). The failure will only be justified if the reason for the failure is both material to the circumstances of the particular case and is substantial.

Employers are therefore under a duty to make reasonable adjustments to the competencies that they apply to disabled persons where the competencies would place the disabled person at a substantial disadvantage. A failure to make such adjustments to the competencies will constitute discrimination unless the employer can show that its failure to make the adjustments is justified.

Small businesses which have fewer than 15 employees are exempt from the above provisions on disability discrimination.

New legislation on disability discrimination will also have to be introduced pursuant to the Directive on Equal Treatment in Employment and Occupation (Directive 2000/78/EC) – see below under "Discrimination on grounds of religion, age, etc".

As at the time of going to press, the indications are that the government is planning to remove the justification defence from claims that an employer has breached its duty to make reasonable adjustments, and also to exclude the small-employer exemption.

Discrimination on grounds of religion, age, etc

There is a new Directive on Equal Treatment in Employment and Occupation (Directive 2000/78/EC). This provides that the member states of the EU must introduce legislation against discrimination in employment on grounds of religion or belief, disability, age or sexual orientation. Member states, including the UK, should pass the necessary legislation by 2 December 2003 at the latest. (However, if necessary, member states may have an additional period up to December 2006 in which to pass the legislation on age and disability discrimination, but not that on religious or sexual orientation discrimination.)

The legislation that the UK is required to enact will have to prohibit both direct and indirect discrimination. Again, the definition of indirect discrimination is broad and will cover a "provision, criterion or practice" that is apparently neutral but that would put persons who have a particular religion or belief, age, disability or sexual orientation at a particular disadvantage compared with other persons unless the provision, criterion or practice can be objectively justified by a legitimate aim, and the means of achieving the aim are appropriate and necessary.

Therefore, under the new legislation, competencies that would place persons of a particular religion or belief, a particular age, a particular disability or a particular sexual orientation at a particular disadvantage compared with others will amount to unlawful (indirect) discrimination unless the competency concerned can be objectively justified by a legitimate aim. Again, such competencies may constitute indirect discrimination even if they are merely to be taken into account rather than being absolute requirements for such purposes as promotion, for example.

As regards age, the UK is permitted to provide in its legislation that differences of treatment on grounds of age shall not constitute discrimination if they are objectively and reasonably justified by a legitimate aim and if the means of achieving that aim are appropriate and necessary. Such differences of treatment may include the fixing of minimum conditions of age, professional experience or seniority in service in relation to advantages linked to employment. It remains to be seen whether and to what extent the UK will avail itself of this general exception when the government frames the legislation required to enforce the Directive in the UK.

Age

There is presently in domestic legislation no prohibition against discrimination on the grounds of age. This will be altered as and when the new Directive on Equal Treatment in Employment and Occupation is brought into effect by UK legislation. However, there is currently a challenge outstanding to the upper age limit for bringing unfair dismissal claims provided by Section 109 of the Employment Rights Act 1996 ("ERA 1996"). That section provides that, in a claim for unfair dismissal, where there is no normal retiring age for the position held by the complainant, there is a default upper age limit of 65 years for bringing a claim. In the case of *Rutherford v Harvest Town Circle Limited*, EAT, 10/7/01 unreported, Mr Rutherford complained that Section 109 amounted to unlawful indirect sex discrimination, in breach of Article 141 of the EU Treaty. The ET found in favour of Mr Rutherford. The employer succeeded before the EAT, and the matter has been remitted for a fresh hearing by a tribunal. However, the general expectation is that the statistics will not show a significant adverse impact on men as compared with women so far as the upper age limit is concerned.

Part-time working

There are certain legal protections offered to part-time workers. The sources of law are the Part-Time Workers (Prevention of Less Favourable Treatment) Regulations 2000 SI 2000 No. 1551, and the EU Directive 97/81/EC of 15 December 1997 concerning the Framework Agreement on Part-Time Work; there are also guidance notes attached to the Statutory Instrument, and the Department of

Trade and Industry has issued a document called the *Law and best practice*, which is a detailed guide for employers and part-timers.

It is helpful to set out the definitions of part-time worker and full-time worker contained in the Regulations. A *full-time* worker is a person who "is paid wholly or in part by reference to the time he works and, having regard to the custom and practice of the employer in relation to workers employed by the workers' employer under the same type of contract, is identifiable as a full-time worker".

A *part-time* worker is someone who "is paid wholly or in part by reference to the time he works and, having regard to the custom and practice of the employer in relation to workers employed by the workers' employer under the same type of contract, is not identifiable as a full-time worker".

A part-time worker has the right to no less favourable treatment than a full-time worker. This right applies only if the treatment is on the ground that the worker is a part-time worker, and the treatment is not justified on objective grounds. In determining whether or not a part-time worker has been treated less favourably than a comparable full-time worker, the pro-rata principle should be applied unless it is inappropriate. The Regulations are able to confer protection on a large variety of matters, for example rates of pay, overtime, contractual sickness and maternity pay, access to training, redundancy, other benefits (such as health insurance, subsidised mortgages, staff discounts, company cars), and recruitment.

As with indirect discrimination in the fields of sex and race, justification is concerned with whether the less favourable treatment is for a legitimate aim, and the treatment is both necessary and proportionate to the aim to be achieved.

Although these Regulations therefore confer a measure of protection on part-time workers, it is significant that they do not confer a right on a worker to part-time work. If a worker is to seek to work part-time, for example in the case of a woman, she may seek to bring an indirect sex discrimination claim under the SDA 1975 for the failure by the employer to permit her to return following maternity leave from an original full-time position to part-time work.

Fixed-Term Work

The EU issued Directive 99/7/EC on 28 June 1999 concerning fixed term work, which forbids employers to treat fixed-term workers in a less favourable manner than permanent workers solely because they have a fixed-term contract, unless the difference in treatment can be justified on objective grounds. The implementation date was 10 July 2001. The government has published draft Regulations, known as the Fixed-Term Employees (Prevention of Less Favourable Treatment) Regulations 2001, and has consulted on their contents. At the time of going to press, the government has not yet brought such Regulations into force.

Learning points

- Competency-related pay is covered, for gender and marital status, by the Equal Pay Act 1970 and the Sex Discrimination Act 1975, Article 141 of the EU Treaty (formerly Article 119) and the Equal Treatment Directive. In terms of ethnicity, it is covered by the Race Relations Act 1976.

- The Equal Opportunities Commission's Code of Practice, which is admissable as evidence, recommends that employers review their pay schemes for bias.

- Equal pay legislation focuses on the work carried out, not how it is performed. It mainly applies to technical/functional competences, and not to behavioural/emotional intelligence competencies.

- For example, "work rated as equivalent" involves an acceptable job evaluation scheme, based on the demands made on individuals under various headings. These cover technical/functional competences, and a scheme using behavioural competencies may not qualify as being "analytical" or "objective".

- Employers may defeat an equal pay claim by showing that the differences are based on a "genuine material factor".

- Discrimination on the grounds of race, sex, marital status and disability is in general unlawful. Race discrimination is outlawed by the Race Relations Act 1976 ("RRA 1976"). Sex discrimination and discrimination on the grounds of marital

---

status are outlawed by the SDA 1975. Unlawful disability discrimination is outlawed by the Disability Discrimination Act 1995 ("DDA").

- The first two of these Acts operate in the same way. They cover less-favourable treatment at work, such as in recruitment, promotion, access to benefits and dismissal. The cause may be overt, or direct, but is often an indirect "requirement or condition". To be unlawful, those that can comply must be "considerably smaller" than a comparator person or group, and the requirement cannot be justified.

- For race discrimination, the requirement must be something that must be complied with. For sex discrimination, it can be merely a factor "taken into account" based on the "application of a provision, criterion or practice". Treating competencies as not being must-haves will probably exclude them from the law on race discrimination (until the law changes on or before July 2003), but not the law on sex discrimination.

- The defence of indirect discrimination is that the requirement or condition is justifiable: it satisfies a legitimate aim, is necessary for achieving that aim, and is proportionate.

- Discrimination against disabled people is governed by the Disability Discrimination Act 1995. There is no distinction between direct and indirect discrimination, and no need for a comparator. The Act includes terms and conditions, recruitment, opportunities for promotion, transfers and access to training, other benefits, dismissal and redundancy. It covers less favourable treatment, based on a reason that relates to the disabled person's disability; and where the treatment is not justified.

- There is a duty on an employer to make reasonable adjustments in its arrangements (and the physical features of its premises) where they would place a disabled person at a substantial disadvantage. Employers are therefore under a duty to make reasonable adjustments to the competencies that they apply to disabled persons where the competencies would place the disabled person at a substantial disadvantage.

- The Directive on Equal Treatment in Employment and Occupation provides that member states must introduce legislation against discrimination in employment on grounds of religion or belief, disability, age or sexual orientation. The legislation will have to prohibit both direct and indirect discrimination. The definition of indirect discrimination is broad and will cover a "provision, criterion or practice" that is apparently neutral. Therefore, competencies that would place persons of a particular religion or belief, a particular age, a particular disability or a particular sexual orientation at a particular disadvantage compared with others will be amount to unlawful (indirect) discrimination unless the competency concerned can be objectively justified by a legitimate aim.

Chapter 6

Discrimination: practical issues

Introduction

Neil Rankin

Less than one in four employers with competency frameworks carry out an equality audit to ensure that they do not discriminate unfairly against individuals or groups in the workforce. This finding from the latest benchmarking survey (Rankin, 2001) is disappointing and gives little reassurance that many employers will be able to provide a confident, robust defence against any tribunal applications under the UK's increasingly assertive discrimination laws.

This is not to say that the competency approach is more liable to discriminate unfairly than any other technique used in the management of people at work. In fact, one of the merits of the use of competencies is that it has the potential to improve diversity and equality practices. Rather, the difficulty lies in most organisations' failure to check that their competencies and the ways that they are applied have this beneficial impact. Without proper monitoring data and validation studies, employers can only trust to luck that the design and implementation of their competency frameworks are free of unfair bias.

The ways in which unfair discrimination can occur in the design and use of competencies are reviewed by Katherine Adams in the first section of this chapter. Katherine has conducted several studies of the ways that bias can occur, and shares these insights with us here. Mee-Yan Cheung-Judge, an equality and diversity expert adviser, then follows up some of Katherine's points, focusing on the design process and how bias can be built in and diversity ignored. Importantly, she relates these issues not only to the principles of equality under the law, but also to the damage that failure to address them can do to organisations' businesses and social standing.

Avoiding discrimination by the back door

Katherine Adams

The rise of the competencies phenomenon has been meteoric. Barely heard of in this country a couple of decades years ago, it is now a strong contender for most-favoured human resource management technique in many British organisations. But when an ideology takes hold so fast, there are bound to be casualties, and there is a danger that equal opportunities could be one of them.

A gaping hole in the literature – astonishing for such an otherwise well-rehearsed subject – attests to an apparent lack of concern about competencies' likely impact on equal opportunities. And yet, as innumerable case studies of practice show, employers are using them as the basis for decisions about recruitment, development, promotion, grading and pay. All of these have obvious "equality" implications, and several of them (especially the last) have legal ones as well. Are practitioners and experts being soothed into complacency by the competency philosophy's claims to scientific rigour and objectivity? Might it not, rather, prove a Trojan horse for subtler and more insidious forms of discrimination?

Potential sources of discrimination

It is easy to see why the competency approach might appear blameless from an equal opportunities point of view. It seems to direct attention away from irrelevant personal characteristics and onto the things that really matter for good performance. So, for example, some of the "fundamental principles and aims" of competence-based National Vocational Qualifications are that they should be:

- awarded on the basis of valid and reliable assessment;

- free from unnecessary barriers restricting access and progression, and available to all those who are able to reach the required standard by whatever means;

- free from overt and covert discriminatory practices of any kind; and

- based on assessment of the outcomes of learning, normally arrived at independently of any particular mode, duration or location of learning (NCVQ, 1995).

In the USA, the competencies movement arguably began when Harvard professor David McClelland began to look for "competency variables" which were better at predicting job performance and less biased against "minorities, women, and persons from lower socioeconomic strata" than traditional academic exams (McClelland, 1993). But to what extent can we accept these statements of good intent at face value? It does not take much digging to uncover a whole range of potential problems. In broad terms, it would seem that bias can enter at any of the following points:

- the design of competency frameworks;

- the assessment of individuals' competencies; and

- the use of competencies for personnel management processes, especially pay and grading.

Designing competencies

When it comes to designing competencies, there are two main approaches to be considered: the one developed by McClelland and his McBer consultancy in the USA, and the other propounded by National Vocational Qualifications and occupational standards in the UK (see chapter 3 for more details of these differences and how they arose). Both are influential with employers in this country.

McClelland is clear (1993) that the methods involved in his "job competence assessment method" should result in a competency framework that is largely free from bias. And yet a close examination of each of these methods reveals ample prima facie scope for bias:

- The use of *criterion samples* means comparing "people who have clearly had successful jobs or interesting lives with those who are less successful," in order to determine which characteristics are associated with success (ibid). Three different types of criterion measure are used to identify the "successful" and "unsuccessful" samples (Boyatzis, 1982): an individual's work output (for example, total sales), supervisors' ratings and peer ratings.

- *Job element analysis* involves group sessions of jobholders brainstorming the characteristics that they regard as distinguishing effective or superior performance, and then checking these with larger samples of jobholders by means of questionnaires.

- During *behavioural event interviews*, "successful" and "unsuccessful" jobholders are asked to describe incidents in which they felt effective and ineffective in the job. These descriptions are analysed to identify the behaviours characteristic of each group, and then the behaviours are further analysed into clusters. Each cluster is given a title (such as "self-confidence") which then becomes a competency.

The problem with all of these methods is, of course, that they rely entirely on the judgments of individuals: jobholders, their peers and supervisors, and those who carry out the research and analysis. And, as with any area of life where judgment is concerned, bias is a possibility.

Richard Boyatzis, an early proponent of competency (ibid), acknowledges this problem when he says: "Of course, the problem with any measure of performance or effectiveness is that it emerges from an individual's or a group's ideal image of an appropriate goal for the organisation, or the people in specific jobs within that organisation. Such a measure, which may be theoretically or philosophically sound, is a relatively subjective judgment. Therefore, it is based on a particular theory or set of values." In his view, however, this kind of measure is the best available; the alternative is to impose some "arbitrary, theoretical or value-based" assumption about what constitutes success in the job.

The question of bias in competency design is a neglected one, but research in other areas does shed some light on the issue, if only indirectly. For instance, a report for the Equal Opportunities Commission from the Institute for Employment Studies (Bevan and Thompson, 1992), which looks at the operation of merit pay in four organisations, concludes that:

- Managers of both sexes value different attributes in men than they do in women. For instance, in one company, intelligence, dynamism, energy and assertiveness were rated as important among male subordinates, whereas thoroughness, organisation, dependability and honesty were valued highly in respect of female subordinates.

- Male managers value different attributes among their subordinates than female managers do. For example, in one company, male managers rated intelligence, logic, energy and creativity more highly than female managers. On the other hand, women managers placed a greater emphasis on organisation, perceptiveness and competence.

This study is not alone in suggesting that people's views of "success" in the job tend to be gender biased (see, for example, Alimo-Metcalfe, 1992). If this is the case, there is every reason to suppose that competency frameworks developed using techniques like behavioural event interviewing and criterion sampling will reflect such bias.

The NVQ approach

The issue of subjectivity is also a potential problem for the government-sponsored approach in the UK which has developed sets of occupational standards and, from them, National Vocational Qualifications (NVQs). This approach focuses on "what" types of competence: the technical and functional skills that are required in a job. In contrast, the behavioural competency approach developed by McClelland, Boyatzis and others emphasises the "how" types of competency: the way in which an individual conducts themselves at work.

The UK approach has involved employer-led "lead bodies" (latterly called National Training Organisations) developing an occupational map to define the domain of a particular occupational area such as management, accountancy or tourism. A small group of industry experts then work with a consultant to produce a functional map of the occupational area, usually on the basis of interviews or surveys of jobholders plus expert analysis. Further small groups of experts and consultants then analyse the resulting functions to define the standard to which they should be carried out in terms of performance criteria and range statements. This means that the occupational standards, and National Vocational Qualifications derived from them, aim to define acceptable performance in a particular occupation.

Once again, however, like the behavioural types of competency, little work seems to have been done on the question of potential bias. But as one of the few pieces of research available says: "[Occupational analysis] is intended to be a value-free process . . . Nevertheless, available guidance on this process suggests that the outcome will depend on the expertise and range of experience of the participants. . . . The technique, then, may be value-free, but the participants, whose contributions will be a result of their own experiences, are unlikely to be. . . . Factors such as gender may also influence results. For example, research in Australia (National Training Board, 1991) suggests that males tend to underemphasise some functions which females identify more readily" (Employment Department, 1992).

Perpetuating the status quo?

Related to the issue of subjectivity – but separate from it – is the question of "cloning". As David McClelland says: "Competencies identified by the job-competency process are context-sensitive (eg they describe what successful Indian entrepreneurs actually do in their own organisations and culture)" (McClelland, 1993).

But similarly, competencies in a male-dominated job, such as senior management, presumably just reflect what these male managers actually do. There is some evidence, especially in the area of management (see, for example, Sparrow and Rigg, 1993; *Personnel Today*, 1995), that men and women tend to have different work "styles". So a competency framework based on the analysis of mainly male jobholders would run the risk of ignoring "female" competencies – the so-called "cloning" effect.

Types of bias

Given the potential problems of subjectivity and cloning, how might bias be reflected in a competency framework? Work in the field of job evaluation (Hastings, 1991), though only indirectly relevant to this area, does offer some clues:

- the omission of "factors" commonly demonstrated by women (for instance, the organisational skills demonstrated in many administrative, clerical and secretarial posts);

- the duplication of male "factors" by including them under more than one heading (such as evaluation – counted under "mental demands", problem-solving – also under "mental demands" – and decision-making – counted under "responsibility"); and

- the elision of female "factors" leading to their being under-valued (for example, "physical effort", including both strength and stamina).

Some of the competencies that are sometimes thought to be more likely to be demonstrated by men than by women are:

- leadership ability;
- self-reliance;
- vigour;
- objectivity;
- logical thought;
- self-confidence;
- reliability; and
- effort.

How can the dangers be minimised?

Given the potential for bias in both the US and UK approaches to competency design, are there any precautions that can be taken? Marie Strebler of the Institute for Employment Studies has said: "Employers seem to have done very little in terms of trying to get fair samples when they do competency development work. There are ways you can improve validity, for example by choosing your sample so that it reflects the gender, race and other aspects of your workforce. But with senior managers, for instance, it can be very difficult to do this without tokenism. An alternative is to have a project team that's representative, and, in my experience, this works quite well. And, of course, when you're producing the framework, it's good practice to consult widely. This is an opportunity to see if there are competencies in the framework that are open to misinterpretation, or less likely to be demonstrated by one group than another."

Clearly, paying attention to samples – of jobholders, their peers and supervisors, and those conducting the analysis – will be very important in helping to reduce bias, such as the tendency of men to value different attributes than women. Equal opportunities training may also help, for example in tackling the thorny problem that people of both sexes may tend to value different attributes in men than they do in women.

As for the problem of "cloning", some would suggest more drastic remedies. A paper by John Sparrow and Clare Rigg (1993) urged that techniques that have been developed to take account of future job requirements should be adapted to consider alternative – such as, "female" – approaches to a job. These techniques include:

- developing business scenarios;

- cultural-analysis techniques;

- visioning workshops;

- hierarchical task analysis; and

- functional approaches.

The problem of vagueness

A final problem under the heading of "design" points the way to our second issue: the question of assessment. There is a danger that competency definitions may be so vague that they encourage biased interpretation in practice. Again, little research has been conducted that directly relates to competency-based assessment. But extrapolating the findings of Bevan and Thompson's investigation of performance-related pay for the Equal Opportunities Commission (Bevan and Thompson, 1992) indicates that there are two potential problems.

First, poorly-defined assessment criteria – in this case, vague competency definitions and examples of performance – can be interpreted differently. Not only can individuals understand them in different ways, but there is evidence that differences also tend to reflect the different outlooks of men and women. For example, an imprecisely defined competency of "leadership" might be understood by men as requiring firmness, while women might give its nurturing aspects more attention.

Second, men and women might be judged differently when vague competencies are applied. For example, a man might be judged to be a good leader if he leads from the front, lays down the law and so on, while a woman demonstrating these qualities might be seen as "pushy".

An Institute for Employment Studies survey (Strebler, 1994; Strebler and Bevan, 1996) on the use of competencies in some 200 organisations found that the interpretation of what competency headings meant in practice does pose problems for managers. Of course, vagueness can be reduced by clear definitions – in the form of performance criteria, behavioural indicators, or examples. But some would argue (Adams, 1993) that very broad competencies like "leadership" are not genuine, assessable competencies; rather, they might be amalgams that need to be broken down into their component parts if they are not to encourage bias.

Assessment

The question of interpretation brings us to my second theme: equal opportunities issues in the assessment of competencies. Unlike "hard" performance measures, such as the achievement of sales targets, competencies are qualitative measures and, thus, at least on the face of it, are more open to subjective judgment when it comes to one individual assessing another. And all the problems of bias that we have already discussed under the heading of "design" raise their heads once again.

Marie Strebler of the Institute for Employment Studies has said: "This whole area is fraught with difficulties. Whenever you deal with performance rating, there is a danger of bias creeping in. It's not clear whether competency is likely to improve the objectivity of performance rating or not. Employers are starting to recognise this as a major issue."

Although there is a great dearth of information about bias in competency assessment, many of the principles of good practice that apply to assessment generally may also reduce the likelihood of bias in competency assessment. These include:

- using more than one assessor per assessee;

- providing equal opportunities training for assessors;

- monitoring assessors' decisions individually and collectively; and

- regularly reviewing the assessment system.

Why does it matter?

Ultimately, of course, the reason why bias in competency design and assessment is problematic is that competencies are increasingly being used for a whole range of personnel management issues that involve decisions about individuals: recruitment, selection for development, promotion and pay. If any of these are based on competencies that have been designed, interpreted or assessed in a biased way, they are likely to be discriminatory. Employers using them run the risk of treating individuals unfairly and wasting the talents of groups in the organisation. They also expose themselves to legal action, particularly (in the case of pay) equal value claims.

Competency-related pay

Of all the competency-based personnel management techniques, competency-related pay is probably the most thorny issue from the equal opportunities point of view. It has become increasingly popular in recent years and a good deal of attention has focused on the potential legal implications of this development (see, for example, Armstrong and Baron, 1995). For further information on competency-related pay, see chapter 9.

Marie Strebler of the Institute for Employment Studies has said: "Many organisations are going for broadbanding [grading schemes with wide salary ranges, often associated with competency-related pay], thinking that competencies will help them to get away from issues of equal value. But there's no reason why they should. Job evaluation won't necessarily be made more rigorous by basing it on competencies."

Fear of equal pay claims under UK or EU legislation may in fact have inhibited some employers from moving towards competency-related pay, on the grounds that this kind of system could result in a pay gap between male and female workers doing work of "equal value". Certainly, in the case of individual performance-related pay it has been found that: "Bias tends to enter the merit pay process when appraisal ratings are being translated into merit pay awards. Typically, men and women at the same job level and with the same ratings received different pay rises" (Bevan and Thompson, 1992).

However, there is as yet no case law directly relevant to competency-related pay. According to the Equal Opportunities Commission, the same principles apply to competency-related pay as to performance-related pay in general. This means that competencies must be genuine requirements of the job; they must not be confined to those that favour one sex in particular, and they must be interpreted consistently and in a gender-neutral way.

The commission says that what is good practice for performance-related pay generally may also be regarded as good practice for competency-related pay. This includes regular monitoring of the allocation of individuals' competency ratings and the subsequent allocation of competency-related pay increases by gender, ethnic group, job level (especially for male- or female-dominated areas) and length of service. Managers who are involved in assessing individuals for purposes that are connected with competency-related pay should be given regular training in conducting objective and non-discriminatory assessments. There should be a regular, formal review of the operation of the competency-related pay system. And, more generally, there should be regular monitoring of access to other resources that could have a bearing on individuals' ratings and pay awards, such as training, development and promotion.

However, Sue Hastings, a job evaluation expert and adviser to trade unions, has said that: "There doesn't seem to be a lot of monitoring of competency-related pay schemes. When you ask about it, management looks at you blankly. It's not deliberate – they've just not thought about it. With competency-related pay, if there is no glaring issue of discrimination, it is often hard to see if there are problems below the surface, so monitoring becomes especially important."

Pay and job segregation

Job segregation is a well-recognised problem for those concerned with equal opportunities, and it is one that can clearly have an impact on competency-related pay. According to Sue Hastings, trade unions have encountered two major problems with competency-related pay. First, the systems do not always cover the whole workforce. In one organisation, part-timers who were cleaners were not covered by competency-related pay and, of course, most of these were women. Second, there is an impression that competency-related pay is being introduced as part of a process of cultural change, where the employer wants to encourage greater flexibility. In some of these cases, employers are giving priority, in terms of the introduction of competency-related pay, to the groups whose flexibility has most importance – and these groups are also being given priority in access to training. It seems that some of these priority groups are male-dominated.

Clearly, the exclusion or prioritising of certain groups in relation to competency-related pay schemes could well have an equal opportunities impact if there is substantial job segregation. A subtler one, perhaps, might be the effect of assessing different, job-segregated groups against different sets of (pay-related) competencies.

However, the impact of competency-related pay may not all be negative. In general, trade unions, for example, see competency-related pay as being an improvement on performance-related pay (Adams, 1998). Often, unions appreciate that it can offer greater transparency than individual performance-related pay schemes, and is accompanied by assessment guidelines that reduce the discretion (and, therefore, subjectivity) of line managers.

Conclusion

The potential for discrimination in competency-related pay schemes is likely to exercise both trade unions and employers over the next few years, but issues of equal value may be just the tip of the iceberg. It is clear that a thorough consideration of the impact of competencies on diversity and equality in personnel management processes is well overdue. Until that has taken place, employers will have to tread cautiously and, apart from the issues highlighted in this and the preceding chapter, ensure that they have effective monitoring and review systems in place to detect unfair discrimination should it occur.

Avoiding discrimination in competency design

Mee-Yan Cheung-Judge

In the section above, Katherine Adams argues that the issue of bias in competency design is an important one, though is often neglected. In this section, I shall expand on her argument, suggesting that organisations that fail to incorporate the principles of equality and diversity into their competency frameworks are running grave business risks.

Before competencies came into fashion, successful performance at work was often described in vague and highly elusive terms. So it was relatively easy, from the "professional" equality and diversity point of view, to dismiss it. But when people began to define explicitly the behaviours of those who are "successful" in an organisation, using the methodology of competencies, what used to be elusive and obviously biased started to appear robust and professional. My fear is that the competency approach can become a tool of discrimination, justifying deep-seated notions of "acceptability" with a veneer of respectability.

The perils of "acceptability"

Let me start by looking at this question of acceptability and the connected one of corporate culture. One of the most important factors determining corporate culture is the organisation's leaders. In the UK, almost all directors and function heads are men. The values they bring to their corporate world are very much those they are at home with, and these are gender- and culture-specific. It is these values that directly shape the corporate mindset. The demarcation of what and who is acceptable in the organisation is shaped by this mindset and institutionalised through the organisation's policies, systems, processes, and reward system. In his research into racial discrimination, Jenkins (1982; 1984 and 1986) found that when individuals are different from those in power, the probability that they will be regarded as acceptable becomes slim.

Anyone who is designing a competency framework – and those who are implementing it or assessing the competencies – needs to be aware of this issue of acceptability. This is because, as Jenkins has shown, the existing gender and racial mix of the workplace significantly influences the collective view of who is acceptable through the process of cognitive and social modelling. Moreover, he argues, although "acceptability" is different from someone's actual "suitability" to do a particular job, views about acceptability have an effect on perceptions about someone's suitability.

The idea of "acceptability" concerns how well someone fits into the existing corporate culture, and how smoothly they can be integrated into the managerial procedures and social routines of the organisation. In other words, it is about one's ability to fit into the organisation's ways of thinking and doing things – not about one's ability to achieve certain tasks in order to achieve specified results. But the questions of acceptability and suitability are very much interlinked. Jenkins found that when staff cross the threshold of suitability, criteria of acceptability will swing into action. Moreover, suitability criteria are often defined within the framework of acceptability. In defining whether someone demonstrates "successful" behaviour, it is the acceptability packaging that really matters.

Given that so much is already taken as read about a person's acceptability vis-à-vis the organisation's culture, what counts as success – who are the successful people and what behaviour they manifest – becomes merely a rhetorical question. Thus discrimination is routinely embedded in the day-to-day life of the organisation: invisible and taken for granted.

Why does it matter?

The danger that competency frameworks, while attempting to identify "successful" performance, merely reinforce ethno- and gender-centric views of "acceptability" ought to alarm employers. For one thing, there is growing evidence of the benefits of an effective equality and diversity policy for organisations that are concerned to keep their competitive edge in a highly complex and fast-changing environment.

For example, in research on both sides of the Atlantic, Hammond and Holton (1991) found direct benefits stemming from such a policy, such as becoming an employer of choice, and getting close to customers. Similarly, others have established a link between managing diversity and organisational competitiveness in terms of cost, resource acquisition, marketing, creativity, problem-solving and organisational flexibility (for example, Cox and Blake, 1991; Cox, 1993; Cox and Beale, 1997; and Tayeb, 1996). And Kandola and Fullerton (1994) have itemised potential benefits (not all of them proven) such as access to talent, organisational flexibility, team creativity and innovation, better decision-making, improved customer service and increased sales to members of minority culture groups.

However, I think that documenting the benefits of equality and diversity at work in this way can be misleading. This is because it suggests that embracing equality and diversity is an add-on which an organisation can opt for if these particular benefits appeal to them – or ignore if they do not. A better approach, in my view, locates the logic of equality and diversity in strategic business issues, such as the environment in which the business functions and the organisation's strategic objectives. The following facts about our environment, for instance, all have an immediate relevance to the question of equality and diversity:

- the labour pool from which business draws its supply is no longer homogeneous;

- worldwide population movement is a reality;

- markets are increasingly diverse, and are all influenced by factors such as gender, class and culture;

- many businesses now operate in a global setting; and

- there are changing social attitudes among younger workers.

In this environment, simply knowing how to manage staff is no longer sufficient. What is needed from all managers is the ability to manage diverse groups of staff and to bring out the best in them. Being non-discriminatory is no longer leading-edge; cultural sensitivity to customers and product range is critical. Furthermore, having all the strategic scanning of the environment being done by a homogeneous group of senior managers is no longer a guarantee of accuracy. What is needed is a diverse group of senior managers with different values who can meet a range of different external challenges.

Getting the message

Focusing senior management's attention on strategic issues can really bear fruit when trying to get commitment to equality and diversity.

An example will help to illustrate this. When I was working with the board members of Sainsbury Supermarkets Ltd, I decided to focus their effort on mapping out all the external factors that influence the way they managed the organisation. They developed a long list, ranging from marketplace conditions for retailers, share price, and profit margins, to product sourcing and environmental issues, and changing gender attitudes, customer demographics, lifestyle changes and public relations. Staffing factors included high labour turnover, employment legislation, the "changing expectation of quality of life among the labour pool", and employee perceptions.

Scanning this list, I realised that all I had to ask them to do was identify those factors whose impact could helpfully be managed by an effective equality and diversity policy, helping the company to capitalise on resources, and minimise potential damage. This was a very powerful exercise, with the board members immediately catching hold of why equality and diversity was important to their business. I then focused their minds upon the "strategic web" they had built and asked whether they could really deliver these strategic objectives without the ethos of equality and diversity. Again, their answers convinced them that these principles had to be integrated into everything they were doing.

Avoiding bias

Once the point of equality and diversity is properly located in the business context, then it becomes very clear that this dimension must be explicitly incorporated when an organisation comes to develop its competency framework.

But how can this be done? There are a number of possible methods, and the first can be illustrated by an example from my own work. A client who works for a public utility company called me one day and said she had just received the first draft of the company's new managerial competency framework, which had been produced by an external consultancy firm. Not only was it macho in tone, but the content of the framework was inconsistent with the "transforming" culture the organisation was trying to develop under the leadership of the chief executive. As a senior manager, she wondered what she could do to intervene.

I asked her what method the consultants had used. She answered: behavioural event interviews with the top 200 managers. Without asking about the gender or ethnic profile of the top 200 managers, I suggested that she should try to push the draft document down to the next two levels of the organisation for consultation. For example, she could run some focus groups, particularly for female and/or black managers, to comb through the document. I also suggested that she should ask the company's "culture-change" team to work through the draft competency profile so that they could identify those bits that did not fit the new culture the company was trying to achieve.

Later on, the client told me that none of the top 200 managers were black, and just 3% were women, while for the next two levels down the percentages were 2% black people and 12% women. How had I guessed? While the action I proposed could only be a matter of damage limitation, it did help to rescue a framework that had previously been derived exclusively from a 97% white male population. Better still would have been to build in equality and diversity principles at an earlier stage. I would suggest that organisations involved in competency design should make sure that behavioural event interviews do not stop at the senior level. It is much better to use a stratified sample to ensure that the resulting competency framework incorporates a diverse perspective on what constitutes "success" at work.

Good practice

Another method is to include in the research specialised staff, such as experts in human resource management, and/or equality and diversity champions. Compare data from these groups with data from the main sample, and bring representatives from the two groups together to work through the similarities and differences, hence increasing understanding of their different perspectives.

In terms of good practice, it is obviously a good idea to encourage a partnership between those who are developing the competencies and a number of other groups: those responsible for strategic planning; people concerned with customer care; the custodians of the culture and of culture change; and those who are internal champions for equality and diversity. In this way, the design of the organisation's competencies will not only be backward-looking, but also visionary, linked to the success of the organisation in the future.

A final suggestion is to benchmark what your organisation has come up with against the framework used by an organisation that is well-known for its commitment to equality and diversity, and learn from their example. To provide a start, box 6.1 lists a number of behavioural indicators that explicitly incorporate the principles of equality and diversity. All these examples have been developed through my work with clients, who have included them, alongside more traditional behavioural indicators, under a range of standard competency headings. I hope these examples will help to dispel the myth that incorporating principles of equality and diversity into a competency framework is an artificial exercise.

Conclusion

My aim in this article has not been to undermine the methodology used to design competency frameworks, nor would I question the value of competencies as a way of developing people to help meet the demands of the modern organisation. My argument is that if competencies are just being used to help maintain an organisation's status quo, then their value in terms of return on investment will be truly limited.

6.1. Equality and diversity in competencies

The following are examples of behavioural indicators that explicitly incorporate equality and diversity principles.

Strategic thinking

- Considers long-term strategic impact and effects on products and services to all types of customers when reacting to short-term demands.

- Ensures equality and diversity issues are included in the business-planning processes and/or any operational/project-planning processes.

Creative thinking

- Prepared not to accept established methods as the only solution and willing to actively seek fresh ideas to meet diverse needs.

- Willing to challenge established assumptions and generalisations with staff and colleagues, so that both operational practices and policies/procedures will move on to effective management of a diverse culture.

Team leadership

- Role-models and leads in a way that will develop within a team a culture where diversity is valued and being "different" is not considered to be a problem.

- Ensures that inclusive dialogues are held with all staff members, acknowledging the diverse needs among the team.

- Encourages discussion and ownership of equality and diversity practice regularly within the team.

- Actively utilises the diversity in a team to increase its creativity and problem-solving capacity.

- Ensures that appropriate equality and diversity issues have a place on the team's agenda.

Development orientation

- Facilitates and coaches each person regardless of their background and membership group, so that they can realise their full potential.

- Values the contribution of all members of staff by involving, listening and giving constructive feedback on their development.

- When assessing individual staff member's professional and career development needs, takes their background, their history in gaining access to such opportunities, their career pattern and their aspirations into consideration.

- Gives unbiased formal recognition to each individual's positive work practices and achievement.

Relationship building

- Actively practises appreciation of colleagues, partners and contractors who are different in background in race, class, ethnicity, religion, disability, etc, and works with their differences to achieve common goals.

- Demonstrates awareness that different people have different levels of access to networks. Sets up appropriate steps to ensure that those who will need help will be given it.

- Demonstrates acceptance of others who are different and who hold different views when working with them to achieve corporate results.

Responsiveness – customer service

- Demonstrates understanding that customers are made up of diverse groups of people who have different tastes, needs and preferences.

- Responds promptly, courteously and positively to different customer needs and requests for services, information and support.

- Actively builds relationships with diverse communities, and extracts key issues from each community when considering what type of services and products the organisation should provide.

- Ensures all changes and improvements in service and products incorporate appropriate equality and diversity standards.

Self-confidence

- Recognises and values one's own diversity and the benefits it can bring to the workplace.

Information management

- Conveys ideas or concepts that are comprehensive and relevant to different levels of staff.

- Recognises the impact of certain information on different staff members, hence is discriminating in choosing the means of communication.

References

Adams, Katherine (1993), "Identifying core competencies: ICI's 10 years of experience", *Competency & Emotional Intelligence Quarterly*, vol. 1, no.1, Autumn.

Adams, Katherine (1998), "Competencies and the unions: 2. pay and grading", *Competency & Emotional Intelligence Quarterly*, vol. 6 no.1, pp.23–27, Autumn.

Alimo-Metcalfe, Beverly (1992), "Different gender, different rules: assessment of women in management" in Barrar, Peter and Cooper, Cary L eds, *Managing organisations in 1992: strategic responses*, Routledge.

Armstrong, Michael and Baron, Angela (1995), *The job evaluation handbook*, Institute for Personnel and Development.

Bevan, Stephen and Thompson, Marc (1992), *Merit pay, performance appraisal and attitudes to women's work*, Institute for Employment Studies for the Equal Opportunities Commission.

Boyatzis, Richard E (1982), *The competent manager: a model for effective performance*, McBer and Co, Wiley.

Cox, T H and Blake, S (1991), "Managing cultural diversity: implications for organisational competitiveness", *Academy of Management Executive*, no.5, pp.45–56.

Cox, T H (1993), *Cultural diversity in organisations – theory, research and practice*, Berrett-Koehler.

Cox, T H and Beale, L (1997), *Developing competency to manage diversity – readings, cases and activities*, Berrett-Koehler.

Employment Department (1992), *Equal opportunities and the development and assessment of NVQs and SVQs.*

Hammond, V and Holton, V (1991), *A balanced workforce? Achieving cultural change for women – a comparative study*, Ashridge Management Research Group.

Hastings, Sue (1991), *Developing a less discriminatory job evaluation scheme*, Trade Union Research Unit.

Jenkins, R (1982), "Managers, recruitment procedures and black workers", *Working Papers in Ethnic Relations*, no.18, RUER, Birmingham.

Jenkins, R (1984), "Acceptability, suitability and the search for the habituated worker: how women and black workers lose out", *International Journal of Social Economics*, vol. 2, no.7, pp.64–76.

Jenkins, R (1986), *Racism and recruitment: managers, organisations and equal opportunity in the labour market*, Cambridge University Press.

Kandola, B and Fullerton, J, *Managing the mosaic – diversity in action*, Institute of Personnel and Development, 1994.

McClelland, David C (1993), introduction, in Spencer, Lyle M Jr and Spencer, Signe M eds, *Competence at work: models for superior performance*, Wiley.

National Council for Vocational Qualifications (1995), *NVQ criteria and guidance.*

National Training Board (1991), *Eliminating gender bias in the development of national competency standards: an addendum to national competency standards policy and guidelines*, Canberra City, Australia.

Personnel Today (1995), article on Abbey National, 5 December.

Rankin, Neil (2001), "Raising performance through people: the eighth competency survey", *Competency & Emotional Intelligence Benchmarking*, 2000/01, January.

Sparrow, John and Rigg, Clare (1993), "Job analysis: selecting for the masculine approach to management?", *Selection & Development Review*, vol. 9, no.2, April.

Strebler, Marie (1994), "Assessing competencies as a fairer way of measuring performance in the public sector", presentation to IIR conference, *Successfully linking pay and performance in the public sector*, March.

Strebler, Marie and Bevan, Stephen (1996), *Competence-based management training*, Institute for Employment Studies.

Tayeb, H (1996), *The management of a multicultural workforce*, Wiley.

179

Learning points

Avoiding discrimination

- The impact of competencies on equality and diversity at work has received little attention, and there is little guidance for employers to follow. However, because employers use competencies in decisions that affect individuals, there are strong equality implications, some of which expose them to legal challenge.

- Competencies appear to be less likely to discriminate unfairly than other personnel-management techniques, and employers may be over-confident that bias will not occur. In fact, it can occur in one or more of three ways: through the design of competency frameworks; the ways in which individuals' competencies are assessed; and their application as part of personnel management processes, especially pay and grading.

- Most design projects incorporate methods that rely on subjective judgments. There is evidence that subjectivity can be influenced by a person's gender; men and women tend to value different attributes. Men and women tend to have different work "styles". So a competency framework based on the analysis of mainly male jobholders would run the risk of ignoring "female" competencies, and vice versa.

- Flawed design can produce several types of bias and discrimination.

- Some of the competencies that are thought to be more likely to be demonstrated by men than by women are: leadership ability; self-reliance; vigour; objectivity; logical thought; self-confidence; reliability; and effort.

- Design can be improved by ensuring that the individuals and groups used for the research reflect the gender, race and other aspects of the workforce. Where this is not possible, it is important to ensure that the project team leading the design process is representative. Wide consultation also broadens the basis. Providing training in equality and diversity issues can also be beneficial. There are also techniques based on analysing future job requirements that can be used to minimise cloning.

- Reducing bias in competency assessment involves applying good practice. This includes: providing equal opportunities training for assessors; monitoring assessors' decisions; and regularly reviewing the assessment system.

- Competency-related pay raises more issues from an equality and diversity perspective than any other application of competencies. Often, competencies are incorporated into existing performance-related pay processes; some of these have been found to be biased against women.

- Reducing such bias involves applying the same principles as apply to performance-related pay. Competencies must be genuine requirements of the job; they must not be confined to those that favour one sex in particular, and they must be interpreted consistently and in a gender-neutral way. There should be regular monitoring of the allocation of individuals' competency ratings and the subsequent allocation of competency-related pay increases by gender, ethnic group, job level and length of service.

- In addition, where job segregation exists, the partial coverage of competency-related pay, in terms of different grades or groups of workers, could have an equal opportunities impact.

Biased design and the business case

- Employers that fail to incorporate equality and diversity in their competency frameworks run grave business risks.

- Competencies should reflect business priorities, yet these are set by business leaders who are nearly always men from an ethnic majority background. Corporate cultures are also influenced by their leaders, resulting in a view that reflects gender and ethnic definitions of "suitability" to work in the organisation. Competencies can reinforce the invisible discrimination that is embedded in the organisation.

- There is growing evidence of the benefits of an effective equality and diversity policy for organisations that are concerned to keep their competitive edge. Instead of a desirable add-on, it is best to see such policies as part of the business's strategic response to its environment, where managing diverse groups of staff, cultural sensitivity to customers and product range are critical.

- Once equality and diversity is properly located in the business context, it becomes clear that this dimension must be explicitly incorporated when an organisation develops its competency framework.

- To avoid cloning where the relevant groups are mainly of one sex or ethnicity, consultation can be broadened to include related, perhaps less senior, groups. However, it is better to use a stratified sample to ensure that the resulting competency framework incorporates a diverse perspective on what constitutes "success" at work. Another method is to include specialised staff, such as experts in human resource management, and/or equality and diversity champions. Data from these groups should be compared with data from the main sample. The draft competency framework can also be benchmarked against the framework used by an organisation that is well-known for its commitment to equality and diversity. Box 6.1 lists a number of behavioural indicators that explicitly incorporate the principles of equality and diversity.

Chapter 7
Emotional intelligence
Anand Shukla

Introduction

The world of work is increasingly concerned with people, not standardised services or batch production, and a concept such as emotional intelligence, that offers a way of helping people to work together more productively, has naturally captured the spirit of the times. Emotional intelligence (EI) is an exciting – yet much misunderstood – means of explaining why some people excel in their work and of helping others to develop in the same way.

The origins of EI

Emotional intelligence as a label for a non-rational form of intelligence has only been used for little more than a decade. It made its first appearance in a seminal academic article written in 1989 by Peter Salovey from Yale University and John D Mayer from the University of New Hampshire (Salovey and Mayer, 1989/90). The ideas behind EI, however, go back to at least the 1930s. And in 1983, Harvard University psychologist Howard Gardner clarified the distinction between intellectual and emotional capacities in his widely-regarded model of "multiple intelligence". His list of seven kinds of intelligence included not just the familiar verbal and maths abilities, but two areas hitherto unassociated with traditional "rational" models of intelligence: knowing one's inner world and social adeptness.

This view of intelligence was echoed in Mayer and Salovey's research in the same decade. An interest in the way that emotions and cognition interact to improve thinking led to the question: could people be helped to understand and manage both their own emotions and those of other people? This then led to their pioneering emotional intelligence theory. Despite these antecedents, it was only in 1995 that the concept of emotional intelligence first came to public prominence as a result of Daniel Goleman's

Emotional intelligence: why it can matter more than IQ (Goleman, 1996). Goleman, a psychologist and a journalist for the *New York Times*, synthesised the work of Mayer, Salovey and others, such as the Israeli psychologist Reuven Bar-On, to popularise the theory of emotional intelligence. Summarising the academic evidence to make it accessible to non-specialists, his book became an instant best-seller.

What is emotional intelligence?

Emotional intelligence describes abilities that are distinct from, but complementary to, the purely cognitive capacities measured by IQ (intelligence quotient). These two different kinds of intelligence express the activity of different parts of the brain. The intellect is based solely on the workings of the neocortex – the more recently evolved layers at the top of the brain – whereas the emotional centres lie in the more ancient subcortex, which is lower in the brain. Emotional intelligence involves these emotional centres working in harmony with the intellectual centres. Put simply, emotional intelligence is the intelligent use of emotions: intentionally making your emotions work for you by using them to help guide your behaviour and thinking in ways that enhance your results. Good levels of EI also enable you to understand other people's emotions, and help you communicate with them, relate to them, and influence them.

In their 1989 article, Mayer and Salovey (1989/90) defined emotional intelligence as "the ability to monitor one's own and others' feelings and emotions, to discriminate among them and to use this information to guide one's thinking and actions". They viewed emotional intelligence as consisting of four separate elements:

- Identifying emotions: the ability to recognise how you and those around you are feeling;

- Using emotions: the ability to generate emotion, and to reason with this emotion;

- Understanding emotions: the ability to understand complex emotions and emotional "chains" – how emotions move from one stage to another; and

- Managing emotions: the ability that allows you to manage emotions in yourself and in others.

Mayer and Salovey's model of emotional intelligence has been adapted in different ways by other writers. Daniel Goleman developed their model into a set of five emotional and social competencies that he included in *Working with emotional intelligence* – his second book on EI (Goleman, 1998). Later, he reduced his model to four domains (see box 7.1) and used these as the basis for a questionnaire that he developed in conjunction with the Hay Group (Watkin, 2000).

Dr Malcolm Higgs and Professor Victor Dulewicz, both from Henley Management College, identify seven elements of EI in their book *Making sense of emotional intelligence* (Higgs and Dulewicz, 1999). These are broken down into the following three areas:

- Drivers: motivation and decisiveness – two traits that energise people and drive them towards achieving their goals, which are usually set very high.

- Constrainers: conscientiousness/integrity and emotional resilience – these control and curb the excesses of the drivers.

- Enablers: sensitivity, influence and self-awareness – three traits facilitating performance and helping the individual to succeed.

There are a number of other such models, such as those of Reuven Bar-On, and of Robert Cooper and Ayman Sawaf.

7.1. Daniel Goleman's model of EI

● **Personal competence**

These competencies determine how we manage ourselves

Self-awareness

Knowing one's internal states, preferences, resources and intuitions

Emotional self-awareness: recognising one's emotions and their effects

Accurate self-assessment: knowing one's strengths and limits

Self-confidence: a strong sense of one's self-worth and capabilities

Self-management

Managing one's internal states, impulses and resources

Self-control: keeping disruptive emotions and impulses in check

---

Trustworthiness: maintaining standards of honesty and integrity

Conscientiousness: taking responsibility for personal performance

Adaptability: flexibility in handling change

Achievement-orientation: striving to improve or meeting a standard of excellence

Initiative: readiness to act on opportunities

● **Social competence**

These competencies determine how we handle relationships

Social awareness

Awareness of others' feelings, needs and concerns

Empathy: sensing others' feelings and perspectives, and taking an active interest in their concerns

Organisational awareness: reading a group's emotional currents and power relationships

Service orientation: anticipating, recognising and meeting customers' needs

Social skills

Adeptness at inducing desirable responses in others

Developing others: sensing others' development needs and bolstering their abilities

Leadership: inspiring and guiding individuals and groups

Influence: wielding effective tactics for persuasion

Communication: listening openly and sending convincing messages

Change catalyst: initiating or managing change

Conflict management: negotiating and resolving disagreements

Building bonds: nurturing instrumental relationships

Teamwork and collaboration: working with others toward shared goals. Creating group synergy in pursuing collective goals.

Source: Emotional Intelligence Services/Hay Group, 1999.

How does EI transfer to the workplace?

Blessed with high self-awareness, emotionally intelligent employees can monitor themselves in action – for instance, being aware if their voice is becoming louder and they are becoming increasingly angry and thus recognising the need to lower their voice and defuse their anger. Being able to manage their emotions, individuals with good EI can understand why they are feeling as they do and use that understanding to deal with situations productively. Thus, in a distressing situation – the restructuring of a department, for example – the emotionally-intelligent employee will be able to think productively and use problem-solving skills to come up with a course of action.

Using their powers of self-motivation, high-EI employees will begin a task, persevere and move to completion, continually dealing with setbacks as and when they arise. Such employees will also use their effective social skills to be able to resolve workplace conflicts. Indeed, such model employees will be able to help their emotionally-deficient colleagues manage their own emotions, communicate effectively, solve their problems, resolve their conflicts and become motivated.

The importance of such skills for organisations has, of course, long been recognised. However, what is new is the rationale. Rather than using vague, imprecise terms such as "people skills", emotional intelligence provides an understanding based on neuroscience of the importance of these character traits for employees. Crucially, subsequent research has demonstrated the value of emotional intelligence precepts to the bottom line, as explained below.

Just how important is EI?

Emotional intelligence writers differ in their views as to the importance of emotional intelligence for organisations in the modern-day economy. Daniel Goleman (1998) has stated that emotional intelligence within organisations will emerge as one of the key factors determining which companies survive – and thrive – and which companies die. In a less hyperbolic fashion, Higgs and Dulewicz (1999) point to the numerous benefits that emotional intelligence can yield for organisations: improved leadership, more effective dispute handling and resolution, improved negotiations, more cost-effective decision-making and better-quality problem-solving.

John Mayer, on the other hand, strikes a more cautionary note about the importance of emotional intelligence. In his view, not every manager or leader needs to have emotional intelligence, though managers should be aware of that understanding in others and value it (Pickard, 1999). One of Mayer's collaborators, David R Caruso (on his emotionalIQ.com website), says that EI "does not, and should not, be thought of as a replacement or substitute for ability, knowledge or job skills. Emotional intelligence – people skills – enhances your success; it does not guarantee it in the absence of suitable skills." Time will tell which of these interpretations proves most accurate.

Certainly, both Higgs/Dulewicz and Goleman have amassed a wealth of evidence demonstrating the utility of the emotional intelligence concept for organisations. In *Working with emotional intelligence* (1998), Goleman describes his research into the relative importance of emotional competence for success as compared to the traditional emphasis upon technical skills and intellect. Using the competence frameworks for 181 different positions drawn from 121 companies and organisations worldwide, Goleman compared which of the competencies listed as essential for each position could be classed as a purely cognitive or technical skill, and which were emotional competencies. He found that 67% of abilities deemed essential for effective performance were emotional competencies. In other words, he argues that, compared with IQ and expertise, emotional competence matters twice as much. An analysis of data from 40 different corporations by Hay/McBer (with whom Goleman is now associated) supported the finding that emotional competencies are considered twice as important in contributing to high performance as pure excellence and expertise. Using data purely from the UK, Higgs and Dulewicz have also discovered "a very clear relationship" between a competency-based measure of emotional intelligence and managers' rates of career advancement over a seven-year period (Higgs and Dulewicz, 1999).

Advocates of emotional intelligence have also provided numerous examples of how emotional intelligence can have a positive impact on the bottom line. The Consortium for Research on Emotional Intelligence in Organizations (chaired by Goleman and Cary Cherniss of Rutgers University) describes the experience of the L'Oreal cosmetics company. Among its sales agents, those who were selected on the basis of certain emotional competencies significantly outsold sales people selected using the old selection procedure. On an annual basis, salespeople selected on the basis of emotional intelligence sold $91,370 more than other salespeople, yielding a net revenue increase of $2,558,360. Goleman has also related how at American Express Financial Advisors, financial advisers who went through an emotional competence personal development programme had sales gains of 8% to 20% (Goleman, 1998). Further, sales gains were significantly more than for the comparison groups who did not get the training, and also more than the average company-wide.

The case for the use of emotional intelligence seems to have been won in the USA. A 1997 survey of benchmark practices conducted among major corporations by the American Society for Training and Development found that four out of five organisations surveyed were trying to promote emotional intelligence in their employees through training and development, when evaluating performance and in hiring (ASTD Benchmarking Forum, 1997).

Uses and non-uses of EI at work

There is no consensus about how emotional intelligence theory should be applied in the workplace. Many different areas of working life have been proposed, including recruitment, selection, reward, team-building, executive coaching, leadership and management development, and career development.

Using EI concepts for selection purposes is perhaps the most contentious area. Buckholdt Associates, a UK-based emotional intelligence consultancy and training provider, says: "Recruitment is one area where emotional intelligence assessment is invaluable. Because there is such a high correlation between EI and successful job performance, the more you test and recruit for this, the better your staff pool is going to become" (taken from its website: www.emotionalintelligence.co.uk).

Certainly, as illustrated above, there is some evidence of a high correlation between EI and successful job performance. There are also illustrations of a link between the use of emotional intelligence assessments in recruitment procedures and a lower labour turnover rate. The Consortium for Research on Emotional Intelligence in Organizations describes how a large beverage firm used standard methods to hire divisional presidents and 50% left within two years, largely because of poor performance. When it started selecting on the basis of emotional competencies, such as initiative,

189

self-confidence and leadership, just 6% left in two years. The L'Oreal case study mentioned above also includes details of turnover rates among the sales agents. Agents selected for strengths in emotional competence had a 63% lower wastage rate during their first year than those whose selection process disregarded their EI competence profile (Goleman, 1998).

However, in an interview with *Competency & Emotional Intelligence Quarterly*, Daniel Goleman said that he is against the use of emotional competencies in recruitment (Adams, 1999). While employers should be alert for these qualities, they should not use his model for any kind of selection test (this is also his view in respect of reward decisions: performance alone should determine pay). Goleman's concern is shared by most in the emotional intelligence world. Only a few of the emotional intelligence tests that are on the market are intended for use in selection, including the EQ-I from Pro-Philes – the North American emotional intelligence consultancy founded by Dr Reuven Bar-On – and the OPQ32 EI, launched by the UK-based, international occupational psychometric consultancy Saville & Holdsworth.

There is, however, more of a consensus regarding the acceptability of the use of emotional competencies in areas such as team-building, the identification of leadership potential and in personal/career development.

7.2. Emotional intelligence in successful teams

Vanessa Drukat's study of 150 self-managed teams in the German chemical company Hoechst-Celanese identified 10 emotional competencies that emerged as the distinguishing capabilities of successful teams:

Empathy or interpersonal understanding;

Cooperation;

Open communication;

A drive to improve;

Self-awareness in the sense of evaluating strengths and weaknesses of the team;

Being proactive and taking the initiative;

Self-confidence;

Flexibility in the approach towards solving collective tasks;

Building bonds with other teams; and

Organisational awareness in terms of assessing the needs of other key groups within the organisation and being enterprising in their use of the organisation's resources.

Source: cited in Goleman, Daniel, Working with emotional intelligence, Bloomsbury, 1998.

EI and team-building

Research has suggested that the single most important element in teamwork is not average IQ but emotional intelligence. Higher quality decision-making in management teams has been shown to result from people who have high cognitive capabilities, diverse perspectives and expertise. But important as intellect and expertise are to effectiveness, team members also need to have healthy interactions with each other. It is this quality of interaction that is key to the eventual success of the group. Too easy a consensus risks a poor decision, while too much contention can result in a lack of unity. The presence of emotional intelligence allows the team to debate heatedly and productively, but enables it to conclude with a strong consensus.

Robert Steinberg and Wendy Williams from Yale University have found that the single most important factor in maximising the excellence of a group's product is the degree to which members are able to create a state of internal harmony. This echoes the study of Vanessa Drukat, professor at Weatherhead School of Management at Case Western Reserve University in the USA (cited in Goleman, 1998), that analysed 150 self-managed teams at the German chemical company Hoechst-Celanese. Ten emotional competencies emerged as the distinguishing capabilities of successful teams (see box 7.2).

EI and effective leadership

Emotional intelligence is also recommended as an effective way of identifying leadership potential among employees. Qualities commonly recognised as constituting good leadership include decisiveness, empowering others, managing change and openness to change – all of which reflect components of emotional intelligence. Goleman also notes that the importance of emotional intelligence increases the higher that an individual climbs within an organisation. Hay/McBer analysed its own competencies database to assess the importance of emotional competence for executive and leadership positions in business. This yielded the finding that just one cognitive ability distinguished star performers from average – pattern recognition, or "big picture" thinking. This is an ability that allows leaders to select significant trends from a mass of information, and to think strategically into the future.

With this one exception, intellectual or technical superiority played no role in leadership success. While everyone requires cognitive skills at top management levels, these cognitive skills are the entry-level criteria for such positions. They do not, of themselves, determine excellence in leadership. Rather, Goleman has found that emotional competence made the crucial difference between star performers and the rest. Successful leaders exhibited significantly greater strengths in a range of emotional competencies, among them influence, team leadership, political awareness, self-confidence and achievement drive. On average, Goleman calculated that approximately 90% of star performers' success in leadership was attributable to emotional intelligence. A number of emotional intelligence questionnaires are specifically designed to identify such leadership potential, among them Mayer, Salovey and Caruso's MEIS Emotional IQ Test, and the Emotional Intelligence Questionnaire, developed by Higgs and Dulewicz.

Can EI be developed?

There is a consensus among experts that emotional intelligence is a trait capable of development; certainly, the tests aiming to promote emotional competence development that many of the same experts have devised would be of little commercial use if this were not the case. Emotional intelligence seems to be deeply embedded from a very early age.

Goleman cites an experiment designed to assess the impulse control of a group of four-year-old American children (Goleman, 1996). The "marshmallow challenge" was devised by psychologist Walter Mischel during the 1960s. The children were told by the experimenter that if they waited until he had completed an errand, they could have two marshmallows as a treat. If they weren't able to wait until his return, they could have just one, but they could have it straight away. Some of the children waited 20 minutes for the experimenter to return. Others, considerably more impulsive, grabbed one straight away. Mischel then tracked down these four-year-olds some 12 to 14 years later, as they were leaving high school. Those who had resisted temptation at the age of four were more socially competent, personally effective, self-assertive and better able to cope with life's frustrations. In general, they were self-reliant, confident, trustworthy and dependable. However, the third of the sample that had grabbed the single marshmallow straight away tended to have fewer of these qualities and were also more likely to have a troubled psychological portrait. These teenagers were more likely to shy away from social contact in adolescence, and tended to be stubborn, indecisive and easily upset by frustrations.

Yet while temperament is, to some degree, a given trait at birth, emotional intelligence writers argue that emotional make-up can be changed by experience. In the context of personal development, they consider that it can also be changed by learning and practising the capabilities and skills that make up emotional intelligence. The workings of the human brain are by no means fully formed at birth. They continue to take shape throughout life, with the most intense growth occurring during childhood. Indeed, several brain areas critical for emotional growth are among the slowest to mature, and continue to develop into late adolescence. Thus, as an infant you might be prone to tantrums but, because of the way you are brought up and the experiences you encounter along the way, you learn to manage and control this tendency.

Indeed, studies conclude that people get better at these capabilities as they go through life and learn from their experiences. As we become more aware of our moods and learn to handle distressing emotions, and as we learn to listen and empathise, emotional intelligence levels increase. Mayer carried out a comparison of adults and adolescents, where adults were found to have higher levels of emotional intelligence across the board. Similarly, in a study conducted by Ronald Ballou of the Weatherhead School of Management of how well MBA students – ranging in age from their early 20s to their 50s – were able to master new levels of emotional competence, the most improvement occurred in those aged 29 or older, compared with those students aged under 25 (Ballou et al, 1997). In this respect, emotional intelligence development is simply a new way of describing the considerably more old-fashioned term – maturity.

How should EI be measured?

There is a variety of methods available for assessing emotional intelligence, with no consensus on the most preferable one. A self-completion questionnaire is the method favoured by Higgs and Dulewicz, where the emphasis is placed upon the individual to reflect upon the behaviour he or she tends to show in certain situations and, where necessary, to practise different behaviour. They recommend that participants actively seek feedback and advocate the use of a trusted mentor or guide.

However, self-report questionnaires have their critics. People are often not good judges of their own emotional intelligence, and they may also succumb to the temptation to answer questions in a way that makes themselves look good. To try and counter these problems, Goleman recommends 360-degree instruments that incorporate ratings from superiors, peers and subordinates alongside input from the individual concerned. He does see potential flaws in this approach, acknowledging that evaluations by other people are susceptible to the machinations of office politics: evaluations can be used as a weapon in political in-fighting, or as a way for friends to exchange favours. Noting that any evaluation will always reflect the evaluator, Goleman believes that the only way to ensure the most accurate assessment is to have multiple evaluations from multiple sources. The overall score is likely to even out any imbalances.

Indeed, Goleman has mooted the idea of 550-degree feedback, where, on top of the assessments from superiors, peers and subordinates, assessment of emotional competencies is solicited from family members (Adams, 1999). Aside from the problems of how reliable such information might be, the questions of intrusion in personal privacy means that this is one assessment method that is unlikely to take off in the UK. Mayer, on the other hand, is a critic of both self-report questionnaires and 360-degree evaluations. He notes that people are not very good judges of others' intelligence and are "horrible judges" of their own (Pickard, 1999). The MEIS/Emotional IQ Test, which he developed with Salovey and Caruso, accordingly consists of a series of practical ability tests.

7.3. A model EI development programme

The Consortium for Research on Emotional Intelligence in Organizations has drawn up a model programme for the development of EI among employees and managers. It involves four basic phases in the learning process:

1. Preparation phase

Crucial here is the motivation of participants to take part in the development programme. This can be a challenging admission. All the competencies required for success in the job should be identified. The personal strengths and weaknesses of the participant should be identified, and feedback should be provided with care. The learner's choice about his or her particular training programme should be accommodated as far as possible.

2. Training phase

Motivation during the learning phase continues to be a crucial element to counter any threat to the learner's self-esteem. A good relationship between the learner and trainer is crucial; the trainer must be genuine and empathic. Clear goals are required; these should be broken into manageable steps. There should be frequent opportunities to practise the learning. Experiential methods, such as role-plays, group discussions and simulations, are preferable to lecturing or reading. The use is recommended of live or videotaped models that show clearly how the competency is to be used in particular situations.

3. Transfer and maintenance

Transferring and maintaining learned skills is always the key challenge from training. Back in the familiar environment, there are likely to be many cues that support the old neural pathways the learning was designed to weaken. Using the learned skills on the job is to be encouraged, and support from management is essential.

4. Evaluation

Ongoing evaluation research should be conducted. Pre- and post-360-degree assessments of those who have gone through the training programmes are advocated, as are follow-up courses after one year.

> Source: *The Consortium for Research on Emotional Intelligence in Organizations, published on its website: www.eiconsortium.org*

Developing EI versus IQ

Daniel Goleman has argued that trying to teach emotional competencies on a course in the same way as, say, teaching a new computer programme, is fundamentally flawed. He draws a distinction between declarative knowledge – knowing a concept and its technical details – and procedural knowledge, which involves being able to put these concepts and details into action. Knowing does not equal doing. For Goleman, helping people to master an emotional competency demands nothing less than a new understanding of how people learn (Goleman, 1998).

His view of emotional competence teaching is shaped by an understanding of how the brain works. He believes that as we acquire our repertoire of thoughts, feelings and actions, the neural connections that support this repertoire are strengthened and become the dominant pathways for nerve impulses. Connections that are unused become weakened or even lost, whereas those that are used again and again become increasingly strengthened. Thus, given a choice between two alternative responses, the one that has the richer, stronger network of neurons will win out, he says. And the more a response occurs, the thicker a neural pathway grows to support it. So when habits have been well learned, the underlying neural circuitry becomes the brain's default mechanism.

Describing competencies as a coordinated bundle of habits, Goleman writes that changing a dysfunctional habit and replacing it with a more effective one requires enough practice of the better habit – and inhibition of the poorer one – to ensure that the neural circuitry for the old habit withers and the circuitry for the better behaviour grows stronger. Eventually, this will lead to the better habit replacing the old habit as the person's automatic response in key situations. Evidently, this cannot be achieved on a two-day course. Goleman says that conventional training and development efforts in industry have confused the methods required for cognitive learning with those that are needed for emotional learning. They have failed to recognise that capacities such as empathy or flexibility differ crucially from cognitive abilities, as they draw on different areas of the brain.

Purely cognitive abilities are based in the neocortex, but emotional competencies bring additional brain areas into play – mainly the circuitry that runs from the emotional centres deep in the brain up to the prefrontal lobes, the brain's executive centre. Learning emotional competence retunes this circuitry. So, whereas cognitive learning is essentially a question of adding information and understanding to the memory banks of the neocortex, learning an emotional competence involves all that and more as it requires the engagement of our emotional circuitry. To change social and emotional habits that are deeply embedded is a far more complex task than to add new information to old.

As well as the underlying neurological differences between cognitive and emotional learning, motivational factors also come into play. Emotional learning will involve ways of thinking and acting that are more central to a person's identity. Someone who is told they require training to learn a new software package is less likely to become defensive than if they are told they need to develop better interpersonal skills or that they need to be better able to control their temper. The prospect of emotional learning is thus more likely to generate resistance to change.

What is good practice?

Goleman's approach involves a few days away from work, taking people through 360-degree feedback. Based on this, participants are helped to produce an action plan. Back at work, they are encouraged to practise the new behaviour immediately, with day-to-day support from a mentor or immediate manager. Goleman believes that it can take "a couple of months at least" (Adams, 1999) to successfully unlearn old behaviour patterns and replace them with new ones.

In their treatment of emotional intelligence learning, Malcolm Higgs and Victor Dulewicz make a distinction between its different categories. They argue that their emotional intelligence components divide into two categories. The first comprises those that people can clearly learn through established learning activities, such as personal development strategies – sensitivity, influence and self-awareness. The second group, by contrast, relates to more enduring elements of an individual's personality that are clearly more difficult to learn – motivation, decisiveness, emotional resilience and conscientiousness/ integrity. For this latter category, the approach to development should consist of training strategies that exploit each individual's characteristics to the full and on developing "coping strategies" that minimise the impact of potential limitations.

The Consortium for Research on Emotional Intelligence in Organizations is undertaking research into best practice in developing EI. It has drawn up a model programme (published on its website at www.eiconsortium.org) – see box 7.3.

Conclusion

Clearly, organisational culture will have a key impact on whether employees possessing high emotional intelligence – or wanting to develop their EI levels – will be recognised and allowed to prosper. While emotional intelligence, as a discipline, is still in its initial phases, the potential impact of emotional intelligence on performance at work outlined above gives personnel professionals a powerful message to deliver to their organisations about the importance of personal development and the methods used to achieve it.

References

Adams, Katherine (1999), "Interview with Daniel Goleman", *Competency and Emotional Intelligence Quarterly*, vol. 6 no.4, Summer, pp.33–38.

ASTD Benchmarking Forum (1997), *Member-to-member survey results*, American Society for Training and Development.

Ballou, Ronald et al (1997), *Fellowship in lifelong learning: an executive development program for advanced professionals*, Weatherhead School of Management, cited in Goleman (1998).

Goleman, Daniel (1996), *Emotional intelligence: why it can matter more than IQ*, Bloomsbury.

Goleman, Daniel (1998), *Working with emotional intelligence*, Bloomsbury.

Higgs, Malcolm and Dulewicz, Victor (1999), *Making sense of emotional intelligence*, NFER-NELSON Publishing Company.

Mayer, John D, Salovey, Peter and Caruso, David (1997), "Emotional intelligence meets traditional standards for an intelligence", unpublished paper, cited in Goleman (1998).

Pickard, Jane (1999), "Sense and sensitivity", *People Management*, 28 October.

Salovey, Peter and Mayer, John D (1989/90), "Emotional intelligence", *Imagination, Cognition and Personality*, vol. 9 no.3, pp.185–211.

Watkin, Chris (2000), "Developing emotional intelligence", *Competency & Emotional Intelligence Quarterly*, vol. 7 no.3, Spring.

Williams, Wendy M and Steinberg, Robert J (1988), "Group intelligence: why some groups are better than others", *Intelligence* 12, cited in Goleman 1998.

Learning points

- Emotional intelligence is the name for a group of interpersonal competencies – involved with understanding and managing one's own and others' emotions and motivations – that have been found to be essential to effective performance at work.

- Discounting some extravagant claims of its importance, it is still clear that the concept of emotional intelligence covers skills that are essential aspects of effective modern organisations, such as good leadership, teamworking, building good relationships and customer care.

- Individuals' levels of emotional intelligence can be measured by one of the range of questionnaires on the market, and there is a consensus among experts that emotional intelligence can be developed. However, some emotional intelligence competencies can be developed more easily than others. Many of them require long-term development, or may be difficult to improve, involving traits that are embedded at an early age.

Chapter 8

Introducing competencies to the workforce

Introduction

Neil Rankin

Ask yourself the question whether you would have been happy to have spent six months of your time developing a set of competencies, traded on the goodwill of colleagues, and risked alienating line managers and board members, if you had known that neither managers nor employees would understand the end result? Consider, too, the fact that two-thirds of employers using competencies report that they have experienced just those problems: falling short of helping employees understand competencies (reported by 65% of users), or of aiding managers to understand them (63% of users) (Rankin, 2001).

The warning is clear: the point at which competencies are introduced to the workforce is crucial in making or breaking a competency initiative. Employers are aware that communication and involvement are important, but, as these findings suggest, often either fail to perceive just how vital they are, or have difficulty in mounting truly effective communication and involvement exercises. The methods in use are well established. According the latest benchmarking survey – the same source as the findings just mentioned – the most commonly used methods among 113 employers contacted are:

- group or team briefings (used by 78%);

- providing training for managers (74%);

- involving managers and/or employees at the design stage (71%);

- producing and distributing a special leaflet or brochure (35%); and

- publishing items in the regular staff newspaper or magazine (34%).

Viewing involvement and communication as a *process* seems to play a vital part in successful initiatives. A competency framework that has been designed with their involvement is less likely to be seen by employees and managers as being imposed on them. The design phase is formative in more than one way, too. It helps to shape the eventual framework, and it also begins to familiarise the workforce with the nature and scope of the competencies. But the familiarisation process needs to be sustained and built on. Time will elapse, memories will dim, and the framework will evolve. So, continuous communication is important, too. And, at the launch phase, proper training and introductions must be provided.

All these themes are explored by Louis Wustemann in the two sections below, where he draws on the experience of many employers that have been through the exercise of designing and introducing competencies.

Employee communication and involvement

Louis Wustemann

"The quality of the framework is important, but how you implement it is more important. It does not have to be the greatest framework in the world but, if it is introduced, communicated and used well, you will get results," said a personnel and development specialist at food manufacturer Golden Wonder, reflecting on the importance of explaining new competencies to the employees they cover. "Communication, communication and communication" is often listed by human resources commentators as the recipe for the success of any new organisational initiative. But simply putting out information and hoping it will be absorbed does not equate to preparing employees effectively for new working practices or performance measures.

Involving employees in the design stage of competency frameworks is a commonly-used method of communication, with almost three-quarters (71%) of employers using it, according to the latest benchmarking survey (Rankin, 2001). The principal reason for the popularity of this early involvement is the other benefits it offers beyond simple communication. Bringing in staff to help define and refine the competencies that will be used to assess their performance, promotion potential or training needs helps ensure the organisational fit of the resulting framework. At Golden Wonder, for example, entrusting the drafting of the descriptions for each of the 12 competencies to a project team of managers from all levels (during a revision of the company's framework for 150 managers in 1998) sacrificed beautiful prose for relevance. "It meant they were couched in local company language. If we had used a consultant to draft them they would have been more elegant and better written, but they wouldn't have been ours."

The most common method of early staff involvement is usually through focus or development groups involving a cross-section of the employees to be covered by the competencies, directed by human resources specialists or consultants. These groups are convened, in most cases, to work on identifying the appropriate behaviours under competency headings already devised by internal human resources staff or consultants. But at Norfolk and Norwich Health Care NHS Trust the behaviours came first. Brainstorming meetings of groups of around eight specialist staff (including gynaecologists, surgeons and anaesthetists) identified the key behaviours for each discipline, and the development staff formulated the competency headings to cover them. "We believed practice should influence competencies, not the other way round," explained an education and development manager.

The Medicines Control Agency developed its framework using separate focus groups of between eight and 20 staff for each of the four disciplinary groups working on competencies for their own specialist areas. These focus groups were supplemented by a core group (some of whose members were drawn from the other groups) which had the task of developing the core competencies. Some of these groups met regularly, others completed their work in a single session. The Royal Society for the Prevention of Cruelty to Animals (RSPCA), for instance, held a single two-day development session with a group of 20 call-centre managers to develop a profile of the behaviours that make an effective team supervisor.

One size does not fit all

There seems to be no consensus among employers on the ideal size of focus groups, but employers accept that, unless the number of employees to be covered by competencies is small, it would be difficult to set the groups up as statistically valid cross-sections. At the Benefits Agency, for instance, the competency framework covers some 70,000 staff, and during a revision exercise in 1996 the consultation stage involved 10 workshops of 12 participants. "We could never consult with everybody," said a spokesperson for the agency, "so we tried to get a representative sample."

At Littlewoods Retail, those who participated in the 12 focus groups of 10 staff (for a set of competencies launched in 1997 covering 6,000 employees) were also selected to be representative as far as possible, reflecting the ethnic balance, job types and ability levels of the larger population. This meant that while the groups were formed of volunteers where possible, employees with something to contribute were "press-ganged where necessary". Medical products manufacturer Ethicon picked the 40-odd people for its competency development group "at random" according to a human resources manager, "though there were some key managers who we knew had to be there".

The most common lead time for the establishment of such focus groups is six months before the launch of new competencies. At the Open University, the groups working on the 1998 framework revision to align it more closely with organisational objectives started meeting only three months before launch. "We didn't need all that long," a development specialist explained, "because we had the existing competencies to work on."

At the polls

Some employers supplement their use of focus or development groups with other means of researching and canvassing opinion. The Open University preceded its focus groups with telephone interviews with up to 30 managers. "We booked appointments," a development specialist said, "and went though a series of questions such as: 'In your view what competencies are required of middle managers to achieve the university's strategic objectives?'." The results led to the formulation of 12 broad competency headings, and three focus groups of 12 managers were then charged with defining behaviours under each heading. At Gloucestershire County Council (see box 8.1), a personnel specialist carried out interviews with key managers and sought the opinions of existing departmental development teams (set up for the purposes of the council's Investors in People accreditation) and the authority's National Vocational Qualification assessor groups.

Employers often gain a double benefit by incorporating employees' and managers' views and expertise into the design process. Not only does this involvement help to tie competencies tightly to the organisational culture and existing best practice, but it also provides an early, informal means of "trickle-down" communication. As a development specialist at the Open University put it: "The grapevine can be very useful in some circumstances. It gives people an idea of what is coming, whereas just throwing out information with no warning can build more resistance."

8.1. Gloucestershire County Council: the writing on the wall

Just before the launch of Gloucestershire County Council's new competencies in April 1999, Personnel Consultant Lise Lewis concluded a thorough communication process, which had included consultation groups and a special newsletter, with a poster campaign publicising the new competencies. The full-colour A4 posters were sent to every department in sets of three to be displayed on local noticeboards. She said that: "I wanted to make them light and not dreary. So I tried to come up with a different, striking image for each one." Each poster was designed to sum up one of the three different competency headings, and she used the following images:

- a picture of huskies drawing a sledge to express "teamwork";

- an ostrich with its head in the sand for "communications"; and

- a Saint Bernard dog with a barrel round its neck for "customer focus".

"It was challenging to find something that was interesting and politically correct at the same time," said Lise, " but the result was good."

8.2. Smooth information transmission at First Data Resources

When electronic payment processing specialist First Data Resources introduced its new competency framework to support training and pay decisions for 2,500 staff in 1996, it was only after an extensive communication and involvement exercise that had lasted more than 12 months. This started with the formation of a working party of 20 people, drawn from all sections of the company, to consult on the overall framework, plus subgroups to focus on specific issues such as the individual competency categories, training and the link to pay.

The company then brought in an external agency to survey staff opinion using focus groups of staff at all levels. The staff were asked questions such as: "What do you think are the pros and cons of appraisal now?". The results provided material for the working party's deliberations, but also introduced the idea of competencies to focus-group members, preparing the ground.

As the framework developed throughout 1995, there were regular updates in the company magazine *FDR Line*. At least one item on competencies was included in each monthly issue. At the point when the competencies were ready to be introduced, personnel specialists issued a pack to all employees containing a set of new pages on the competency system to insert into their staff handbooks and a sample performance agreement form. All staff were briefed at face-to-face sessions.

8.3. Top-down involvement at Marley Building Materials

At Marley Building Materials, the competency roll-out started with around 90 sales staff in 1998, but preparations had been in train for up to two years before. The organisation started by gaining the agreement of senior management to the competency principle, then asked the middle managers to carry out self-assessments and task assessments in the proposed key competency areas. The results were then discussed with those managers and the competencies revised. The managers were expected to discuss the competencies with the staff in their sections and gather feedback. The company found this approach to be an invaluable means of transferring information about the system through the organisation and preparing staff for the subsequent introduction of competencies lower in the hierarchy. One "quick win" in gaining acceptance for the new framework was the immediate use of the competencies to identify training needs, then making sure the training was provided.

Voices in unison

Another, more formal, way of involving staff at the design stage of competency structures is via their union representatives. Organisations such as the Benefits Agency, the Medicines Control Agency, Hinchingbrooke Health Care NHS Trust and Gloucestershire County Council were obliged to consult recognised unions or negotiate their new frameworks with them.

"We would never have moved forward if we had not had their support," said a spokesperson at Hinchingbrooke NHS Trust of its dealings with the Royal College of Nursing and Unison. Its personnel director supervised the development of a new unified competency-based grading scheme for two previously separate groups of operating theatre staff in early 1999. "Communication with staff and the unions from the beginning was essential to getting agreement," the spokesperson explained. "As we were developing the new structure to recruit and retain people in the face of national shortages, we needed them to support it." Union representatives were involved in fine-tuning the new grading structure in the design stage – refining and clarifying the descriptions of responsibilities, skills and competencies needed to progress from one grade to another.

Apart from the necessity of involving unions where membership levels are high, a spokesperson for the Benefits Agency pointed out that unions can be a valuable part of the whole communications exercise. "They helped by providing information to their members," noting that all the different communication channels were valuable because the agency could not justify the cost of sending personalised information to its 70,000 staff.

In the press

Existing staff publications, such as company newsletters, seem the most obvious communication conduits for raising awareness of new or revised competency structures among employees. Yet only a third of the respondents to the annual benchmarking survey (Rankin, 2001) said they had taken advantage of their internal publications for this purpose. Some employers have said that there is no strong reason for this low level of use; rather they have preferred to put their efforts into other communication methods. However, a few employers consider that competencies might be too complex or detailed a subject to be dealt with adequately in brief newsletter articles.

Among the few who have used their internal publications, both Royal Bank Invoice Finance and the Open University simply included small articles trailing the new frameworks during the later development stages. "We just put in an article telling people what we are doing and why we are doing it," said a recruitment and development specialist at Royal Bank Invoice Finance. "We put in a small piece explaining the concepts when we rolled out to middle managers, and now we have decided to go down to the level of the 400 first line managers, I expect we will put something in again," said a development specialist at the Open University.

In contrast, the Medicines Control Agency produced a monthly newsletter dedicated to the new competency framework, starting eight months before its introduction. "It was called *Competency Newsletter* and went to all staff members, with details on what the focus groups were discussing, where we were against targets, and progress on training," a spokesperson said. "It also allowed us to invite comments and feedback on drafts." The agency found that the *Competency Newsletter* was a valuable means of referring staff to information on the developing framework that they might have missed elsewhere, and an "opportunity to reinforce key messages". The newsletter continued after the framework's launch, at a reduced six-weekly frequency, during its post-implementation evaluation stage, and was sent as an attachment to the agency's main e-mailed staff newsletter.

Gloucestershire County Council also used e-mail for the bi-monthly information sent to each department's managers to incorporate into their own local newsletters. "We started with very basic information on why we were doing this and what competencies were. But as time went on, I got focus-group members to contribute pieces on their perspectives and gave information about other well-known employers using competencies – everyday names such as W H Smith – to give confidence in the process. It's important to do that, to add confidence, while being careful not to oversell it," a personnel specialist said.

Special editions

Few employers produce special brochures or leaflets to explain competencies to employees. One exception was Bass Brewers, where the Head of Management Development produced a 30-page colour brochure which was then distributed to all the 200 senior managers, the first group covered by the new competencies in autumn 1999. A development specialist at Bass said that: "We wanted to ensure consistency of approach across the divisions, so each competency was described in detail, with descriptions of on-target and superior performance. It should be a reference point during appraisal meetings."

The growth of organisations' internal electronic publishing activities is reflected in the distribution of competency news updates via e-mail (as mentioned above). The training and development section of the Open University's intranet was used to provide several pages of information on its competencies when they were being introduced, and used other material to direct employees to them.

Person to person

The most popular method of communication for new competencies among the latest competency benchmarking survey sample (Rankin, 2001) was face-to-face briefing sessions for groups of employees and managers, used by 78% of respondents. However, employers approach the use of briefings in many different ways. For example, at Littlewoods Retail, where the new framework covered 6,000 staff, members of the HR team briefed staff in groups of 40 in what it called a "sheep-dip" fashion.

Ethicon used a "belt-and-braces" approach to briefing staff, combining special company-wide sessions to explain the general competency issues and principles with the existing structure of fortnightly briefings by team leaders to deliver targeted information on the local impact of the new structure. Royal Bank Invoice Finance also doubled up its briefings. A recruitment and development specialist led informal meetings of groups of six to 10 staff at all the company's regional offices late in 1999 (for a competency roll-out in February 2000), giving them the opportunity to ask questions, then provided more information via the cascade briefings held by managers.

Involving managers in the briefing process is generally seen by employers as a valuable way of ensuring the principles and practice of competencies are well understood by those who have to administer and evaluate them (as well as taking some of the communication pressure off the personnel and training specialists).

At Gloucestershire County Council, a personnel specialist worked with the authority's various departments to find what briefing methods suited each of them best. "Some had group briefings and I would attend to answer questions," they said. "Others would use normal team-briefing sessions and I would provide them with materials or vet whatever they drew up. One had a single massive meeting for all staff. It was better than foisting one approach on all departments."

Final words

There is no one best way of conducting a communication exercise when introducing competencies; this must be related to the needs and circumstances of the organisation. Often, though, employers look back and find that they could have given more attention and resources to communication. Those who have been through this process advise using as many different communication media as possible, and providing information on a frequent basis. There are limits, too, to what communication and involvement can achieve; they can prepare a receptive welcome for the use of competencies, and help ensure that the framework is relevant and well-designed. But this foundation must be built on through the provision of training.

Training employees to use and accept competencies

Louis Wustemann

Even where employees are already familiar with the principle and practice of performance assessment, adding competencies to the equation can require real adjustment on their part. As one training manager puts it: "Competencies changed the review structure here fundamentally, from a chat with a colleague to a rigorous interview with serious implications, good or bad." In the section above, I looked at the process of embedding competencies into the corporate culture through involvement and communication. Here, I review the experiences of a cross-section of employers in training their managers and/or employees to make their frameworks effective in practice.

All but one of the organisations that I contacted have provided some form of training for competency assessors or those workers being assessed. The exception was British Steel (now part of Corus), where the development of a system based on National Vocational Qualifications (NVQs) followed extensive work by staff at shopfloor level and above to develop the new standards of competence. According to a training and development specialist, this "ground-up" development process meant that staff were already so familiar with the standards that when NVQs were introduced they needed no extra training. Nevertheless, though many other organisations had similarly involved staff in the design of their competencies, to a greater or lesser extent, they also provided training of some sort to support their launch.

Managers go first

In the seventh competency benchmarking survey (Rankin, 2000), staff at managerial level were found to be the most likely focus for competency training. Almost three out of four respondents had prepared managers and supervisors in this way. Those who I interviewed for their experiences reflect this finding – almost all offer training in competencies to managers.

There are similarities between these organisations' approaches to management training – all but one (the Medicines Control Agency: see box 8.4), for instance, used internal trainers – but there were also strong differences. One of the greatest variations lies in the time allotted to training. Although the most common training period is half a day – a timespan used at Aylesbury Vale Healthcare NHS Trust, Bass Brewers and food manufacturer Golden Wonder – others provided training that lasted from as little as one hour up to 18 weeks.

8.4 Going outside: The Medicines Control Agency

External consultants were brought in to train staff in the Medicines Control Agency's new competency framework, when it was launched in April 1999. Several factors led to its decision to outsource the training. There was a perception that participants would have more confidence in what they saw as external experts and help to overcome the cynicism about the competencies project prevalent within the organisation. Outsourcing would also lighten the load on internal training staff and provide a source of specialist expertise in a technical area.

All staff, both appraisers and appraisees, were issued with a comprehensive manual explaining the system, which was described as "good for self-instruction if they worked through it properly". The manual included a "frequently-asked questions" annex with answers to queries such as: "Is this going to affect my pay?" and: "What if I disagree with my manager's assessment?".

These materials were backed up by formal on-site training by the consultants who offered two-hour sessions for appraisees and a half-day for appraisers. Finally, they provided a helpline for anyone whose questions were not answered elsewhere – an offer that many participants took up afterwards.

The lower of these figures was provided by the UK division of Dutch airline KLM, where the competency hour formed part of a half-day session on appraisals. A personnel specialist said that competencies were "not a holy grail for us", being seen as one an element in the total appraisal process where target achievement is the main measure. Also at the end of the spectrum where shorter training times have been used lies engineering consultancy the Babtie Group, whose two-and-a-half hour sessions for managers before the introduction of a new competency framework for 2,500 staff in July 1999 covered the aims of the system and managers' role as appraisers. "In two-and-a-half hours, you can get a hell of a lot over," a development specialist said. Nevertheless, additional training on how to appraise staff was carried out separately a year later.

At the other end of the spectrum lies the 18 weeks' off-the-job training that was provided by the Lincoln Co-operative Society for work-based assessors – most of them store managers – for the society's NVQ programme. The impact on the business was reduced by spreading the training for each manager over a year and by introducing the whole programme gradually over several years.

Content providers

The variety and scope of the different approaches to competency development and assessment among the organisations contacted is reflected in the content of their training sessions. Nevertheless, there are features common to many training sessions whether they were for a new system or revisions to an existing one. These points of similarity include:

- **Dealing with difficult appraisees** or challenges during appraisals. "How do you resolve it if someone says 'I am a level four' and their manager says 'You are a level two'?" said a development specialist at Canon UK. "You have to prepare for that because it is one of the most common questions."

- **Ensuring consistency**, making sure managers apply the same standards to competency assessment across the board. "It's a lot easier to deal with it at the training stage than when the assessment appeals start coming through later," comments one HR manager.

- **Filling in the form**, preparing managers for the new paperwork associated with competency assessment by going through a sample appraisal form.

- **Observing behaviours** and correlating them to the appropriate part of the competency model. This was the main thrust of the three-day sessions at assessment centres for senior managers in the run-up to the relaunch of the Benefits Agency's framework in 1996. The sessions – which formed part of the agency's management development programme – were valuable according to a spokesperson for the agency, "because the focused act of observing and assessing behaviours gave them better understanding of what competencies were all about".

Utility first

There is a remarkable consistency in the format of the training sessions for competency assessors. Most organisations use off-the-job, but on-site, training for small groups, commonly of eight to 12 staff. Training organisers agree on the importance of keeping the groups small. Limiting the size cuts down the impression of classroom teaching, and allows the courses to be more practice-based and interactive. These two features, *practicality* and *involvement*, were emphasised very strongly and were the most common priorities cited by interviewees when asked what they would advise other organisations to include in their competency training.

Canon UK stressed the need to make the training as relevant to individual managers as possible. "We don't want a blanket approach," a development specialist said. "It has to have a practical basis. With competencies you are always trying to bring them alive, to see how they would manifest themselves in someone's daily work life." On the subject of interactivity – that is, the need to involve managers in the sessions – some employers have used role plays to allow managers to carry out dry runs in using a new appraisal process. For example, at Aylesbury Vale NHS Trust, trainees paired off for practical exercises. They used profiles and were asked to think of the questions they would pose if they were doing a real assessment interview.

The two-day training sessions held in 1998 for managers at NEC Technologies were "very, very participative", with many one-to-one practical exercises. The company had, in any case, been moving away from "chalk-and-talk" training to more participative, learner-centred provision. It approached the implementation of competencies in a new light, because of this shift in thinking. Instead of providing training in order to gear people up to implement a new framework, it involved them in a practical way and adapted the competencies to ensure they met managers' needs. In NEC's view, if an organisation does not pay attention and respond to the experience of those working day-to-day with the competencies and make appropriate changes to the framework, "then it dies".

Finding the time

The more in-depth the training that is offered to appraisers, the longer the time commitment expected of them in most cases. A thorny issue for several training and development managers is that of balancing the needs of managers to fulfil their existing obligations with the organisational need for thorough preparation for, and a consistent approach to, any new structure.

In its days as an independent bank, NatWest relaunched its competency framework in 1997 and provided a one-day workshop for managers. The framework was to cover 60,000 employees, reducing the number of competencies from 22 to 15, and introducing a behaviourally-anchored rating scale. Individual divisions of NatWest were left to decide whether or not the training was mandatory, which resulted in varied levels of preparation. Some areas said "here's the paperwork, get on with it"; some were very prescriptive about the workshop; and others made it an option. An insider said that: "If it was my business, I would have made it obligatory. You can have the greatest set of competencies in the world, but if people don't know how to use them, it is useless."

At Lincoln Co-operative Society, the heavy 18-week training commitment for the NVQ assessors brought resistance, according to one of its personnel specialists. "These are busy managers or supervisors, and you get a lot of pressure from departments that they don't want to release them for a whole day at a time, so we came to a compromise." The compromise involved training days running from midday to 7 pm, so the time was split between work and personal time.

Help from above

The problem of management commitment to the training process also arose at Aylesbury Vale Healthcare NHS Trust where competencies were gradually introduced for almost all of the trust's 1,100-strong workforce over a period of four years. The project team developing the competences had to undertake a "selling" or marketing campaign to persuade reluctant line managers of the need for training provision. "You have to make any fliers you produce or any e-mails you send as attractive and relevant as possible," one of the project team said. "And it helps if you can get senior managers on board to encourage people to attend."

This point about top-level encouragement was echoed by a personnel specialist at RAC Motoring Services, where the training for the launch of competencies for call-centre staff in 1997 involved team leaders in a hefty 10 days' classroom training (though these sessions took in a whole revision of the management training process, not just competencies). The training was mandatory, "but we never needed to make that explicit because we had a high level of buy-in". The presence of the customer service director on the committee overseeing the competency launch was seen as particularly useful.

Employees on board

The annual benchmarking surveys carried out by the *Competency & Emotional Intelligence* journal reveal that training for employees covered by competencies is less common than training for their managers, with around half the organisations surveyed offering training below managerial level. This finding was reflected among the organisations interviewed, of whom around half have trained employees below managerial level. In all cases, this training was shorter and less intense than for managers in the same organisation.

The Babtie Group simply ran the same sessions for appraisees as for appraisers, with the omission of the element covering how to appraise. At Gloucestershire County Council, where competencies were introduced for 12,000 employees in 1998, the training varied from department to department, but one section gave the appraisers a day's training, then trainers helped them present a morning workshop for their own subordinates. Similarly, Lexmark rolled out training to senior then middle managers, who then worked with local training staff to prepare sessions for their own staff. NEC Technologies offered employees a one-day session (compared with the two or three days for managers) focusing on how competencies would feed into their performance reviews.

Light refreshment

Once the initial education programmes for a competency launch or relaunch is over, most organisations seem to take the view that "practice makes perfect", and that little further training is needed unless the framework is revised. Refresher training offered is usually available only to those who ask for it. One easy, and common, approach is to allow people to opt back into the training they previously received when the course is being re-run for new arrivals.

Following its 1997 relaunch, NatWest's one-day workshop was subsequently made available to managers for refresher training at the same time as it was being offered to new recruits. However, it found that managers were unlikely to participate for a second time, as, by then, they were actively involved in the new system and had learned by experience. However, other trainers are less convinced of this point of view. Rather than simply undergoing the same experience and learning all over again, they believe that the most valuable learning comes from the questions, real-life examples and pooled experience that participants themselves bring to a workshop – and these differ every time a workshop is run.

AXA Sun Life Services first introduced competencies at the beginning of the 1990s, and has found that: "Alongside some form of refresher training, the other common approach is to use training staff as a source of personal assistance to those who feel they need extra help – and to encourage them to seek it out. If people need more support, they will self-nominate. They can go to the training staff in their business area and get some one-to-one coaching."

NEC Technologies is unusual in taking a highly structured approach to refresher training. All appraisers go through a half-day updating session in groups at the company's training centre once a year before the annual performance reviews. The company wants to be sure that managers are still on top of the assessment procedures, and believes that providing the sessions helps to remind managers of the importance of competency evaluation. On a practical level, the sessions also provide the opportunity to inform managers of any changes that have taken place, such as amendments to the assessment form.

Overall, organisations seem convinced of the need for competency training, especially for assessors, to give those at the "front line" confidence to implement new systems effectively. But several organisations said that, however valuable formal training before and during the introduction or revision of competencies, the most valuable learning comes afterwards when they are working day-to-day with the system.

References

Rankin, Neil (2000) "Performance through people: the seventh annual competency survey", *Competency & Emotional Intelligence Benchmarking*, 1999/2000, January.

Rankin, Neil (2001), "Raising performance through people: the eighth competency survey", *Competency & Emotional Intelligence Benchmarking*, 2000/01, January.

Learning points

Overview

- Employers often underestimate the importance of ensuring the effective introduction of competencies; as a result, there are widespread problems connected with employees' and managers' lack of understanding.

- The point when competencies are introduced should be linked to the provision of training and further familiarisation, but proper commitment and understanding depend upon the use of a process that starts from the point when the competencies begin to be designed.

- The most common communication methods in use are: group or team briefings; training for managers; involving managers and/or employees at the design stage; a special leaflet or brochure; and items in the regular staff newspaper or magazine.

Communication and involvement

- Early involvement from the design stage onwards begins the process of communication and "buy in". Focus groups or project groups are often used as a means of involving a cross-section of the workforce in the design work. However, most organisations are too large for such groups to be truly representative, so they cannot provide the only means of communication and involvement. The most common lead time for the establishment of such focus groups is six months before the launch of new competencies.

- Other methods used at the design stage include conducting interviews with managers, teams and other staff. Interviewees can act as information channels. Trade unions can be influential in supporting a competency initiative, and/or they can be effective communication channels with their memberships.

- Specialist booklets and leaflets, and articles in staff newsletters, are used as ways of keeping the workforce informed. E-mails and intranets are growing in importance.

- Face-to-face briefings are the most common method in use, although they are used in different ways. Often, the involvement of line managers who will run the new competency process is found to be valuable.

- There is no one best way of conducting a communication exercise when introducing competencies; it must be related to the needs of the organisation. In retrospect, employers often consider they could have given more attention and resources to communication.

Training

- Provision of training linked to the introduction of competencies is widespread, particularly where the competencies will be formally assessed. Priority is usually given to the managers that will conduct these assessments, with employees often either receiving less training, or none at all.

- The training provision is often of short duration, typically half a day, although this depends on the organisation's requirements.

- Many courses cover a core of subjects: dealing with difficult appraisees or challenges during appraisals; ensuring consistency in competency assessments; completing assessment forms; and observing behaviours and correlating them to the appropriate part of the competency model.

- It is important to gain top-level endorsement for the training course, as this encourages line managers to release staff for the training and to attend themselves.

- Few organisations offer refresher training, although many ensure that training is available for later recruits. Many employers believe that the most valuable learning comes afterwards when managers and employees are working day-to-day with the system.

Chapter 9

Reward and competencies

Introduction

Neil Rankin

Reward management has experienced its own "velvet revolution" over the past two decades. Incrementally, rather than convulsively, organisations have changed the way they reward their employees and managers. Instead of the almost universal use of across-the-board pay rises and rigid incrementally-based movement through narrow grades, many employers now link base pay or bonuses to individual performance, and have moved towards fewer, broader grades (known as "broadbanding").

The willingness to innovate in reward is proven, and the rapid, large-scale implementation of competency frameworks would seem to provide an ideal launch pad for new approaches to pay. If an employer shows that competencies are important, why not put the final link in place and relate some part of the reward system to them? Yet, as this chapter shows, reward is the "final frontier" for the application of competencies. Recruitment, development, appraisal and most other aspects of people management have all been reformed in organisations that have adopted competencies, yet pay is usually the notable exception.

Benchmarking research among 113 employers (Rankin, 2001) shows that while 87% of competency users have linked their training and development processes to competencies, only 24% have adopted any form of competency-related reward. In the public sector, the practice is rarer still, with only 17% of employers using it. Moreover, careful analysis of a matched sample of employers shows that while competency frameworks are increasingly being adopted by employers, the proportion of them relating competencies to reward is shrinking (Miller, Rankin and Neathey, 2001).

The relatively low usage of competency-related reward among organisations with established competency frameworks is an indication of both the difficulties that have to be overcome in making such a link and the controversial nature of this approach. There are, in fact, two diametrically opposed schools of thought about the merits of paying for competencies.

The supporters argue that forging a link between competencies and reward is eminently sensible, in that pay is the most fundamental reason that people seek out paid work. Without such a link, the organisation's commitment to competencies will be seen as hollow and half-hearted. Moreover, the "discordant voices" of personnel practices that are based on different methods mean that employees will be torn in two or more ways. Their experience of the organisation's training and development, for example, will tell them that competencies are important. But their differently operated pay system will contradict this, and draw their attention towards targets and objectives.

Equally forcefully, the opponents of competency-related pay maintain that any link of this nature is extremely unwise. In terms of effectiveness, it will fail, because individuals are unlikely to willingly and honestly discuss their performance, and take part in the necessary remedial learning, if they fear that this very honesty will rebound on them in terms of an unfavourable pay award. And in respect of cost control, opponents argue that it makes little sense to reward employees for new or improved competencies if this personal growth does not lead to increased financial performance. The organisation is laying itself open to pay drift, in other words, with no commensurate rise in income to justify higher pay or finance it.

The low usage of competency-related pay has created a vicious circle. There are few role models for other organisations to examine and evaluate. And the lack of a critical mass means that no single best way of linking pay to competencies has so far emerged. This reduces the visibility of competency-related pay and presents yet another obstacle to its adoption, as employers have to choose between a bewildering array of competing methods.

The final straw for decision-makers, though, is fear of legal action: there is widespread concern that the UK's and EU's laws on equal pay make competency-related payments open to legal challenge. These fears are not groundless, but they must be put in perspective. In chapter 5, Barrister Paul Epstein draws on his wide experience of equal opportunities law to highlight the key issues that must be addressed to ensure that pay systems are as fair and robust as possible. His points apply with equal force to any form of reward that moves away from across-the-board payments (pay rises, bonuses or automatic, incremental progression). And many, many employers have made such moves in recent years without any legal action from their staff or trade unions. In fact, competency-related reward is potentially fairer and more defensible than many other individually- or team-based pay practices.

It compares particularly well against performance-related pay systems, which are often cloaked in secrecy, and prone to subjective judgments about individuals. The bases for many performance-related systems are unclear, and proving their rationale would be difficult indeed in a court or at a tribunal. Competency-related systems, in contrast, should be objective, transparent and relatively consistent, *providing they have been properly developed, designed and implemented.*

If fear and lack of information are the barriers preventing the implementation of competency-related reward, then this handbook will provide a key resource. Paul Epstein's guidance on the law appears in chapter 5, and general equal opportunities issues appear in chapter 6. The remainder of this chapter focuses on practice. Competency-related reward is frequently introduced as part of a move to broadbanded grading systems, and Claire Muhiudeen draws on her expertise gained in advising many employers on their reward systems to highlight the key issues that are involved. Katherine Adams analyses the findings of her large-scale research into the various forms of competency-related reward that employers have adopted. And we also feature a case study of one employer's approach, which has taken the form of team reward linked to competencies.

The use of competency models in a broadbanded structure

Clare Muhiudeen

Over recent years, changes in the commercial environment have been characterised by changes in organisational structures, such as moving from hierarchical to flatter, more flexible structures intended to improve process cycle efficiency. The management of people has shifted from the old division of labour to the "one-stop shop" and multiskilling. The emphasis now is on the customer and knowledge worker, rather than those that act as service providers. Competitive pressure is increasing the business focus on the critical capabilities that will most contribute to competitive differentiation and performance in the marketplace. Similarly, business success is increasingly dependent on the speed at which people can learn new skills, abilities and behaviours, and can adapt to changing organisational and market requirements.

Many organisations have found that traditional approaches to job evaluation using "points" and "grades" within a defined set of criteria tend to:

- reinforce a hierarchical structure where the emphasis is more on the job and task, rather than the role and range of skills required in a flatter structure;

- focus on sizing the job and not sizing the contribution;

- ignore the competencies of the individual in the job;

- be based on static and dated criteria that do not take account of the critical capabilities and drivers of business performance;

- be based on a few measures related to market value rather than multiple factors; and

- operate separately and not be integrated with other human resource processes.

Many organisations have used competency models to articulate to their employees the key values, skills, attributes and behaviours expected of them. These models have acted as the cornerstone of many training and development programmes or performance management systems (see box 9.1).

Research conducted by the American Compensation Association (1996) showed that 48% of companies surveyed use competency-based human resource tools to establish expectations of performance standards, and that 42% utilise them to emphasise the capabilities of employees and how these link to organisational success. This is further supported by the findings from the *Competency & Emotional Intelligence Benchmarking* reports which show that the overwhelming rationale for introducing competencies is to support a performance management system.

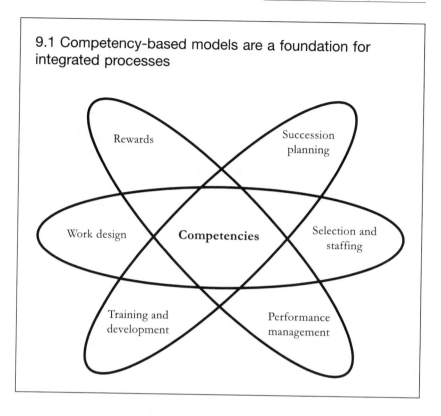

9.1 Competency-based models are a foundation for integrated processes

The points above very accurately describe the use of competency models in articulating *how* employees should do things. However, my own organisation, Watson Wyatt, has uncovered a further trend through our work with organisations. These enterprises also wish to use competency-based models to support *what* should be done. This is especially the case when a traditional job-evaluated structure is felt to be inappropriate for that organisation.

Impact on human resource processes

Companies that have adopted a broadbanded structure typically want to break the focus on the job and a grade and to create a greater emphasis on individuals' contribution and flexibility. However, moving to fewer levels means more than simply changing the number of grades. It means changing the human resource processes relating to job sizing, salary management and the way that career opportunities are communicated. Typical questions asked by employers and employees in these situations include:

- How do we manage career progression?

- How do we maintain motivation?

- What are we rewarding?

- How do we manage salary costs?

The answers to these questions are to a large extent dependent on the way that the broadbanded structure is designed, managed and communicated. A survey by Watson Wyatt (1996) indicated that over half of the companies that have introduced a broadbanded structure still use a method of job evaluation to position and explain job demands within the bands. However, a few organisations have chosen to use competency-based criteria in place of traditional job evaluation factors, and Watson Wyatt has found that this trend is increasing. An example of the use of competencies in underpinning a broadbanded pay structure is shown in box 9.2, while a typical method of progression within bands and the role that market rates can play in such structures are illustrated in box 9.3.

The benefits

Using competency-based models to underpin a broadbanded structure has many advantages, beyond those relating specifically to reward:

- it allows organisations to develop a clear rationale for the number of bands (that is, not simply collapsing an existing grade structure);

- it means that such a competency-based rationale can replace one derived from traditional job evaluation, while at the same time continuing to provide a logical framework to explain organisational structures;

- it allows organisations to reinforce the linkage between organisation levels and performance expectations;

- a similar or comparable vocabulary can be used, reinforcing the linkage between the requirements of the job and the person – both what you do and how you do it;

- it provides a tool for communicating to employees what they have to do in order to progress, such as the nature of the changes in skills and behaviour that are required at the different levels; and, finally

9.2. An example of a broadbanded approach using competency delineators

Teamwork	Band 1	Band 2	Band 3
Sharing	• Willingly shares workload to assist team members.	• Shares ownership and visibility of the project.	• Ensures all team members are involved.
		• Builds team spirit through sharing.	• Assumes other responsibilities when required.
		• Willing to share recognition of results.	• Places team success first.
Coordination	• Knowledge of other team members' roles and responsibilities.	• Takes responsibility for coordination, implementation and functioning of the team.	• Establishes responsibilities and accountabilities.
	• Seeks clarification.	• Seeks and provides clarification.	• Monitors results of the team.
	• Sees role as an equal player.	• Is available to others.	• Provides clarification when needed.
			• Is approachable.
Cooperation	• Supports team decisions.	• Accomodating of diverse points of view.	• Accomplishes goal with support of others.
	• Has constructive approach.	• Makes sacrifices for team.	• Places team needs ahead of personal needs.
	• Involved with other members in problem-solving.	• Builds rapport well.	• Builds effective relationships.
		• Has ability to find common ground.	

- it supports the creation of competency-related reward systems, paying for contribution and not simply job size.

Key considerations

There are, however, a number of considerations that need to be highlighted. First of all, the competency model needs to be simple in design and content, so as to facilitate communication and its application in practice. It may be that a broadbanded structure is designed around core organisational competencies, each of which may constitute a cluster containing a number of specific related competencies. These sub-sets are more likely to be used in support of a performance management process than in shaping a grading structure (see box 9.2 for an example).

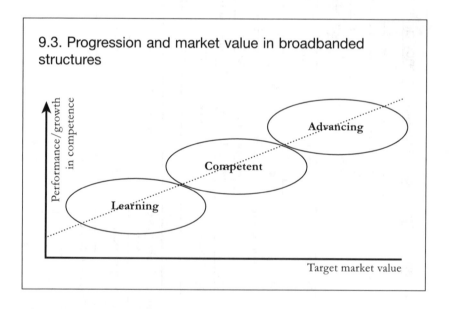

9.3. Progression and market value in broadbanded structures

The measures used in the model need to be reviewed for potential bias or discrimination in the same way as job evaluation factors. Organisations have traditionally used analytical job evaluation schemes as a means of providing evidence of compliance with equal pay legislation. It is unclear at this stage how structures based on competency models would be viewed by tribunals and courts, but the advice to date has been:

- ensure the criteria selected are equally applicable to all jobs (the difference being one of scale);

- do not bias the competency model with measures that overtly reinforce characteristics typically associated with one gender more than the other;

- ensure appropriate involvement of and communication to employees; and

- ensure that users are appropriately trained.

The way that implementation of broadbanding is managed is also of crucial importance. Our experience of working with employers suggests that any direct linkage to pay awards should be introduced gradually. The initial focus should be on explaining the requirements and expectations – in other words, focusing on getting the communication and performance management process right before attaching pay awards to the process. The mechanisms for maintaining reward systems that take account of competencies should be decided in advance, and a suitable mechanism chosen for updating pay ranges and any control points within broad bands. The availability of market data, in particular, will need careful consideration. Broadbanded systems rely heavily on such data but, to date, most information sources are linked to job-based, not competency-based, measures.

The objectives for a broadbanded structure and its impact internally should not be overstated. Replacing job-evaluated gradings with a competency-based broadbanded structure is not the panacea for all grading problems. Realistically, it is likely to increase flexibility, reinforce individual contribution and improve communication about career opportunities. It also provides the means of supporting and integrating contribution-based reward systems. Success is not assured: without an effective and credible performance management process, good internal communications, effective training of line managers, and robust market data for job pricing, broadbanding will not make its hoped-for contribution to the organisation's achievement of its goals.

Case study: competency-related pay for teams at Pet Plan Group

John Warner

Providing a range of insurance policies for animals such as cats, dogs, rabbits and horses, Pet Plan is a wholly owned subsidiary of Cornhill

Insurance. It has 260 employees and an annual turnover of about £60 million. For its part, Cornhill Insurance employs 3,500 people throughout the UK, and introduced a competency framework in 1997. This was rolled-out to include Pet Plan a year later.

During 1997, a strategy group of senior Cornhill managers and human resource managers formed a competency working party. After considering alternatives, it decided to devise its own framework without outside intervention or help. The aim of the competency framework was, and remains, to provide a single base for all human resource activities throughout the Cornhill operation, including Pet Plan. The company believes this prevents a disjointed response and is helping to keep in step appraisal, job descriptions, training and development, and decisions about pay.

Range of competencies

The framework consists of eight competency headings that are broken down into further subheadings:

1. Task planning: organising of self, organising of resources, managing projects and business planning.

2. Decision-making: researching and deciding.

3. Creativity: enterprising and innovating.

4. Motivating others: teamworking, leading, training and coaching, and developing of others.

5. Personal effectiveness: achieving, adapting and persevering.

6. Communication skills: speaking, writing, listening, presenting and influencing.

7. Business skills: key business processes, understanding customers, understanding/developing markets and understanding finance.

8. Technical skills: acquiring knowledge and applying knowledge.

For guidance, each of the subheadings is provided with a statement of the characteristics and actions to describe performance. For example, "training and coaching" (part of the "motivating others" cluster of competencies) is defined as: "Creates and maintains a personal development plan. Is involved with the induction and training of others through one-to-one or group training. Develops colleagues through the coaching process. Identifies and develops potential."

Weighting and grading

These two examples and all the other descriptors do not include negative statements. However, there is a weighting system that shows the relative importance, on a scale of 1 to 5, of each competency area to each role in the organisation. For example, call-centre staff have a weighting of 5 on their "communication skills" competency, but "personal effectiveness" assumes a lower importance. For any job role, the total weighting is limited to a score of 20. In addition, as part of the appraisal process, line managers assess performance by using the following personal grading boundaries:

1 or 3: below standard;

5: normally expected performance; and

7 or 9: above standard.

Using a grid, with the personal grading on the horizontal axis and the eight competencies on the vertical axis, scores are calculated by multiplying the weighting by the personal grading. A total for the eight competencies is determined for each employee. This score is added into team totals. This determines an overall remuneration "pot" for specific teams and is divided according to employees' individual performance totals. This process takes place in an annual cycle, but appraisals are carried out on a quarterly basis. During the appraisal, employees may negotiate with their line managers for a change in their job specification. In consequence, this may result in changes to the weighting score and performance targets. Training and development targets are determined as part of the annual cycle. Normally, three are training-related and the rest relate to personal objectives linked to the business plan. The company believes that employees should aim to develop in one or two competencies per target, if appropriate.

Some reflections

"We've found it a bit difficult to put an objective judgment on call-centre behaviour, which forms an important part of our business," says Philip White, Human Resources Manager. "Clearly defined standards are set out in our training manuals, and the team leaders are quick to pick up on inappropriate behaviour during the year. But we are able to generate empirical measures by monitoring the speed of response to telephone calls and employees' call-wrap-up rates."

Philip says the most taxing part of adopting the competency framework was in writing an appropriate job specification for every role at Pet Plan that matched the eight competencies. This was done by individual employees working in conjunction with their line manager in order to prepare a specification. In the case of generic job roles, line managers considered what needed to be included in the specifications, drafted descriptions and consulted representatives from the relevant teams before final agreement was reached. "Prior to 1998, we were considering introducing our own competence framework. When our parent company offered one that was already devised and in use, it made a great deal of sense to adopt it too," says Philip. "This is particularly true as pay negotiations are conducted collectively for the whole group and the scoring used in the framework influences remuneration."

Employers' practices

Katherine Adams

The question of competency-related pay is important because it can be seen as a kind of litmus test for competencies as a whole. If employers are confident enough to link them to the sensitive issue of pay, this would seem to confirm competencies' apparent pre-eminence in the world of human resource management. Conversely, enough is known about the potential dangers of making these links – including spiralling pay bills, excessive time and cost implications, and equal pay issues – to suggest that, if the attempt goes horribly wrong, the effects might send shock waves through the whole competency movement.

To my knowledge, there has been no major research on competency-related pay in the UK that could shed light on these important issues. To fill this gap, I conducted a large-scale survey in May 1999 into UK employers' practices and experiences on behalf of *Competency & Emotional Intelligence Quarterly* in association with the Fourth International Competency Conference. The survey uses data from 77 organisations, 25 of which use one or more forms of competency-related pay, grading and progression, to uncover some of the detail that has until now been missing. In particular, it tackles the issue of what organisations are hoping to achieve by paying for competencies.

Commentators tend to see the link between competencies and reward as a response to the changing nature of work. In particular, it is thought to encourage employees to be more flexible, working to broad roles rather than narrowly defined jobs, sometimes in teams, often with a greater focus on "the customer", and very often within flatter organisations that afford far fewer promotion opportunities. This survey offered the chance to test these assumptions by asking employers what they saw as the main reasons for taking this step. Most important of all, perhaps, the survey was an opportunity to ask employers how well they believed their system was working in their organisations. I discuss the problems they have faced, and pass on their advice for other organisations planning to make such a link.

One surprise is that those organisations using competency-related pay have been doing so for so long, given the relative newness of the whole competency approach. Over a third (39%) had been using it for two to three years, and a quarter (26%) for four or five years, or even longer. So, all in all, a total of nearly two-thirds (65%) had used it for two years or more. The evidence suggests that there is a greater wealth of experience of competency-related pay among the employers taking part in the research than might have been expected.

Coverage

The sample of 25 organisations that use competency-related pay is split roughly half and half between those who use it for all groups of staff (48%) and those who use it for just some (52%). Roughly half of those using it selectively apply it to specific groups, such as sales staff, IT specialists or healthcare workers. The remainder apply it on the basis of people's level in the organisation – for instance including or excluding blue-collar workers, first line managers, senior executives or those with high potential.

The link to pay

In essence, competency-related pay is a simple concept: the idea is to link an individual's pay to the competencies he or she demonstrates at work. And yet it seems to mean different things to different people. Even in the mid 1990s, when there was much less experience of incorporating competencies in reward schemes, Dr Michael Cross was able to enumerate some 60 variants when he spoke at the 1994 annual conference of the Chartered Institute of Personnel and Development. To try to make sense of this disarray, the survey defined what seemed to be the four main ways that competencies can be linked to pay, and asked employers about each. The four types of link are as follows:

- grading structure design: jobs are assigned to grades according to the competencies they require;

- promotions/demotions: employees move between the job grades according to an assessment of their competencies;

- pay rises/cuts: employees move within their pay band according to an assessment of their competencies; and

- annual pay rise allocations: an overall annual pay rise is divided among employees according to an assessment of their competencies.

In the sections that follow, I examine each of these links in turn.

Design of the grading structure

Perhaps some of the most thoroughgoing systems are those that use competencies to help design the grading structure itself. As practice in Xerox (UK), the Royal Bank of Scotland, the Bank of Scotland and Fine Tubes illustrates, there are a variety of ways in which this can be done. They include:

- dividing the organisation into job families on the basis of pre-defined competencies;

- dividing a particular job family or role into levels on the basis of pre-defined competencies;

- defining the competencies required for a pre-determined set of job families or roles; and

- assigning existing jobs to a new grading structure according to the competencies required.

The first two of these are akin to a job evaluation process, using competencies as the "factors" that underlie the whole grading system;

the second two are processes that are, logically, further down the road of designing a grading system. Of course, organisations can use any number of these methods, in any combination. The survey shows that a surprisingly high proportion of those using competency-related pay say they are using it in this thoroughgoing way: to help design the grading system. Over three-quarters (76%) of the organisations said they do so – though just 8% said that competencies are the only factor determining the grade of each job. The remaining 68% said that other factors also help to determine job grades – in particular job "complexity" (mentioned by 52%), level of responsibility (40%) and job "size" (36%).

Interestingly, 36% said that their organisation uses a job-evaluated pay and grading structure. And 52% said that they use a broadbanded pay and grading structure. (As Claire Muhiudeen explains above, "broadbanding" is a term used to describe a system that features a few pay bands/grades, with a wide pay range for each band.)

Given the scepticism of some commentators about competency-related pay, it was thought important to ask those respondents that also used other factors to determine grades what weight they attached to competencies, vis à vis these other factors. Most (59%) said that competencies are of roughly equal importance as the other factors, while 35% said competencies are the most important factor, and just one organisation (6%) said competencies are the least important factor. So, although it is true that most organisations that use competencies to design the grading structure also use other factors, it can be said that competencies are almost always of at least equal importance as these other factors.

Promotions/demotions

The second type of link between competencies and pay is also a fairly radical matter, whereby an employee's promotion (and demotion) prospects depend on an assessment of their competencies. Rather than just allowing movement within a particular pay band, these moves typically offer the employee access to a new, higher pay band, so this kind of link is not to be embarked on lightly by employers.

In Fine Tubes, ScottishPower Generation Division, the Bank of Scotland and other organisations, promotion to a higher grade may be automatic once an individual attains a certain competency rating, or it may just be that the individual is put forward or can apply for promoted positions once he or she attains that rating. Very often – as in these three companies – the competency assessments will be being made anyway, to determine individuals' progression within their pay bands, so that pay progression and promotion issues are, in effect, part of a seamless whole.

Again, a surprisingly high proportion of competency-related pay users in the survey said that they make the link to promotion and demotion. Four-fifths (80%) had made this link, though, again, just 12% of organisations said that competencies are the only factor that determines how people are promoted or demoted. The remaining 68% of organisations said that other factors also help to determine promotions/demotions – in particular the achievement of objectives/targets (mentioned by 60%).

In terms of the relative importance of competencies and these other factors, a similar picture emerges to the one for grading system design. Most of the organisations using competency-related pay said that competencies are of roughly equal importance as the other factors (67%), 27% said that competencies are the most important factor and just one (7%) said that competencies are the least important factor. So, once again, it can be concluded that for almost all the organisations that link competencies to promotions and demotions, competencies are as important or more important than any other factors.

Pay rises/cuts

The third type of link between competencies and pay – pay rises (and pay cuts) – is in many ways the "classic" approach. So it is not really surprising that this kind of link is the most widespread of the four that was examined, with over four-fifths of users (88%) linking competencies to pay rises/cuts. Generally speaking, an individual's competency assessment is used to determine a usually consolidated, often annual pay increase within their pay band – sometimes supplemented by other increases (such as performance bonuses or cost-of-living increases) determined by other factors.

Interestingly, the survey found that the proportion of those saying that competencies are the only factor determining people's place in their pay band was considerably higher than for the other kinds of link between competencies and pay. Nearly three in 10 (28%) of those using competencies for pay rises/cuts said that competencies are the only factor involved here. Still, twice as many (60%) said that other factors also help to determine pay in their organisations – in particular achievement of objectives/targets (used by all 60%) and market comparisons (44%). Of the 88% in total that link competencies to movement within a pay band, it is interesting to note that most of them (68%) have broad bands with wide pay ranges.

In terms of the relative weight attached to competencies when it comes to determining pay rises/cuts, once again a similar picture holds as for grading system design and promotions/demotions. Almost all of those using competencies along with other factors said that competencies are of roughly equal importance (86%). Of the remainder, 7% said that competencies are the most important factor, and another 7% said that competencies are the least important factor.

Division of annual pay rise

The fourth, and final, type of link between competencies and pay investigated by the survey concerns dividing up an overall annual pay rise among employees according to an assessment of their competencies. Of course, given that many organisations operate an overall pay budget, there is inevitably some overlap between this kind of link and the previous link that was looked at: people's progression through their pay band.

None of the organisations that I interviewed in depth for the study operated a straightforward "pay share" system, though Specsavers Optical Group operates a system that is somewhat akin to it. It determines the total "pot" available for bonus payments, and then awards bonuses based on individuals' competency ratings. A different approach is exemplified by the case of Registers of Scotland (Adams, 1999). This organisation translates its overall annual pay increase into a total paybill for each grade. Each of these pay "pots" is then divided into "equity shares", the value of each share depending on how many shares are earned by all employees in that grade. And the number of shares that individuals earn is determined by their competencies plus their achievement of objectives.

The survey found that this type of link – the division of an annual pay rise into shares of an annual pay "pot" – is the least popular of the four reward systems investigated. Still, more than half (56%) of the organisations in the study said that they used it. Of course, some of these responses may have simply referred to the operation of overall pay budgets, rather than to a thoroughgoing "pay share" system such as that run by Registers of Scotland, so it is important not to overemphasise this finding.

Once again, only two of the 14 organisations using this method (8% overall) said that competencies are the only factor that determines people's share of annual pay rises. For the remainder, other factors also determine pay shares – in particular the achievement of objectives/targets and market comparisons. Again, over half of the organisations that said they use other factors alongside competencies reported that competencies are of roughly equal importance as the other factors.

How "deep" does it go?

An important finding of the survey is that virtually all the users linked competencies to pay in more than one of the ways discussed above. In fact, just one organisation made a single link – namely pay rises/cuts – while the largest group (40%) said that they make all four of the different types of links between competencies and pay. A further 32% made two links, and 24% made three. This finding – and in particular the fact that so many organisations are linking competencies to the design of the grading system and to promotions/demotions – is a strong indication of the depth of competency-related pay in the participating organisations.

And this fact, along with some of the others discussed above, may perhaps be used to counteract some of the scepticism that is expressed about it.

It is clear that competencies have been making inroads into the very structure of the grading system and influencing promotion decisions, as well as affecting pay progression and annual pay increases. Nearly half of those using competency-related pay have applied it to all their staff. And, even when competencies have been used alongside other factors, they have almost always been of at least equal importance as those other factors. But the position should not be exaggerated. The research also found that few organisations have been using

competencies as the sole determinant of pay – just one of the
organisations studied said that competencies represented the only
factor in all the aspects of the pay systems that were investigated.

Why use it?

As I explained at the beginning of this section, the survey was seen
as an ideal opportunity to test some of the assumptions that are
made about competency-related pay's apparent rise in popularity.
Received wisdom is that it is a good way of rewarding employees for
their performance, in particular for showing greater flexibility,
working to broader and more customer-focused remits, and as a way
of compensating for the scarcity of promotion opportunities.

Certainly, the research's findings tend to support this view. The two
most frequently mentioned reasons given by respondents are
encouraging better individual performance (80%) and rewarding
people for developing the competencies needed to work flexibly
(72%).

And this finding holds good whatever the nature of the
pay/competency link that the organisation has adopted. In fact, 64%
of respondents mentioned both of these reasons. Furthermore, these
two reasons maintain their pre-eminent position when it comes to
the question of what are the most important objectives for
competency-related pay: 32% cited encouraging better individual
performance and 23% rewarding the competencies needed to work
flexibly.

In terms of the other reasons, 60% mentioned showing that the
organisation is serious about the need to change behaviour, 52%
giving employees access to job progression in the absence of
promotion opportunities, 36% giving employees access to pay
increases in the absence of promotion opportunities and 24% to
reinforce other competency initiatives.

All these responses were in reply to a pre-set list of options. In
addition, 36% (nine organisations) mentioned other reasons not on
the list. These are:

*"Ensure pay positioning is more objective, promoting fairness and
equity*."*

239

"To maintain a control on wage drift by separating length of service from the equation*."

"To align different pay practices/competency levels."

"To provide a measurable standard of employee behaviour and performance."

"Development is seen as an important factor."

"To reward people for what they achieve*."

"To recognise high potential*."

"To support the company's values in the way results are achieved."

"Aligning individual performance with organisation's vision/values/mission*."

(* These reasons were cited as the most important for introducing competency-related pay.)

And why not?

The survey findings also offer a valuable insight into the question of why organisations have chosen not to introduce links between their competency frameworks and reward. The most noticeable finding is how few organisations have what one could regard as settled objections to competency-related pay. Most (53%) said that they are at too early a stage of introducing competencies. Fewer, but still a significant number, said that their organisation had not yet thought about it (18%). In fact, more than two-thirds (68%) of the organisations favoured one or both of these reasons – suggesting that the pay linkage might be at least a future possibility for the majority of the "refusenik" organisations that were studied.

Of the substantive reasons against this approach, concern about adversely affecting other competency initiatives was the most frequently cited reason, mentioned by 26%. This is an interesting finding, suggesting that competency-related pay's potential to disrupt the whole competency scene has not been lost on UK employers. However, as shall be seen below, these fears do not appear to be borne out by the experience of those employers who have actually introduced it. Another reason for not introducing it involves concerns about employees' reactions (21%). Interestingly, though, concerns about the likely costs, and fears about the potential for equal pay claims, only troubled two organisations in each case (5%) – none of them were those with settled objections to competency-related pay. All these responses were in reply to a pre-set list of options. In addition, however, 42% mentioned other reasons not on the list. A fifth (20%) clearly had doubts about the whole idea of competency-related pay (most of these employers being among those with settled objections) and 5% mentioned other changes taking place in their organisations that rule it out, at least for the time being. Altogether, nine of the 12 organisations with settled objections gave other reasons, including:

"Roles too diverse to make link straightforward, and benefits of this approach would be too limited to make it worthwhile."

"Never seen a truly successful competency-based pay scheme that actually records competencies, not skill levels. Our competencies drive outputs, why change?"

"Used to support development as a basis for achievement – reward is based on achievement."

"Focus competencies on developmental uses, rather than pay."

"We keep things simple in a medium-sized firm."

"We pay for results, not for ability."

"It doesn't fit with our reward system."

These comments give a flavour of the genuine concerns that appeared to be steering some employers away from competency-related pay. But perhaps the most important finding of this part of the survey is that only a third of the "refusenik" organisations appeared to have settled objections to it; the rest hinting that it might at least be an option at some future date.

How successful is it?

Perhaps the most important issue covered by the survey is whether competency-related pay is working in practice. Employers were asked for their views on its success, about the problems they had experienced, and the lessons they felt their organisations had learned in the course of implementing the approach.

On the crucial issue of its success to date, respondents' answers showed a marked degree of unanimity: most of the organisations using competency-related pay (64%) said that, in general, their organisation had been "quite successful" in achieving the objectives that it set out to achieve. Just one organisation said it has been "very successful", and one "not successful". The remaining 28% said that it was too soon to judge success: all of these have had competency-related pay for two years or less.

Problems: costs are not an issue

However, two-thirds of respondents (64%) reported problems. In common with most performance-related pay systems, competency-related pay usually relies heavily on line managers' assessments – in this case, assessments of the competencies of their staff – and managing pay decisions in such a decentralised system clearly presents some difficulties. The problem most commonly mentioned among the survey's respondents was ensuring consistent pay decisions (cited by 50%).

Although this was not covered by the pre-set list, 12% said they had had problems with managers' assessments of competence. And, perhaps linked to these first two problems, 12% said there had been concern about equal pay claims – underlining the point that organisations need to take care that the pay decisions resulting from competency-related pay do not show any gender bias.

Predictably, several organisations said that it has proved complex and/or time-consuming to run (44% and 37% respectively). Employees' concerns have also been a problem: 25% of organisations said that they had experienced resistance from employees, 6% from unions, and 6% from managers.

Given the high profile that has often been given to the danger of "pay drift" in such systems, it is surprising that only 12% of employers had experienced increased pay costs – and none said that competency-related pay had been costly to run (despite this reason being included in the pre-set list) – although 12% remarked, unprompted, that it was difficult to "manage expectations" under competency-related pay. This apparent lack of concern about the issue of pay drift echoes the finding in the section above that fears about the likely costs involved troubled only 5% of those organisations that were not using competency-related pay.

It is also instructive to make another comparison between the reasons that non-users gave for not making a link between competencies and reward and the problems actually experienced by users. It was seen above that fear of adversely affecting other competency initiatives was the most frequent substantive reason why "refusenik" organisations did not use it, mentioned by 26%. And yet none of those organisations that used competency-related pay said that it had actually been a problem (again, despite this reason being included in the pre-set list), suggesting that its potential for wreaking havoc in the competency world may have been exaggerated.

Advice to other employers

Employers were asked what lessons they have learned from the experience of introducing competency-related pay, so that this could be passed this on to others. In all, 68% of the users replied to this question, some of them outlining the difficulties they had faced:

"Due to the wide range of staff covered by the competency-based pay structure, it was very difficult to achieve a consistent, fair and universally accepted method of implementing and monitoring the process."

"The people who manage the system do not have an adequate knowledge of competencies to make the system work."

"In a traditional [organisation] that has had a grade and spine system for 30 years, it has been hard. Face-to-face, regular communication is the key to successful implementation."

Others were more upbeat:

"There have been positive responses from employees, who now see a clearer career progression linked to competitive salary increases. There is much more of a focus on developing customer-focused behaviour and less on achieving statistical targets – which was the goal."

"A very good fit with a knowledge-worker company."

243

"More motivated and better-skilled workforce. Implementation and management of the system takes much more time than originally planned."

And others were keen to share the lessons they had learned:

"Do not link to pay and grading immediately. Introduce competencies then subsequently make linkage."

"Keep it simple. Don't try to get too mechanistic; communicate in a language people can identify with."

"Keep it simple – once it becomes complex, the value of the approach is lost. Develop it in the context of a very clear reward strategy which the senior managers in the business own and are committed to."

"Ensure competencies are relevant to all staff – some key performance indicators prevented some staff from progressing as they were not able to demonstrate consistent behaviour against them in their job roles."

"Key learning has been to demonstrate and communicate to affected staff the strength of evidence that links competency model to success. The more understandable the behavioural indicators, the greater the acceptance. Honesty, and training of managers that this process remains one of judgment on observable evidence."

"One important factor, I feel, is that the limited resistance [we have experienced] is due to the fact that all employees had an input into developing the competency document."

"First, make sure people have an understanding of competencies. Second, link to pay to ensure importance. Third, have a good process to ensure buy-in/involvement in developing competencies."

Next steps

The final issue addressed by the survey was the question of how competency-related pay systems were likely to develop in the future. All the indications are that this is a rapidly developing area, and the survey confirmed this. Nearly half (48%) of users said they were planning changes to their system. A quarter of these were organisations that had experienced problems with competency-related pay, but few of the planned changes seem to suggest deep problems with it. Indeed, some organisations said they were planning to extend the scope of their systems to other staff. Some others were planning to validate, refine or rationalise their competency frameworks. A couple of employers mentioned technical changes:

"Move to broad banding – use of competencies within grade movement."

"Likely to leave competencies as determinant of job grade and pay band, but have bonus payments instead of salary points for achievement of objectives."

And finally, some hinted that the decision to operate competency-related pay requires organisations to be constantly on their toes:

"Full review research required to implement intelligently."

"Development is continual."

"Constantly reviewing against best practice."

In conclusion

At the beginning, I referred to the sceptics who argue that very few organisations are basing their reward systems solely on competencies. Certainly, the survey did nothing to prove them wrong: virtually none of respondents would have agreed that competencies have been the sole determinant of all aspects of pay. But perhaps this is a red herring. What single factor, after all, could be used to the exclusion of all others, and used as the sole basis for pay?

The organisations in the survey appear to be taking a pragmatic approach, mixing and matching a whole range of factors – competencies, achievement of objectives or targets, market comparisons, and traditional "job evaluation" factors such as job size, complexity and level of responsibility – to design the pay and grading systems that ultimately determine pay.

Some organisations, moreover, said that competencies were the sole determinant of some aspect of pay – whether it be the grading system, or promotions, or pay progression, or shares of an annual pay rise – for at least some groups of staff.

Of course, the sceptics are right to point to the problems when it comes to getting competency-related pay to work: the survey confirms that it can be complex, time-consuming and difficult to manage. But it also suggests that some of the supposed problems – in particular "wage drift" and the danger of it "contaminating" other competency initiatives – may actually be taxing employers less than has been thought.

References

Adams, Katherine (1999), "Performance, development and reward at the Registers of Scotland", *Competency & Emotional Intelligence Quarterly*, vol. 6 no.3, pp.10–15, Spring.

American Compensation Association (1996), "Competencies under the microscope", *ACA News*, June, pp.6–10.

Miller, Linda, Rankin, Neil and Neathey, Fiona (2001), *Competency frameworks in UK organisations*, Chartered Institute of Personnel and Development.

Rankin, Neil (2001), "Raising performance through people: the eighth competency survey", *Competency & Emotional Intelligence Benchmarking*, 2000/01, January.

Watson Wyatt (1996), *Survey on broadbanding*.

Learning points

Overview

- Despite the extensive changes made to reward practices, and the widespread take-up of competencies, few organisations have forged links between their payment systems and their competency frameworks.

- The scarcity of competency-related reward reflects practical difficulties in finding a suitable system, principled objections, and concerns about possible legal challenges under equality legislation. However, competency-related reward is potentially fairer and more defensible than many other methods of reward.

Competencies and broadbanding

- Competitive pressures are encouraging employers to focus on the impact of each individual's performance, and to find ways of rewarding effort and contribution. Broadbanding is being adopted to facilitate this; it provides a few, broad pay ranges. Competencies are often used to help locate individuals' positions within a broad grade, and help determine the extent to which they should move along it.

- Moving to fewer pay levels means more than simply changing the number of grades. It means changing the human resource processes relating to job sizing, salary management and the way that career opportunities are communicated.

- Using competency-based models to underpin a broadbanded structure has many advantages. It provides a rationale for the number of bands, reinforces the link between organisation levels and performance expectations, and means that a similar or comparable vocabulary can be used, reinforcing the linkage between the requirements of the job and the person. It provides a tool for communicating to employees what they have to do in order to progress.

- Competency frameworks used in broadbanding need to be simple in design and content. The measures used in the model need to be reviewed for potential discrimination.

Case study of the Pet Plan Group

- Competencies can provide the means of creating a single base for all human resource activities, helping to keep in step appraisal, job descriptions, training and development, and decisions about pay.

- Guidance is essential on the meaning of each competency, and on the ways that it can be assessed in practice. A series of performance levels may be required to allow assessors to rate competency performance.

- Where a single set of competencies is used for the whole workforce, a system may be required to enable it to be applied flexibly across different roles and responsibility levels.

- For pay purposes, there needs to be a mechanism linking individual competency assessments and the person's pay award, such as a total score based on the assessment ratings for each competency. Usually, performance targets (personal objectives) are included alongside competencies in pay awards, so a weighting system for each element is also required.

- Establishing objective criteria to assess behavioural competencies (soft skills) can be difficult, and it can be time-consuming to identify the competencies relevant to each role.

Employers' practices

- The crucial, highly visible position of reward means that initiatives to link it with competencies must be sure of success, as failure can damage all uses of competencies within the organisation.

- Many employers do not use competency-related reward for the workforce as a whole, but confine it to certain groups or roles.

- There are four main ways of linking reward to competencies: (1) using competencies to help design the grading structure; (2) employees move between the job grades according to an assessment of their competencies; (3) employees move within their pay band according to an assessment of their competencies; and (4) an overall annual pay rise is divided among employees according to an assessment of their competencies.

- Employers usually link competencies to reward for two prime reasons: as a way of encouraging better individual performance, and as a means of rewarding people for developing the competencies needed to work flexibly.

- While users report that competency-related reward is reasonably successful, they also frequently experience problems with it. The problem most commonly mentioned is ensuring consistent pay decisions. It has also proved complex and/or time-consuming to run, and employees' concerns have also been a problem. However, few employers have experienced increased pay costs.

- Employers advise that consistency and fairness are important, as is effective training and familiarisation with the competency-related pay system. Simple, business-relevant competencies are vital, as is gaining line managers' support. Competencies must be seen to be relevant to individuals' roles, and the organisation's priorities.

- Benefits reported by employers include clearer communication about the requirements of roles, and what is required to progress; attitudes and culture have changed towards being more customer focused; motivation and skills levels have improved.

Chapter 10

International organisations

Introduction

Neil Rankin

One of the great advantages of the competency approach lies in its ability to articulate business priorities in terms that have a meaning at the level of the individual employee. Competencies help to impart an understanding of what a job or role involves, and what an ambitious person needs to do in order to succeed within an organisation. For organisations that operate across the boundaries of cultures or nations, competencies can be a vital constituent in the "glue" that helps to bind together a culturally or geographically diverse enterprise.

Yet, the very differences that make some type of coordinated approach necessary can also be its undoing. An inflexible "one-size-fits-all" set of competencies is highly likely to ignore the cultural and national differences that makes the management of a multinational such a challenging task. At best, offending local sensibilities will ensure a muted reception for a competency initiative issued from corporate head office. At worst, it will exacerbate tensions and divisions within the company, and do more harm than good.

In this chapter, we consider the role of competency frameworks that attempt to bridge these cultural and national divides. Managing in diverse organisations represents a real challenge, and Katherine Adams examines the growing need for managers to have, at least, some cultural sensitivity and, at its broadest extent, an ability to manage international teams, work as an expatriate or run one or more foreign operations from another country. Her analysis is followed by a case study of BASF, the international chemicals company, where John Warner shows that it is developing an international framework through a flexible, incremental approach.

International competencies for managers

Katherine Adams

Now that businesses are becoming increasingly global in their operations, the people working in them need to become more international in outlook, to work with people from different backgrounds and to manage across cultures. This applies especially to managers. When it is said that globalisation, mergers and acquisitions, joint ventures and outsourcing are leading to greater internationalisation of the manager's role, this can mean a number of different things. In particular, it may refer to:

- the increasing use of expatriates: people who are sent abroad by international head office to manage a local operation;

- the appointment of international managers who are responsible for operations in one or more foreign countries, but are not physically located outside the parent company's home territory on a full-time basis – they manage "virtually" through teleconferencing, e-mails and occasional visits, or by means of frequent visits, spending much of their time on the move;

- the formation and management of international teams, whose members come from, or work in, different countries; and

- the management of multicultural organisations, whose employees, systems and structures are truly international.

What all these trends have in common is that they require people to work with, or manage, individuals from a variety of different backgrounds: backgrounds that are different to their own. The competencies thought to be necessary in this context range from the obvious and practical – such as foreign language ability – to the subtle and intangible – "cultural awareness", "sensitivity", "adaptability" and so on. In addition, the extra layer of complexity that comes from managing across different time-zones, languages and business cultures may require special management skills, such as being able to see the wood for the trees, coping with stress, and having effective communication skills.

Despite the increasing interest in this area, however, employers' policies may be lagging behind developments: many companies have not yet analysed the competencies required for their international assignments. Clearly, if the international dimension of managers' jobs is becoming more important, and if it strongly affects the way that they perform their roles, then ignoring cross-cultural competencies may have serious consequences. Many international organisations suffer from cultural difficulties that lead to misunderstanding, hostility and reduced profits. Failed assignments are a common feature of organisations that use expatriate managers: a tour of duty has to be brought to a premature end, the individual performs below expectations, or the experience is so unsatisfactory for the person that their long-term commitment to the company is damaged.

Do cultural differences really matter?

A word that crops up very frequently in any discussion of international competencies is "culture". This is a slippery concept, but the basic premise is that people in different countries, continents, business sectors or organisations can have noticeably different approaches to the way they live, work, think and communicate. If this is so, then "culture" is something that expatriates, members and managers of international teams, and managers who oversee international organisations will need to be aware of, adapt to and, perhaps, use to their advantage. According to Chris Brewster, Professor of European Human Resource Management at Cranfield School of Management, "Every manager in UK industry is aware that the Japanese, for example, do things differently, particularly in the way they manage their people" (Brewster, 1995). However, he goes on to warn that: "Of course, most UK managers will not be very clear what the differences are in any detail, and the dangers of this form of anecdotal stereotyping are clear."

Putting cultural differences at their strongest, one could argue – as some people do – that employees who work internationally need to develop and use different competencies depending on where, and with whom, they are working. What research there is could certainly be used as ammunition for this argument. For example, the Cranfield *Executive competences survey* (Kakabadse, 1993) established a number of cultural differences. For instance, "the French, although more sensitive to people, are slightly more into power/political styles of management, but less disciplined than the Germans who freely admit less sensitivity to people but a greater adherence to organisational discipline and systems." Another study (Okechuku, 1994) found that, while a number of managerial characteristics are significant predictors of effectiveness in both Eastern and Western cultures, there are also some differences. For instance,

251

"self-actualisation" is the most important predictor of managerial effectiveness in Canada, "self-assurance" in Hong Kong, and "intellectual ability" in the People's Republic of China.

A survey of succession planning and the use of competencies in 19 major international companies (Wallum, 1993) found that "international differences were very real, and the competence model was sometimes used differently in certain countries." Finally, a study of six European telecommunications companies (Hogg, 1993) tentatively suggested that "competence is not generic across Europe". Asked what were the vitally important competencies, managers in the six organisations differed about the importance of technical and professional knowledge and leadership. They also disagreed about learning, analysis, interpersonal communication, financial awareness, oral communication, planning and organising, written communication and decision-making.

Some think not

However, not everyone is convinced that competencies do vary in this way across national or other cultures. Researchers at US consultancy Hay/McBer – one of the pioneers of the competencies approach – have developed a database of many different competency models from around the world. Analysis of this vast mass of data has tended to support the view that the competencies required for similar jobs are essentially the same everywhere in the world (Adams, 1995/96).

On the British side of the Atlantic, too, there appears to be some faith that management competencies are indeed "generic across Europe". CECIOS, the name for the European Council of Management, investigated ways of encouraging other countries to adapt the UK's home-grown management standards that were originally developed by the Management Charter Initiative (MCI) as part of the National Vocational Qualifications system. A simplified form of the standards was used to produce job/person profiling software for use in the UK and several continental European countries. Ultimately, CECIOS would like to see pan-European accreditation of management education, and sees the widespread use of the MCI standards as a useful step in this direction. According to Gene Crozier, who provides the technical assistance to CECIOS: "People make a lot of commotion about cultural differences – maybe they forget that most management is about bottom-line stuff: budget management, team management, obtaining information, and so on."

The opposing camps who feel that management competencies are culturally relative or who think they are generic may find a possible compromise position in a study from Hay/McBer (1995). This argues that, as well as a number of generic competencies that all effective executives possess, there are significant cultural differences in leadership styles. I shall touch on this study's suggested generic competencies later. As far as cultural differences are concerned, the research claims that successful global leaders adapt their style along three "continuums" consisting of "culturally-driven" competencies. For example, the "building business relationships" continuum runs from "personal relationships" at one extreme to "contractual relationships" at the other. Whereas successful chief executives operating in Asia prefer to build strategic alliances through the gradual development of mutual respect and trust, those in North America tend to subordinate personal relationships to more explicit contractual goals, according to the research. To operate in Asia, the important competencies are "developing mutual respect" and "building relationships"; in North America "objectivity" is more important. To be a successful global leader, the chief executive must be able to adapt his or her competencies as circumstances dictate. The other continuums in the Hay/McBer analysis are "basis for action" (extremes: planning, implementation) and "exercising authority" (extremes: centralised authority; participatory leadership).

Intercultural competencies

Whether or not one accepts the strong form of cultural relativism that says international workers need different sets of competencies depending on where and with whom they are working, there is widespread acceptance that cultural differences are important. In many analyses, what international workers are said to need is not so much a series of different sets of competencies as a specific competency or cluster of competencies that will enable them to deal with cultural differences. Such "intercultural" competencies are a common feature of the frameworks now being developed by researchers and employers in order to define the roles of particular types of international workers. A number of these frameworks that emerged in the mid 1990s have been analysed and are shown in boxes 10.1 and 10.2. As these analyses show, competencies such as "cultural sensitivity", "intercultural effectiveness" and "cultural adaptability" have been frequently cited.

For example, the Ashridge survey (Barham and Wills, 1992) of managers who exercise leadership across several countries lists "acting as intercultural mediator and change agent" (see box 10.1) as an important competency. This is defined as:

- switching one's frame of reference rapidly between different cultures;

- being aware of one's own cultural underpinnings and of the need to be sensitive to cultural differences;

- managing change in different contexts and pushing the boundaries of different cultures; and

- balancing the need for speed and the need for sensitivity.

A survey for the then Institute of Personnel and Development on international personnel managers (1995) (also in box 10.1) found that "intercultural effectiveness" is perhaps the most important competency. This is said to include:

- understanding the key cultural differences between one's own country and other countries and adapting one's behaviour to these different circumstances;

- recognising, respecting and valuing differences, making these differences work together, and balancing the needs of different people and/or groups; and

- working in multicultural teams.

As mentioned above, the Hay/McBer survey (1995) of "global leaders" (also analysed in box 10.1) is couched in terms of the different competencies that need to be adopted in different circumstances. But it, too, talks of the need for "international adaptability": the ability to identify and use these different competencies in the appropriate circumstances. (The other competencies listed under Hay/McBer in box 10.1 are those generic competencies that its researchers feel are required by all chief executives.) A study by UMIST, the CBI Employee Relocation Council and the Centre for International Briefing (1995) found a number of common elements in employers' competency frameworks for expatriates (see box 10.1). "Cultural sensitivity and adaptability" is one – though, interestingly, it tends to be prized more among expatriates themselves than among their employers.

Research into managers in multinational companies by John Bristow and Christopher Ridgeway (1994/95) has revealed the importance of a number of competencies, including "emotional competencies" (see box 10.1 and chapter 7). By this is meant:

- understanding and working with differences;

- sensitivity or cultural empathy; and

- emotional strength to work through tensions to arrive at a mutual understanding of these differences.

Finally, in his book on "cultural competences", Chong Ju Choi (Choi and Kelemen, 1995) identifies four generic competencies required for international managers (see box 10.1). One of the four is "cultural windows", defined as:

- the ability to enter and work effectively in a different business environment;

- the ability to develop cultural knowledge and information that can allow a manager to be more easily accepted into the foreign environment and hence to gather information more effectively; and

- a willingness to accept and accumulate knowledge along with an appreciation of, and sensitivity and responsiveness to different cultures.

Employers' intercultural focus

As box 10.2 shows, it is not just researchers who are emphasising the importance of intercultural competency: a number of employers are also incorporating it into their frameworks. For instance, according to a 1995 study of the Tetley Group (Atack, 1995/96), the organisation had a framework of 12 competencies including "cultural adaptability" and "cultural sensitivity". The latter was defined in terms of the following:

- respect for local value systems;

- sensitivity to other people's needs, position and feelings, and ability to work with these;

- being non-judgmental; not making personal criticisms;

- acceptance of cultural differences; and

- recognition that people are different, not inferior.

Boots Pharmaceuticals (Atack, 1994/95), prior to its sale to BASF later in 1994, had a worldwide framework of top management competencies, designed to be sufficiently flexible to accommodate cultural differences (see box 10.2). It featured "interpersonal sensitivity and communication skills", including "the ability to demonstrate cultural sensitivity to the way things are done in different parts of the business and of the world". Also shown in box 10.2 is Fiat's framework (Barham and Oates, 1993), which includes "quality of know-how", defined as professional expertise but also "intercultural competence". Examples of the latter include:

- a particular sensitivity to the correct understanding and interpretation of other cultures; and

- the ability to identify the values that influence managerial behaviour and company approaches in different cultural settings.

Another competency identified by Fiat is "a strong identity": the ability to reconcile the necessary flexibility and openness needed to communicate effectively with other cultures, with a firm grounding in the home culture. Finally, Price Waterhouse Europe (Barham and Oates, 1993), prior to its merger with Coopers & Lybrand, included in its framework for international managers "the ability to adopt perspectives other than one's own".

There are striking similarities between many of the definitions of "intercultural competency" provided by employers and researchers. In essence, one might say that intercultural competency is primarily a question of understanding or being sensitive to cultural differences, and respecting those differences. These differences are often thought to include traditional styles of leadership; different systems of business ethics (for example, different attitudes to gift-giving); different concepts of space and time; differences in non-verbal communication, such as body language; and concepts such as the importance of not "losing face" in the Far East.

Communication: the crux of the matter?

The analyses presented in boxes 10.1 and 10.2 list a number of other competencies that are frequently identified as necessary for people who work in an international context, especially: strategic awareness; language ability; communication; resilience; and cognitive skills. Language ability and the related competency of communication are especially interesting. "Language ability", in this context, often encompasses more than simple fluency in a foreign language. For instance, the Institute of Personnel and Development's survey (1995) defines this skill to include:

- the ability to look beyond the actual words that people are using to understand what they are really trying to say;

- listening, checking understanding, empathy; and

- the ability to communicate appropriately, such as by speaking clearly and simply, and avoiding jargon.

And on the related issue of intercultural "communication", there is now a burgeoning research industry that has so far analysed at least three levels of competency (Martin, 1993):

- higher-order cognitive and behavioural processes (for example, understanding the cultural, social and relational rules governing interaction);

- mid-range constructs, including clusters of specific behaviours (for example, interaction management, social relaxation), traits (such as empathy, assertiveness), functions (being friendly, and so on) or rules; and

- lower-level behaviours (for example, head nods, eye gaze, interruptions).

Of course, the issue of communication is, in some ways, the crux of the matter: working with people from different cultures is difficult largely because of the problems of communication. And as the list above makes clear, there are large overlaps between intercultural communication and the intercultural competencies discussed earlier. However, in a final twist, the problems of intercultural communication also present a particularly tough challenge to the whole exercise of developing international competencies. If the business of developing competency frameworks for small, homogeneous groups is difficult enough, how much more difficult must it be when these are complicated by the problems of translation, interpretation and communication from one language and one culture to another?

10.1. Competencies for international managers: research findings

	Barham, and Wills (1992)	IPD (1995)	Hay/McBer (1995)	UMIST/CBI/ CIB (1995)	Bristow/ Ridgeway (1994/95)	Choi (Choi and Kelemen 1995)
Intercultural awareness/ effectiveness	Acting as intercultural mediator and change agent	Intercultural effectiveness	International adaptability	Cultural sensitivity and adaptability	Emotional competencies (including sensitivity or cultural empathy)	"Cultural windows" (the ability to work effectively in a different business environment)
Strategic awareness	Championing international strategy	Strategic grasp of the business as a whole	Broad scanning		Conceptual competencies (including the ability to see things in both a global and local perspective)	
Language ability	Cognitive complexity (including language fluency)	Languages		Linguistic ability		"Language expectation" (linguistic skills and knowledge of the language preferences of other cultures)

	Barham, and Wills (1992)	IPD (1995)	Hay/McBer (1995)	UMIST/CBI/CIB (1995)	Bristow/Ridgeway (1994/95)	Choi (Choi and Kelemen 1995)
Resilience	Managing personal effectiveness for international business (including thriving on challenges); emotional energy	Resilience		Personal resilience	Emotional competencies (including emotional strength)	
Cognitive skills	Cognitive complexity		Analytical thinking; conceptual thinking		Conceptual competencies	
Influencing skills	Operating as a cross-border coach and coordinator (including using persuasion)		Impact and influence		Ability to influence and network	

	Barham, and Wills (1992)	IPD (1995)	Hay/McBer (1995)	UMIST/CBI/CIB (1995)	Bristow/Ridgeway (1994/95)	Choi (Choi and Kelemen 1995)
Communication		Excellent interpersonal/ communications ability		Communication skills		
Flexibility		Flexibility		Flexibility of management style		
Maturity	Psychological maturity				Personal security and maturity	
Managing complexity		Ability to manage complexity and diversity			Ability to manage complexity	

	Barham, and Wills (1992)	IPD (1995)	Hay/McBer (1995)	UMIST/CBI/CIB (1995)	Bristow/Ridgeway (1994/95)	Choi (Choi and Kelemen 1995)
Other		Knowledge of local country employment law and conditions; understanding of the international business environment	Leadership; decisive insight; organisational know-how; good judgment of people; social responsibility; initiating action; self-confidence; need to achieve		Behavioural competencies (including ability to convey one's view as being relative, not absolute; using appropriate non-verbal behaviour); ability to handle risk, uncertainty and change	Negotiation; business ethics

10.2 Competencies for international managers: employers' frameworks

	Tetley Group (Atack, 1995/96)	Colgate-Palmolive (Solomon, 1994)	Boots Pharmaceuticals (Atack, 1994/95)	Fiat (Barham, and Oates 1993)	Price Waterhouse Europe (Barham, and Oates 1993)
Strategic awareness	Strategic thinking	Strategy	Strategic perspective		Ability to think strategically; ability to work in both strategic and operational modes
Communication	Communication	Communication	Interpersonal sensitivity and communication skills (including the ability to communicate clearly, concisely and with impact)		Good communication; ability to develop communication networks
Leadership	Good team-playing and leadership	The ability to form and manage routines and global teams	Leadership	Winning leadership	

	Tetley Group (Atack, 1995/96)	Colgate-Palmolive (Solomon, 1994)	Boots Pharmaceuticals (Atack, 1994/95)	Fiat (Barham, and Oates 1993)	Price Waterhouse Europe (Barham, and Oates 1993)
Intercultural awareness/ effectiveness	Cultural adaptability; cultural sensitivity		Interpersonal sensitivity and communication skills (including cultural sensitivity)	Quality of know-how (including intercultural competence)	Ability to adopt other perspectives
Results orientation	Results orientation		Results orientation	Winning leadership (including results orientation)	
Resilience	Personal strength		Tough-mindedness	Personal qualities (including management of stress)	
Cognitive skills		Conceptual creativity	Intellect		Analytical ability; creativity; imagination
Language ability	Linguistic skills				Language skills
Flexibility	Flexibility				Mobility and flexibility
Teamwork	Good team-playing and leadership	Teamwork			

	Tetley Group (Atack, 1995/96)	Colgate-Palmolive (Solomon, 1994)	Boots Pharmaceuticals (Atack, 1994/95)	Fiat (Barham, and Oates 1993)	Price Waterhouse Europe (Barham, and Oates 1993)
Business awareness	Sound business acumen		Business awareness		
Vision		Vision			Vision
Knowledge of the organisation			Organisational perspective		Knowledge of the company as a whole
Other	Self-confidence; lifelong learning ability	Presentation skills; planning and execution; long-term planning	Personal style and values	A strong identity; professional competence; managerial abilities; intercultural competence (including communicating and representing the company's image abroad; successful negotiation)	Knowledge of competitive markets and technological dynamics; political sensitivity; realism; the ability to propose and implement change

Case study: Achieving European accord at BASF UK

John Warner

German-owned BASF's operation in England is concerned with the sale and manufacture of chemicals. It employs 2,500 people at its sites in Cheshire, Derbyshire, Teesside, Nottinghamshire and Oxfordshire. Selling business-to-business, it has an annual turnover of about £650 million, and supplies chemicals and plastics to the automotive, packaging, pharmaceutical and building industries, among others. BASF introduced its competency framework in 1996 as part of a performance management approach. This sought to establish at a corporate and individual level how certain activities were achieved, and how individual effort was rewarded. BASF seeks to capitalise on individual performance by providing a clear focus on what is expected of employees in such areas as teamwork and leadership.

Cross-sectional teams were formed from different levels and different functions including management, sales, engineering and secretarial. Using brainstorming techniques, the teams determined what represented successful and unsuccessful behaviours for all of the different groups represented. With this input from the teams, the original framework was designed by Hay Management Consultants.

International developments

The British set of competencies was updated in 1999 so that it could form part of a Europe-wide framework. Staff from BASF's UK operation undertook the work in conjunction with the German-based corporate personnel function and representatives from a number of countries. The revised framework has drawn on past UK experience, together with the information gleaned from behavioural event interviews with business directors, and a range of different ideas from across Europe.

Chris Holroyde, Learning and Development Manager based in Cheadle Hulme, Cheshire, has been leading the working party for this development and has been involved in a series of workshops and feedback sessions across Europe. "We've picked out the best from a number of our businesses, but it's much more complicated implementing an international competency framework than one that applies to only one country," says Chris. "There are different cultural influences, business practices and a wide variety of job roles to consider – not to mention document translation into seven or eight different languages. Also in the UK, we've linked performance to remuneration, but this is being considered in the rest of Europe."

The framework consists of five clusters of competencies (see box 10.3), each of which is subdivided into competency headings to make a total of 18. The entrepreneurial cluster is the largest with 10 competencies. The professional and intellectual clusters have only one competency and the remaining two clusters have three each. The 18 competencies are described in outline, together with descriptions for four levels of behaviour. Each of the job roles in the company takes the most relevant competencies from the full list – usually between six and eight – and the appropriate levels of behaviour are identified. However, employees are encouraged to seek the support of their human resources department locally if it is felt necessary to customise the framework to describe the behaviours more specifically in different countries.

10.3. BASF's European competencies

Entrepreneurial competencies

Change orientation

Customer focus

Decisiveness

External and business awareness

Initiative

Innovativeness

Planning and organising

Responsibility and ownership

Result-orientation

Strategic orientation

Leadership competencies

Leadership

Developing others

Influencing

Professional competencies

Sharing expertise

Intellectual competencies

Analysing and solving complex problems

Cooperation and communication competencies

Interpersonal communication

Transnational orientation

Teamworking

Snowballing

Chris Holroyde recalls the early days of the UK framework and the degree of concern that managers had at the time about making employee assessments of performance. He attributes this to a lack of understanding of what could be achieved through performance management and the competency framework. Over time, it has turned the other way, and managers have extended the use of the competency framework into areas such as team selection, promotion, development centres and as a useful tool in managing reorganisation.

The revised European framework is already being used in international career development and other workshops. The corporate human resources department in Germany has been developing a similar competency framework for top-level management positions worldwide, for "development area assessment" purposes. Chris says that the roll-out of the European framework for non-production employees is being continued, by working through each country's human resources department. This can involve negotiations with works councils to secure agreement for implementation.

References

Adams, Katherine (1995/96), "Competency's American origins and the conflicting approaches in use today", *Competency & Emotional Intelligence Quarterly*, vol. 3, no.2, Winter, pp.44–48.

Atack, Wendy (1994/95), "The international dimension: Boots Pharmaceuticals", *Competency & Emotional Intelligence Quarterly*, vol. 2, no.2, Winter, p.2.

Atack, Wendy (1995/96), "Competencies for international managers: Tetley GB", *Competency & Emotional Intelligence Quarterly*, vol. 3, no.2, Winter, p.2.

Barham, Kevin and Oates, David (1993), *The international manager*, Pitman.

Barham, Kevin and Wills, Stefan (1992), *Management across frontiers: identifying the competences of successful international managers*, Ashridge Management Research Group/the Foundation for Management Education.

Brewster, Chris (1995), "National cultures and international management", in *Strategic prospects for HRM*, ed. Shaun Tyson, Institute of Personnel and Development, 1995.

Bristow, John and Ridgeway, Christopher (1994/95), "Competence in managing internationally", *Competency & Emotional Intelligence Quarterly*, vol. 2, no.2, Winter, pp.34–36.

Choi, Chong Ju and Kelemen, Mihaela (1995), *Cultural competences: managing cooperatively across cultures*, Dartmouth.

Hay/McBer International (1995), *Mastering global leadership*.

Hogg, Bridget A (1993), "European managerial competences", *European Business Review*, vol. 93, no.2, pp.21–26.

Institute of Personnel and Development (1995), *The IPD guide on developing an international personnel career*.

Kakabadse, Andrew (1993), "The success levers for Europe: the Cranfield executive competences survey", *Journal of Management Development*, vol. 12, no.8, pp.12–17.

Martin, Judith N (1993), "Intercultural communication competence: a review", in Intercultural communication competence edited by Richard L Wiseman and Jolene Koester, *International and Intercultural Communication Annual*, vol. 17, Sage Publications.

Okechuku, Chike (1994), "The relationship of six managerial characteristics to the assessment of managerial effectiveness in Canada, Hong Kong and People's Republic of China", *Journal of Occupational and Organizational Psychology*, vol. 67, no.1, March, pp.79–86.

Solomon, Charlene Marner (1994), "Staff selection impacts global success", *Personnel Journal*, vol. 73, January, pp.88–101.

UMIST/CBI Employee Relocation Council/The Centre for International Briefing (1995), *Assessment, selection and preparation for expatriate assignments*. See also Ruitenbeek, Diane van (1996), "The competent expatriate: how to ensure success in the global marketplace", *Competency & Emotional Intelligence Quarterly*, vol. 3, no.3, Spring, pp.25–30.

Wallum, Peter (1993), "A broader view of succession planning", *Personnel Management*, September, pp.42–45.

Learning points

International competencies

- The increasingly global nature of business means that managers working in them need to become more international in outlook, work with people from different backgrounds and manage across cultures. This means that the competencies relating to success in managing in this way should be identified, and suitable development opportunities provided.

- "Culture" is a slippery concept, but the basic premise is that people can have noticeably different approaches to the way they live, work, think and communicate. Managers who work internationally need to develop and use different competencies depending on where, and with whom, they are working, in order to reflect these cultural differences.

- There are two opposing views about the implications for competency frameworks of cultural and national differences. One viewpoint believes that these differences mean that different sets of competencies are required; the other viewpoint believes that the competencies themselves do not vary across national or other cultures. The latter has led to the development of competency frameworks that apply across borders, both by multinational companies and by international associations.

- However, there is widespread acceptance that cultural differences are important and a frequent response is to identify and describe a specific competency or cluster of competencies that will enable managers to deal with cultural differences. Boxes 10.1 and 10.2 compare several such models.

- Often, the competency or cluster relates to "intercultural competency", and there are similarities between many such definitions

- The competency of "communication" is crucial: working with people from different cultures is difficult largely because of the problems of communication. There are large overlaps between intercultural communication and other intercultural competencies.

Case study of BASF UK

- The use of a single competency framework for an organisation's operations in several different countries can have business advantages, particularly in ensuring coordination and consistency in areas where personnel processes cut across national borders. It can also help to extend effective business practices and the elements of highly effective performance from one local operation to the international organisation as a whole.

- Developing an international framework is often more complicated than one applying to one country or culture, as it will probably have to take account of differences in cultures, local business practices and a wider range of job roles. The framework and accompanying documentation may also need to be translated in the various local languages.

- Building in flexibility to an international framework is often advantageous, as it helps to accommodate local differences, and gain local managers' commitment to the framework's use.

- The scale of the task of developing an international framework may mean that a pilot programme and/or a rolling introduction of its use are desirable.

Chapter 11

Assessment

Introduction

Neil Rankin

The business relevance of competencies depends upon ensuring that they articulate the performance expectations of the organisation, defined in a meaningful way that uses the language of the organisation and reflects its culture and values. These expectations can have no existence, however, without some form of assessment taking place. Employees and managers will not take competencies seriously if there is no attempt to assess their performance against them. And improvements in individuals' and teams' competency levels depend upon assessment of development needs, and regular assessments that the development intervention has had the desired impact on raising performance.

Assessment of existing employees and managers – as opposed to job applicants – focuses on their current performance levels, their development needs and, in some organisations, on their potential for progression to more demanding roles. The past two decades have seen growing emphasis on individual contribution to the business and, with it, new mechanisms to assess it and act as symbols that it is being treated seriously. Performance-related pay for individuals has grown, as a consequence, as have appraisal and performance-management processes.

However, the desire to assess performance has not meant that its execution has proved to be an easy task. Creating a performance-management process that line managers consider represents a benefit – rather than a burden – has been a major challenge for personnel and development professionals. Without this commitment, though, the process can easily become a sham, with both manager and employee conspiring to neutralise it. The goal is lost of delivering a productive, yet challenging, review of achievements and personal strengths (behavioural competencies), and the creation of a development plan to tackle significant shortfalls and weaknesses. Instead, assessments are anodyne, and, where rating systems are used, a safe and unthreatening middle-ground mark is awarded.

It is no surprise, therefore, that many employers using competency frameworks find that assessment presents an area of difficulty. In the latest benchmarking survey from the *Competency & Emotional Intelligence* journal (Rankin, 2001a), over half (59%) of the 113 organisations contacted reported assessment problems. Based on their feedback and other contact that myself and my colleagues at IRS have had with users, the following are the key issues that can make or break an effective competency-related assessment process:

- gaining the commitment of line managers to conduct assessments in a thorough way. This is a difficult, painstaking process that should start at the point when the competencies are first being developed, through employees' and managers' involvement in the design phase, continue through a communications process, and be reinforced by the provision of training in understanding and assessing competencies;

- consistency: ensuring that the requirements of a competency are interpreted in the same way by different line managers; ensuring that performance in a competency is assessed and/or rated in the same way;

- objectivity: avoiding as much subjectivity in assessments as possible; in particular, ensuring that line managers do not display favouritism, or discriminate unfairly;

- guidance: provide good, clear guidance to employees and managers about each competency's requirements (its definition; how it can be seen in action; and, where performance levels are used, examples of each level being performed in action to show how the levels differ from one another);

- NVQs: where competencies take the form of National Vocational Qualifications, Scottish Vocational Qualifications, or standards based on them, the assessment process needs to be documented in clear English, and the attendant bureaucracy reduced as much as possible.

The assessment of competencies is more complicated than the assessment of other aspects of individuals' performance, such as the achievement of objectives, because not only does the design and application of the assessment process have an important bearing, but, so, too, does the design and use of competencies themselves. The competency framework will be difficult to assess in practice if is poorly developed, with inappropriate competencies, poor definitions, or insufficient or over-complex documentation. If individuals are not committed to using competencies, through insufficient involvement and/or training, then even the best-designed framework is likely to suffer from the assessment "conspiracies" that I mentioned above.

So, how have employers approached this taxing issue of assessing competency? Below, John Warner reviews current practice, and the themes involved. Then, Peter Goodge, Sharon Atchley and Jane Coomber examine one of the latest trends in assessment, the use of 360-degree feedback, and the ways that competencies can be assessed by means of this process to gain maximum impact on those being assessed and the organisation itself. Finally, we provide a more detailed example of employer practice in John Warner's case study of Smith and Nephew Wound Management.

First steps in assessing individual competence

John Warner

Nothing is as crucial to the use of competencies as the assessment of individual performance. Without it, there is no possibility of making an objective judgment of an employee's or manager's training needs, their suitability for promotion, or the size of their pay award. There may be marginal benefits if competencies are used as yardsticks against which individuals measure themselves on an informal basis, but mainstream organisational life is unlikely to take a competency framework seriously if its standards are not backed up by formal assessment practices. But putting assessment into practice is no easy task – particularly when most organisations' frameworks emphasise "soft skills" or behaviours that, by definition, are not dependent on hard results or outcomes for their legitimacy.

Different organisations have tackled the identification and definition of their competencies in different ways, but, whatever the method, the result should be relevant to the needs of the business and the individuals working for it and – crucially – accepted as such by employees and line managers.

Choosing appropriate headings is essential to ensure that assessment is made against competencies that really contribute to the success of the organisation. For example, an ability to communicate effectively may be desirable in all employees, but becomes critically important for people employed in a call centre, or in a selling or leadership role. High buy-in rates to competencies, and assessments based on them, are far more likely if the consultations to determine competency headings have been conducted widely among the workforce. Arbitrarily imposed competencies may be poorly received by the workforce because they are perceived as not recognising existing commitment to high performance.

Number of headings

No matter how acceptable and attractive a set of competencies can look on paper, they still have to be capable of easy implementation. Here, the number of competency headings is a crucial factor; too many can be off-putting and unwieldy, too few can create ambiguity.

Huhtamaki Van Leer, a Finnish/Dutch-owned packaging-materials business, features only three main headings in its competency framework (Warner, 2001a). These involve "people; thinking; and personal effectiveness". This approach is intended to help understanding and provide employees with a few memorable headings on which they can "peg" their drive for higher performance. On the other hand, Union Fenosa, a diverse group of Spanish companies with origins in the utilities sector, has created a framework that has a total of 60 competency headings for its 20,000 employees (Warner, 2001b). This sounds daunting, but the framework is predominantly based on technical skills – "knowledge competencies" – and only includes five core behavioural competencies: "manage; lead; plan; interact; and communicate".

Many organisations have adopted frameworks that include about 10 to 12 competency headings, which are often grouped together in three or four related clusters. An example of this is the framework developed by Aventis Pasteur MSD, a pharmaceuticals company (Warner, 2000a). The company's framework applies to all staff and consists of 12 competency headings arranged into four clusters:

- use of resources: action planning; technical expertise; information processing; and project management;

- professional relationships/communications: customer orientation (internal/external); influencing others; and written or oral expression;

- people management: effective delegation; teamwork; and development of others; and

- personal development: creativity and innovation; flexibility; and self-development.

When headings are being chosen, it is important to decide whether or not they are intended to apply to all roles in the organisation. Increasingly, employers are creating flexible behavioural frameworks that encapsulate a few core competencies that apply to all employees, within a system that can be tailored to the needs of different roles and functions/departments. Sets of technical competences, based on tasks and outputs, are often dealt with separately, being developed as standalone lists of requirements for each role or function.

These flexible systems may be more difficult to develop and design, but they often improve the ultimate usefulness of the framework. Employees and managers have some control over the choice of headings that apply to themselves, and can identify those that are of greatest relevance and usefulness. This means that personnel processes based on competencies are, in turn, more likely to be relevant and accepted internally. When it comes to individuals developing their competencies, it is advisable that they only concentrate on two or three at a time.

Giving life

The crucial first steps are, thus, establishing the mechanism by which behavioural competency headings are determined, resolving the issue of how many should be included, and settling on the format and coverage of the framework. But for most organisations, this is only the beginning of the process that leads to performance assessment. If they are to have validity, competencies should become the focus for assessment of individual performance. But when making an assessment of, for example, "personal effectiveness", a purely objective judgment is simply not possible. Personal interpretations of what the competency means will be as many and as varied as the assessor and assessed. Competencies on their own are several steps away from bringing a framework to life and being ready for the real world of opinion, bias and general human perversity! To overcome problems of ambiguity, employers develop further "layers" in the competency framework.

The first of these might be a description that gives a sharper focus to the interpretation of each competency. "Personal effectiveness" may be described as "How we manage ourselves". "Group and interpersonal effectiveness" may be described as "How we effect desired responses in others and relate to those around us" (from the competency framework for the Irish Civil Service; (Warner, 2000b)). By qualifying the competency with an explanatory statement, interpretation of meaning becomes a little more precise in the mind of an assessor and closer to the original intention.

Brief but effective

Some frameworks are little developed beyond their competency headings, as is illustrated by that used by Hanson Quarry Products (Warner, 2000c). The company's framework is used in its sales operation and is concerned with one key competence: "persuasive communications". Rather than being defined in behavioural terms, six aspects of the competency are identified instead: "preparation; opening; need-finding; knowledge of the offer; objection-handling; and closing". In each case, the framework then details the various elements of achievement that are involved.

To make an assessment of performance, a manager joins one of the company's sales staff as a passive observer at a meeting with a potential client. The manager considers the performance in a couple of the fields (more if the manager is very experienced), and starts to formulate ideas about the level of success, using a 1–5 scale. Following the client meeting, the manager will give immediate feedback to the sales person on what was observed, and record an agreed performance rating in a workbook held by the employee. Alternatively, he or she will prepare a written report overnight, and meet the employee the following day.

Depending on the manager, such assessments take place every three to six months, and the manager is issued with a manual to back up his or her judgments. Assessment is biased towards actions and outcomes, but implicit in "persuasive communications" are behaviours that are conducive to the closing of a sale.

Other layers

More widely used than the approach taken by Hanson are frameworks that include "behavioural indicators". As the term implies, these give examples of behaviours that can help establish whether or not the employee is meeting the requirements of a competency. Most frameworks with behavioural indicators concentrate on positive examples of behaviour, although some include negative or unacceptable ones as well (see below). Frameworks can rely on the degree of detail provided by single sets of behavioural indicators, but, most go further by differentiating each competency according to a series of performance levels. In these cases, each level is provided with its own series of behavioural examples. The levels themselves are little or no different in approach to those found in traditional appraisal systems, and may be denoted by numbers, letters or given titles.

A less conventional example can be found in the levels applied to "sales advisers" at the House of Fraser department stores, which are: "trainee; bronze; silver; and gold" (Warner, 1999). Line managers' assessments are guided by explanatory statements. At the silver level, for example, they are told that: "This level equates to an advanced-driver status, and signifies [that] the sales adviser performs well in all basic job tasks as well as using specialist skills to maximise sales and influence profitability."

Going into the negative

When competency frameworks are being devised, a decision has to be made as to whether they should include negative descriptors, or should only seek to highlight positive behaviours. Negative behavioural indicators can be freestanding, and illustrate examples of poor behaviour generally in relation to the competency concerned. Or they can be attached to a specific level of performance, so that the range of possible assessment levels goes below the bare minimum to the "unacceptable", to use one of the labels in common use.

One organisation that took on board negative descriptors when devising its framework is West Yorkshire Police (Warner, 2000d). For example, when describing a core competency of how both officers and civilian support staff should respond (positively) to the needs of customers, the force also includes negative statements. These include: "Fobs off and makes excuses; fails to respond to requests, or leaves enquiries unattended; and adopts a take-it-or-leave-it attitude."

Slightly less harshly, the negative indicators developed by West of England tubing manufacturer Fine Tubes includes for its "problem-solving" competency: "Supplies solutions without studying the problem; ignores problems hoping they will go away; investigates problems and does nothing about it; big mouth, small ears, charges over the wrong hill" (Rankin, 2001b, p.35).

Employers adopting adverse indicators such as these provide their assessors with a more complete, and realistic, spectrum of behaviours as a basis for their decisions, than those confined to "the good news". However, their use must be consistent with the culture of the organisation concerned. In some instances, employees will view their inclusion in a less constructive light, and interpret their presence as an indication that the organisation implicitly condones under-performance.

Living without ratings

However, not all employers make use of rating scales, with or without negative indicators. They prefer instead to use some statements about behaviour arranged in what may loosely be described as performance gradations. Rating scales do not therefore apply, and the assessor must try to match the observed behaviour with the closest descriptor.

Bedfordshire Police has such a system included in its framework (Warner, 2001c). Under the competency of "oral communication", level 2 includes: "Talk to people on their level and check they have understood. Contribute without interrupting others . . .", and level 3 includes: "Speak confidently in large groups. Convey ideas and issues reflecting the way the force operates . . ." The two are not connected, but stand as separate descriptors in their own right. These "levels" are specified in job-role descriptions and, during performance reviews, line managers try to evaluate with the employee how closely their behaviour matches the descriptor. The process of matching forms the basis of a discussion and is followed by decisions about related development needs.

Consistent influence

Designing a framework that has widely supported competency headings, clear descriptions of the meaning of the competencies and a range of behavioural descriptors assists line managers in making consistent assessments. The initial design of the framework can determine what form the assessment process will take (for example, the contrasting approaches of Hanson Quarry Products and Bedfordshire Police) and also the format of performance review sessions. The initial design of a competency framework should always support organisational goals, and it should also recognise how line managers will assess performance and provide effective feedback. The framework's structure should not be the master of practice, but rather it should be its complement.

Variety

Assuming an ideal framework is in place, enjoying popular support and complementing practice and procedures, what other steps, besides those already outlined, can be taken to assess competency?

Assessment of performance by line managers tends to rely on forming a match between observed behaviours and those defined in a framework or job-role description. But employers' approaches to this process can come in many different forms. During performance review, managers at Enterprise Oil match observed behaviours with those set out under the company's core competencies. It uses a scale of 0–5 to determine a level of performance, and regards the framework as a focus for development-need discussions between appraiser and appraisee. A performance review is seen as a "local" event (Enterprise Oil has an extensive international presence) that assists by encouraging people to take time out to think about competencies and individual performance. Although it offers no formal training to assist managers in assessing competency, it does provide back-up development courses that support the framework (Warner, 2000e).

The Halifax Group, the UK-based banking and financial services company, has a network of succession planning committees, made up of senior managers, that review the competencies of employees who are deemed ready for promotion. As part of an executive assessment and development programme, eight employees at a time participate in assessment centres. This involves two teams of four running a simulated business, while a number of trained observers watch on. The intention of the simulation is to draw the best out of people and for the observers to assess the behaviour of participants over a sustained period. The process is regarded by participants as being realistic, enjoyable and involving. Assessment derived from the events informs decisions on promotion and development needs (Warner, 2000f).

The assessment process used for middle and senior managers at Ladbrokes, a major high-street betting chain, consists of four stages. First, a portfolio of evidence of competence is gathered, followed by psychometric questionnaires that gather information on personal and interpersonal values. The third stage provides 360-degree feedback (multirater assessment), and the final stage involves an assessment centre. The managers undertake a business simulation – generally computer-based – over several days, and in teams selected by the participants themselves. Those in charge of the company's betting shops have a different procedure applied to their assessment. Technical and managerial competencies are assessed at the end of the managers' initial training programme. After six months in a post, they receive 180-degree feedback from a line manager on their competence. The process of assessment is helping Ladbrokes to identify people who are ready for more responsibility and promotion (Warner, 2000g).

Working with external consultants, the multinational pharmaceuticals company Eli Lilly assists its managers in making their assessment of employees' competence through the STAR system. STAR is an acronym for "situation – task – action – result", and has been devised by Development Dimensions International (DDI). As part of a performance review process, critical incident interviews are arranged. During these, the STAR system becomes the focus of a discussion about what was achieved under given circumstances and how the employee went about tackling a task or specific incident (the behaviours). This structure also helps to draw up an appropriate development plan for an individual (Warner, 2001d).

Social housing provider Liverpool Housing Trust (Warner, 2000h) has designed a 1–10 rating scale for competencies, which is completed by employees prior to a performance review meeting. During the meeting, a line manager annotates the self-assessment document with his or her own judgments about competence. Discussions about performance tend to concentrate on areas where there is misalignment between the line manager's and the employee's views of performance. The aim is to form an agreed position and identify the competence areas requiring further development.

The Valuation Office Agency, which is an executive arm of the UK's Inland Revenue, makes use of narrative statements about competencies and observable behaviours, without performance levels.

During the framework's design, the statements were formulated with wide staff participation. In six core competency areas, members of staff were asked what behaviours they would anticipate being displayed by an outstanding performer, and then carried out a similar exercise for their line manager's behaviours. Participation has ensured that the narrative statements are valued and this contributes to the success of the assessment process (Warner, 2000i).

Eastleigh Borough Council in Hampshire wanted its competency framework to emphasise the leadership roles to be adopted by managers. Under the appraisal system, behaviours are compared with competency-based job profiles to assess the degree that they match. Appraiser and appraised discuss performance and come to agreement on this judgment. A formal development interview takes place to determine a training programme to be undertaken during the forthcoming review period. Without a deliberate emphasis on development needs, the local authority was finding that this area tended to "get lost" during performance appraisals. Where disputes arise between appraiser and appraised on performance, an informal arrangement is made for arbitration with a senior manager, but a previous more formal "grandfathering" system has been dropped from assessment procedures (Warner, 2000j).

Reflections

To assist the process of assessing competency, the view of most of the organisations featured in this article is that the fundamental design of the competency framework must be correct. It should reflect organisational goals, accurately detail behaviours, be a prompt for a development review, and enjoy the wide support of employees. If these elements are in place, then assessment becomes a more valued and beneficial process. Putting structure into performance management procedures, such as completion of self-assessment forms and detailed behavioural descriptors, provides managers with essential tools to support their assessment of employees' competence. It also gives a platform for comprehensive feedback and for a review of development needs.

Most of us find criticism of what we do and how we do it difficult to take. But with a good design, support and training, assessment of competence can be made into a positive experience for an employee. In turn, this can only help to raise their performance and ensure that individuals reach their full potential.

Gaining maximum impact from 360-degree feedback

Peter Goodge, Sharon Atchley and Jane Coomber

One of the surprising things about 360-degree feedback or multi-rater appraisal is that it is old – at least three decades old! But, for much of that time it was little used; it is only in the past few years that 360-degree feedback has become popular. And, according to surveys, it is destined to become increasingly popular. The growth of 360-degree feedback is partly explained by the falling costs of computing, increasing recognition of the importance of performance feedback, and the tool's huge range of applications. And, it is explained by 360's immense value in delivering the benefits of competencies.

As a result of its delayed development, it is only recently that we have discovered what works well in 360-degree and what does not work at all. Increasing use has highlighted the features of successful 360-degree projects, and some unhappy mistakes. And, new research has challenged some of our assumptions and ways of doing things. Combining all the lessons of the recent past into a powerful, integrated approach to 360-degree feedback, we have developed an approach that we call "maximum-impact" 360-degree feedback.

Job performance, not competencies

A questionnaire has maximum impact when it asks about the particular tasks contained in a specific job. For example, the questionnaire used by Standard Life's salespeople asks about the planning of sales campaigns, quality of technical advice provided to customers, use of sales support staff, and similar specific issues. The Standard Life questionnaire is 100% relevant to job performance, and is written in language that jobholders understand. (It is no surprise that salespeople designed most of the questionnaire.)

But many 360-degree questionnaires contain "generic" questions based on competency definitions (not job tasks), and their relevance (often marginal) has to be worked out. A particularly bad example is a question relating to the statement "Fully commits his/herself to achieving according to circumstances". The recipients of feedback have to work out what that, and other generic questions, mean to them (if anything). Generic questions often result in vague, poorly

282

substantiated ideas about strengths and development needs. If the scores for most competencies are similar for most people, that is a reliable indicator of poor questions (and perhaps poor competencies). Generic questionnaires can of course be used across a variety of jobs – but lack of relevance, and impact, is the price paid. Off-the-shelf questionnaires can be a particular problem. Yet, modern 360-degree feedback software is so flexible it is possible to create a set of high-impact questions for each employee group, and do so quickly.

A useful method of creating relevant questions is simply to ask a small group of good-performing jobholders to list the important tasks of the job, then group the tasks under the company's competency headings. A questionnaire designer then only has to "word smith" key job tasks into questions.

Engineered critical feedback

Many, perhaps a majority of, 360-degree projects suffer from the same problem: almost all the feedback is favourable. If a questionnaire uses a "poor" to "excellent" rating scale, 90% of the feedback can consist of "good" and "excellent" ratings. Everyone appears to be good at everything, and it is just about impossible to identify development needs. The recipients of overwhelmingly positive feedback are understandably and pleasantly surprised by the high ratings and praise. But positive feedback encourages "more of the same"; little change occurs; and the impact upon most individuals' performance is nil – although their egos might benefit. Uncritical feedback is a widespread problem; it is probably the key reason why some UK companies stop using 360-degree feedback. Senior managers argue that the company's feedback reports lack credibility – "people are not that good".

Changing the rating scale to one to 10, or rating "how often" rather than "how well", does not solve the problem, although many companies still tinker with their scales and questions in attempts to fix a deeper problem. And it is a curiously British problem – other cultures are much more critical. To produce real impact, some of the feedback an individual receives has to be critical. That can be achieved by "forced-choice" questionnaires that require respondents to select better descriptions of the individual – or, more commonly, by requiring a proportion of critical ratings.

For example, the directors of a Whitbread company sought feedback with a 60-item questionnaire answered with ticks and crosses. Respondents were asked to give at least 15 crosses. This ensured that at least some, about 25%, of the feedback was critical, and it highlighted each director's development needs very clearly. But, the requirement for some critical feedback alters how we can interpret the results. For example, low scores were not "weak" competencies, but the things the director did less well compared with his/her other competencies. From a development perspective, that is exactly what people want to know. They want to know which competencies to work on.

The requirement also means we are unable to compare one individual's feedback with another person's, but that has advantages in terms of removing competition between individuals and encouraging openness. However, if we cannot compare individuals, we cannot use maximum-impact 360-degree for performance review, identifying potential or appointment decisions. (Not that it is wise to use 360-degree feedback for such applications anyway.)

Respondent choice and anonymity

Maximum-impact 360-degree assessment asks individuals to choose whom they seek feedback from – in other words, to choose their own respondents. It is crucial that respondents are not selected by others on behalf of the individual, or imposed by some rule. Respondents have to be credible to the individual – not to senior managers, the HR function, or someone else. If respondents are not credible, the feedback will not be credible to the individual. It is that simple. In fact, imposing respondents upon individuals is a classic mistake made by many 360-degree programmes. Doing so invites individuals to dismiss unfavourable feedback with arguments such as "they would say that", "they don't really know the job I do", and "they are unimportant to me".

Restricting the respondent sample produces similar problems. For example, a senior manager successfully argued that the company's policy of omitting his direct reports from the 360-degree process produced a biased, incomplete and unfair view of his skills. Individuals are only really convinced if they choose they own respondents. Of course, we want individuals' managers to be convinced too, so meetings between them and their managers to agree respondents are a smart move.

Both major recent surveys of 360-degree use in the UK reported some anxiety among respondents. About 75% of junior staff are a little threatened by a 360-degree questionnaire, and feel they can not be entirely honest. Completely anonymous questionnaires lessen respondents' concerns, and encourage frank feedback. But, that diminishes the impact of feedback – knowing who said what is an important part of making sense of the feedback. That is one reason why the use of average scores, although they protect respondents' anonymity, are of limited value. Hence, there is a balance to be struck, and we suggest the balance that achieves maximum impact is to:

- ask respondents to place their names on completed questionnaires, so that late or incomplete questionnaires can be followed-up;

- guarantee that respondents' names will not be revealed; and

- provide feedback in terms of what different types of respondents said. For example, feedback could report that three colleagues at a similar management level were critical of the individuals' planning, but not to report who those individuals were.

Simple, striking, informative

Most 360-degree questionnaires are analysed by spreadsheet software, such as Excel or Lotus 123, and the feedback reports produced in this way are very limited. Often, the report is a collection of graphs and averages – the things spreadsheets are designed to produce. There might be lots of graphs and statistics, but they might not mean much. Much better software is available, using database programs like Access, to produce reports that are simpler yet much more informative. An example is the sample report for the competency of Proactive achievement shown in box 11.1. It was produced by a database – it is just about impossible with a spreadsheet.

The report shows the questions used to measure Proactive achievement against the ratings given by individual respondents. Designed to have maximum impact, the original report shows high ratings – scores of four and five – with green backgrounds, and low ratings – scores of one and two – in red (shown as dark and light tints here). Note how easy it is to conclude that this >p.287

11.1. Presenting feedback results

An example, based on the Proactive achievement competency.

Proactive achievement	Reports			Peers			Boss	Self
Tackling difficult problems with real enthusiasm	4	5	3	3	4	4	2	4
Giving exceptional time and energy to projects	5	4	4	4	5	5	3	5
Taking the big risks	2	3	2	2	2	3	1	3
Taking personal responsibility for risky decisions	2	2	2	3	2	2	2	2
Taking action without waiting to be asked to	2	3	3	3	2	2	1	2
Applying "best-practice" methods from elsewhere	4	5	5	4	5	3	2	4
Finding imaginative ways of doing things differently	4	4	5	4	3	4	2	5
Experimenting with new ideas	4	5	4	4	5	4	3	4

individual is not so good at risk-taking, and that his boss has a significantly more negative view. That is a lot of important findings produced very quickly.

Averages (and graphs that use averages) frequently reduce the impact of feedback. For example, averages for groups of respondents, such as peers and direct reports, often hide important differences between respondents. No manager treats his or her direct reports in the same way as each other, or has the same relationship with all his or her peers – so what sense is there in averaging them? Research suggests that there are often big differences between respondents, and that averages make no sense at all. (See Goodge and Burr, 1999, for a review of the research.) For maximum impact, use as few averages as possible, know the assumptions that averages make, and where possible present the raw data.

A feedback report has little impact if the recipient does not have a clear purpose in mind. If we provide feedback to those who do not want it, then they register passing interest before filing and forgetting the report. For 360-degree feedback to have real impact, the recipient has to want it, and has to want it for a particular purpose, such as answering a career question, improving performance, or planning their own training. Hence, a central principle of maximum impact is to define the individual's purpose before they receive feedback. Then, the individual does not merely read the 360-degree report – he or she actively uses it. The GROW coaching process (see box 11.2) is a useful strategy for achieving maximum impact. Use the Goal-setting stage of the process to define the individual's purpose, the 360-degree feedback to lead the Reality-checking stage, and the Options and What next stages for action planning.

The paperwork associated with a 360-degree project is substantial. If 100 managers each ask 10 respondents to complete a three-page, 60-item questionnaire, the project involves 3,000 pieces of paper, 60,000 ratings to be inputted, and at least 2,200 document movements. Of course, things never go as planned, and the workload involved in chasing things up and getting them done properly is probably double what the these figures suggest. The huge administrative workload associated with every large 360-degree project means that reports arrive late, incomplete or not at all. The effectiveness of the project is significantly diminished.

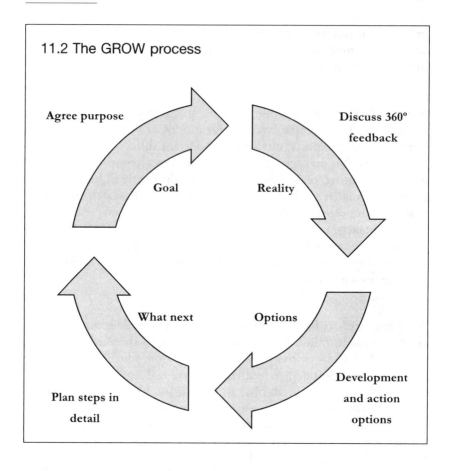

11.2 The GROW process

Agree purpose

Discuss 360°
feedback

Goal   Reality

What next   Options

Development
and action
options

Plan steps in
detail

Hence, the final principle of maximum impact is to remove all the paper, the inputting and the document movements by running the 360-degree project on the internet (or intranet). The internet and 360-degree feedback were made for each other.

Case study: Removing horns and halos at Smith and Nephew Wound Management

John Warner

At its site in Hull, Smith and Nephew manufactures medical devices for three general business units: Wound Management, Casting and Bandaging, and Consumer Products, with the main bulk of production being concerned with Wound Management. The company operates worldwide and the Smith and Nephew Group has an annual turnover of over £1 billion. There are around 1,000 employees at the Hull site, and about 500 staff and managers are included in the behavioural competency framework; it does not cover production workers.

Initially, the competency headings and descriptors were devised by a group of human resources and line managers from the Hull site and other locations in the UK. The group was advised by external consultants, and the development phase was informed by the outcomes of a series of brainstorming workshops. During the sessions, members considered what competencies were needed by various grades of managers and staff. They also answered how, what and why questions, considered examples of good and bad behaviours, and what actions were more (or less) effective in given circumstances. The first year of the framework was seen as a pilot during which employees could comment on it, and modifications could be made based on the feedback. The workshops also devised a five-point numerical grading system for use with the competency descriptors.

Evolving framework

Over the years, the basic competency headings of the original framework have spread from the company's UK sites into Europe and then to the rest of the world. While other sites use the headings, many have adapted the descriptors to meet specific local circumstances or the needs of different groups of employees, such as a sales force. The company has also moved away from its initial numerical grading to grades expressed as statements:

- exceeds expectations;

- meets expectations;

- partly meets expectations; and

- fails to meet expectations.

The framework consists of four main headings, which are sub-divided into 14 further categories.

- Future orientated: strategic direction; business planning;

- Business awareness: developing customer partnership; commercial awareness;

- Task-focused: critical analysis; decision-making; achieving results/orientation; improvement focus; personal effectiveness; and

- Empowering: teamwork; participative leadership; coaching and development; self-projection; influencing others.

The company believes that it is important to be precise about the competencies that have to be demonstrated in a particular job. It says that there is no point in assessing a competency if it is not really necessary for success, and that attempts to cover too many competencies can discourage the person being assessed.

Calibration procedures

In the past, Smith and Nephew experienced inconsistencies in the grading of performance by line managers, not just on the earlier numerical scale but also in the subsequent approach based on statements. To address this issue, the human resources director introduced a moderation procedure originally used by Seagram – the media, spirits and wine company.

Since then, following performance reviews, line managers have met to help iron out grading anomalies. "Calibration discussions" take place, during which the managers' perceptions of team members and their provisional grades are considered by the group. The company believes this consensus approach leads to fairer and more objective grades, and that the "horns and halos" bias is removed. The moderated grade, and not the line manager's grading, is the one conveyed to the employee post-review.

Following induction and before their first review, all new staff and managers take part in performance management training programmes. Staff follow a one-day course familiarising them with the competency framework, and the positive role it plays in personal-development plans and performance review. Managers are taken through a similar programme, but their three-day learning period also provides training to help them carry out and write up reviews, use calibration procedures and communicate the outcomes to their staff. Both training programmes have been developed in-house and are delivered by members of the human resources team.

After its introduction in 1995, the framework was allowed to operate for some years before it was fully reviewed. In 1998, the company underwent restructuring, and changed from a manufacturing focus to one that is more customer oriented and has a global perspective. The core company values have been redefined in terms of "performance", "innovation" and "trust", and the competency framework has been changed to reflect the new values.

References

Goodge, Peter and Burr Jo (1999), "360-degree feedback – for once, the research is useful", *Selection & Development Review*, vol. 15 no.2, pp.3–7.

Rankin, Neil (2001a), "Raising performance through people: the eighth competency survey", *Competency & Emotional Intelligence Benchmarking*, 2000/01, January.

Rankin, Neil (2001b), "Employers' competency frameworks", *Competency & Emotional Intelligence Benchmarking*, 2000/01.

Warner, John (1999), "A competency framework is the vehicle for radical change at the House of Fraser", *Competency & Emotional Intelligence Quarterly*, vol. 6, no.4, Summer, pp.12–16.

Warner, John (2000a), "French connection: Aventis Pasteur MSD", *Competency & Emotional Intelligence Quarterly*, vol. 7, no.3, Spring, p.6

Warner, John (2000b), "A new national performance management and development system: the Republic of Ireland Civil Service", *Competency & Emotional Intelligence Quarterly*, vol. 8, no.1, Autumn, pp.9–14.

Warner, John (2000c), "Moving mountains, adding value: Hanson Quarry Products Europe", *Competency & Emotional Intelligence Quarterly*, vol. 8, no.1, Autumn, p.5.

Warner, John (2000d), "Shared values bring officers and staff together: West Yorkshire Police", *Competency & Emotional Intelligence Quarterly*, vol. 7, no.4, Summer, pp.10–16.

Warner, John (2000e), "Web-based roll-out: Enterprise Oil", *Competency & Emotional Intelligence Quarterly*, vol. 8, no.1, Autumn, p.2.

Warner, John (2000f), "A common language of competencies: Halifax Group plc", *Competency & Emotional Intelligence Quarterly*, vol. 8, no.1, 2000, p.4.

Warner, John (2000g), "Separating competence from performance: Ladbrokes Limited", *Competency & Emotional Intelligence Quarterly*, vol. 8, no.1, Autumn, p.8.

Warner, John (2000h), "New approach; new framework: Liverpool Housing Trust", *Competency & Emotional Intelligence Quarterly*, vol. 8, no.1, Autumn, p.6.

Warner, John (2000i), "An holistic approach: Valuation Office Agency", *Competency & Emotional Intelligence Quarterly*, vol. 7, no.4, Summer, p.8.

Warner, John (2000j), "Changing culture: Eastleigh Borough Council", *Competency & Emotional Intelligence Quarterly*, vol. 7, no.4, Summer, pp.3 and 36.

Assessment

Warner, John (2001a), "Keep it simple: Huhtamaki Van Leer", *Competency & Emotional Intelligence Quarterly*, vol. 8 no.2, Winter 2000/01, p.4.

Warner, John (2001b), "Responding to market liberalisation: Union Fenosa", *Competency & Emotional Intelligence Quarterly*, vol. 8 no.2, Winter 2000/01, p.3.

Warner, John (2001c), "Choose a descriptor: Bedfordshire Police", *Competency & Emotional Intelligence Quarterly*, vol. 8 no.2, Winter 2000/01, p.7.

Warner, John (2000d), "Seven keys: Eli Lilly and Company", *Competency & Emotional Intelligence Quarterly*, vol. 8 no.3, Spring, p.2.

Learning points

Overview

- Competencies are definitions of performance expectations; assessment is essential to ensure these expectations are treated seriously, that development is provided, and that performance improves as a result.

- However, any form of performance assessment is difficult, and liable to be avoided or undermined by those involved. Assessment of competencies is as difficult as conventional assessments, and probably more so. Over half of competency users report problems with assessing competency.

- The key issues in ensuring the successful assessment of individuals' and teams' competencies are: gaining the commitment of line managers to conduct assessments in a thorough way; ensuring that the requirements of a competency are interpreted in the same way by different line managers; ensuring that performance in each competency is assessed and/or rated in the same way; avoiding as much subjectivity in assessments as possible; provide good, clear guidance to employees and managers about each competency's requirements; and the assessment process for National Vocational Qualifications needs to be documented in clear English, and its bureaucracy reduced as much as possible.

First steps in assessment

- Choosing appropriate competency headings is essential to ensure that assessment is made against competencies that contribute to the success of the organisation. High buy-in rates to assessments are more likely if there has been wide consultation when identifying the headings.

- The competency framework has to be capable of easy implementation; the number of competency headings is a crucial factor.

- It is important to decide whether or not the behavioural competencies are intended to apply to all roles. Sets of technical competences, based on tasks and outputs, are often dealt with separately. Flexible systems improve the usefulness and ease of assessment of the competency framework(s).

- Competencies on their own are insufficient for assessment purposes. To overcome problems of ambiguity, employers usually develop further "layers" in the competency framework: definitions; behavioural indicators and, in many cases, performance levels, each with its own series of behavioural examples.

- Assessment can be helped if negative indicators are included, illustrating examples of poor behaviour alongside the positive examples. However, their use must be consistent with the culture of the organisation concerned.

360-degree feedback

- 360-degree assessment has become increasingly popular. It has the potential to be of great value in realising the benefits of using competencies.

- A 360-degree questionnaire has maximum impact when it asks about the particular tasks contained in a specific job. Generally, questions must be well-designed and seen to be relevant. If the scores for most competencies obtained from 360-degree feedback are similar for most people, that is a reliable indicator of poor questions (and perhaps poor competencies).

- To produce real impact, some of the feedback that an individual receives has to be critical. This can be achieved by "forced-choice" questionnaires, or by requiring a proportion of critical ratings.

- It is crucial that 360-degree respondents are not selected on behalf of the subject.

- Anonymous questionnaires encourage frank feedback, but have less impact. A balance should be struck by providing the feedback in terms of what different types of respondents said.

- Averages (and graphs that use averages) frequently reduce the impact of feedback. As few averages as possible should be used, and raw data provided instead.

- For 360-degree feedback to have real impact, the recipient has to want it, and has to want it for a particular purpose.

Case study of Smith and Nephew Wound Management

- Smith and Nephew Wound Management involved line managers in devising its competency headings and descriptors; the framework was piloted for its first year.

- The company believes that it is important to assess only competencies directly relevant to a job; attempts to cover too many competencies can discourage the person being assessed.

- Assessment was initially based on a five-point numerical grading system, which was replaced with grades expressed as statements. However, both approaches suffered from inconsistencies in line managers' assessments.

- A moderation procedure addressed this issue. "Calibration discussions" take place, during which line managers' perceptions of team members and their provisional grades are considered by the group. The moderated grade is the one conveyed to the employee.

- Following induction and before their first performance review, all new staff and managers take part in performance-management training.

Chapter 12

Maintaining and revising competencies

Introduction

Neil Rankin

It is vital that competencies and the processes linked to them are maintained and, where necessary, updated. Organisations change constantly. There are pressures from the marketplace, government and society that require a response. Products and services change; new structures emerge; workplaces are closed or opened, and so on. Given that competencies represent the translation of organisational priorities into the expectations of individuals and teams, there would seem to be an unanswerable case for the effective long-term management of an employer's competency framework.

Yet, many organisations seem content to expend all their energy on devising and introducing competencies, and none on the equally important processes of maintenance and revision. Research carried out for the Chartered Institute of Personnel and Development (Miller, Rankin and Neathey, 2001) found that four in 10 employers (38%) in the matched sample investigated had not revised their frameworks. Indeed, "few frameworks included a date or issue number; from this, it can be inferred that there is not always an intention at the design stage to issue updated frameworks at regular intervals – for which, some form of identification would be required if users were to be confident that they were using the latest version," the research report added.

The design process can hinder or help an organisation's subsequent ability to maintain its competencies. Professor Adrian Furnham's investigation of competencies for the Careers Research Forum, which he describes in chapter 2, led him to conclude that successful competency initiatives comprise three phases: planning and development; implementation; and maintenance. However, he also found that the money and energy are exhausted in the first phase, which takes longer and proves more difficult than anticipated.

Feedback from employers analysed in the latest benchmarking report from the *Competency & Emotional Intelligence* journal (Rankin, 2001) shows that more than four in 10 users of competencies (45%) report problems in keeping them up to date. Professor Furnham identifies three prime reasons for these difficulties:

- lack of time, money and motivation;

- an over-elaborate or over-produced (expensively printed documentation) framework and documentation that acts as a deterrent to subsequent maintenance and revision; and

- in-built obsolescence, through the exclusion of forward-looking competencies.

The first two defects are linked, he believes. If the planning and development phase is poorly managed, not only will it tend to run late and over budget, it will also lead to an unrealistic end-result. There may well be a set of competencies that are too detailed, too fully documented, and too expensively produced for ease of revision.

The third defect involves a failure to look ahead at the likely needs of the organisation. Without an attempt to take account of emerging challenges and changes, a competency exercise will be entirely backward-looking. It will have been designed solely on the basis of what effective performance has meant in the *past*. Below, Katherine Adams explains why many of the techniques used to identify and define competencies look backwards in this way, and what can be done to improve on them. John Warner then provides a case study of how Barclays Contact Centres – the telephone banking operation of Barclays Bank – went about updating its own framework.

Looking ahead – can competencies predict the future?

Katherine Adams

Turbulence and competencies go hand-in-hand. During the years that the competency approach has come to prominence, the notion of continual change has become a cliché of business life. Successive benchmarking surveys from the *Competency & Emotional Intelligence* journal have shown that organisations see competencies as a way of speeding up change by encouraging their employees to behave differently. Many of the frameworks now being used explicitly list competencies like change management, innovation, flexibility, adaptability, and strategic thinking. Yet despite the apparent affinities, the prospect of more change poses a real problem for competencies. Though such competencies as "improving performance through change" may reflect an uneasy awareness that further upheaval is likely, just how clear are organisations about what the future will bring? Apart from the ability to deal with change itself, what other competencies are likely to be needed in the years ahead? And how can these be determined?

The danger with competencies based on the behaviour of successful performers is that they may perpetuate what *yesterday's* top players did in yesterday's circumstances. Tomorrow may require something quite different. Approaches that focus on the requirements of particular jobs may be even more susceptible to this danger, since jobs, too, are changing rapidly in the face of business shifts. Indeed, the very notion of what a job is is under threat. If competencies are to be effective in doing what they are designed for – recruiting the right people, encouraging appropriate behaviour, helping the organisation keep up with the competition and act strategically – they need to focus on the future rather than the past. And yet the most commonly used techniques for designing competencies produce lists that begin to age almost as soon as they are published.

Beyond the "snapshot"

Classically, the way that organisations derive the competencies they plan to use for human resource management involves identifying their best staff – and often average and poor performers, too – and then interviewing them about their work. These interviews generally use one of three well-tried methods: the critical incident technique, behavioural event interviews or repertory grids (these three methods are explained in chapter 3). All three techniques can claim some degree of rigour in that they all systematically gather information about people's behaviour from a number of concrete, detailed examples of actual events or individuals.

But of necessity, all three provide only a "snapshot" of behaviour that has proved successful in the past. This will be of questionable relevance if the organisation concerned is undergoing any kind of major change. At one end of the spectrum, this could include changes to current jobs because of new technology; at the other, it could mean the emergence of entirely new jobs in response to a new business strategy, a merger, or changes in the political, social or economic environment. A number of solutions have been proposed to this problem, but, broadly speaking, they all appear to fall into three categories. The first is an extension of the "benchmarking" idea used in much competency design work; the second is to give competency interviews a more forward-looking focus; and the third is to use a variety of forecasting techniques to build speculation about the future into competency design.

Benchmarking revisited

For many organisations, an early step in devising their own competency frameworks involves obtaining the lists used by other organisations, particularly their competitors or companies that are seen as being in some way similar to their own. Known somewhat grandly as "benchmarking", this can often provide a useful starting point for competency design. Selecting a suitable comparator organisation and looking at its competencies is also often suggested as a way of getting around the "snapshot" problem. If someone else is already dealing with the same challenges, then looking at their competency frameworks can offer a fruitful jumping-off point.

Rosemary Boam is one of the few people to have gone into print with suggestions for designing future-looking competencies (Sparrow and Boam, 1992). Putting organisations in touch with each other is important, she found, as a means of stimulating thinking, rather than transferring one organisation's competencies to another in a mechanical way. Benchmarking that is based on the problems shared, rather than the industry, size or other attribute, provides the best approach.

An alternative approach is to identify a leading-edge department, division or business unit within one's own organisation. The idea is to find those parts of the business which are facing issues that will soon loom large for the company as a whole, or where people are already doing the kind of jobs that will become more important. Competency research can then be carried out from scratch with successful performers, using behavioural event interviews or interviews based on the critical incident technique or the repertory grid. Given cooperative partners, this approach could also be extended to external organisations, the idea being to develop fresh competency frameworks for groups of staff in the comparator organisation that are of particular interest to one's own organisation.

If no helpful comparator organisations can be found, then a compromise might be to conduct interviews with staff in one's own organisation about the way other companies operate. Many employees will have personal knowledge of working for a competitor, have contacts in them, or know their industry or market so well that they have developed considerable insight into the likely direction of future trends.

Adapting competency interviews

It is clear that this suggestion – using competency interviews to speculate about behaviour in other organisations – marks a step away from the classical use of techniques like behavioural event interviews, the critical incident technique and the repertory grid. Typically, these focus on actual examples of behaviour – whether the interviewee's own or that of other people. Here, though, the interviewee is being asked to imagine behaviour that they have not actually experienced.

A further step away from the concrete can also be made by asking interviewees to speculate about possible future behaviour. Viv Shackleton (1992) argues that interviews based on the critical incident technique can be "pushed" into a "forward-looking frame of reference" by asking interviewees "to imagine what incidents of critical success or failure are going to be increasingly seen in the future. And what successes and failures of the past or present the respondent thinks will become rarer or irrelevant."

He suggests that repertory grids, too, can be adapted to provide a more forward-looking focus. Where this technique would typically use a number of actual people as the "elements" to be discussed, a future-oriented interview could instead, he suggests, ask about the behaviour of "an ideal person for the newly-created role" or "someone who is most likely to be successful in the future" or "someone who is good at seeing future requirements in the role". If, as seems likely, this means that interviewees were be asked to think of actual people who they considered to be "an ideal person for the newly-created role", this is in fact akin to the extensions of benchmarking discussed above. Viv Shackleton accepts that these uses of the critical incident technique and repertory grids "rely largely on hypothesising". And it is clear that the more that "imagining" comes to the forefront, the more tenuous becomes the claim of these techniques to be able to provide a "scientific" or "objective" way of deriving competencies.

Uncertain futures

However, the attempt to capture the future necessarily involves a degree of speculation. Indeed, the less certain the future, the more speculative the techniques needed to capture it will have to be. Benchmarking perhaps lies at the least speculative end of the spectrum. But it is clear that this technique is limited to those organisations that have a fairly clear idea of the kind of jobs people will be doing in the future, and of the future environment, so that they can select suitable comparator organisations or leading-edge business units. For many organisations, however, the search for competencies takes place in the context of considerable uncertainty, which may necessitate the use of more speculative techniques. For these organisations, it may be necessary to take a step back and consider wider issues about the future before tackling the question of competencies, and it is here that the third group of techniques comes into play. Scenario planning, the Delphi technique and "visioning" workshops have all been suggested as ways of getting at wider futures issues to feed into competency design.

Business scenarios

Originally developed by Royal Dutch/Shell in the turbulent days of the late 1960s and early 1970s, scenario planning explicitly recognises that uncertainty is endemic in business life. Rather than attempting to predict the future, this method aims to describe a number of possible alternative futures and, most importantly, to open the minds of senior people in an organisation to a range of possibilities as a way of enabling them to make crucial business decisions. One of the originators of the method, Pierre Wack, has described (Wack, 1985) how he and other corporate planners at Royal Dutch/Shell analysed the various economic, social and political challenges facing the company. The aim was to decide which elements were "predetermined" and which uncertain, and to examine the connections between each. The planners then presented Shell's top management with four or so internally-consistent possible futures or "scenarios".

The aim was not for executives to choose between the different scenarios, but simply to recognise the processes at work and the possible consequences, to "question their own model of reality and change it when necessary, so as to come up with strategic insights beyond their minds' previous reach". As the technique developed, interviews with senior managers were introduced at an early stage of the process "to find out what was on their minds and to illuminate the existing decision framework".

Explaining how this technique can be applied to competency design, Viv Shackleton (1992) says that: "Business scenarios involve asking senior managers to imagine possible future events, good or bad, such as high growth, declining growth, turnaround situations, a merger, high profit, low profit, and so on. For each of these scenarios, the key managerial characteristics and competencies can be guessed at." The problem with this, though, is that it would presumably result in several different sets of competencies, each corresponding to a different scenario. The question would then be: "Which set should we try to develop?". Such an approach seems to lose some of the subtlety of the scenario-planning technique, in particular the ability to open managers' minds to new strategic insights. Rather than trying to predict the likeliest scenario, and an associated set of competencies, perhaps a more fruitful approach would be to think about competencies at the same time as the managers were focusing on the interrelations between predetermined and uncertain aspects of the various possible futures. In this way, more general strategic insights about the competencies required might also emerge.

The Delphi technique

Named after the oracle at Delphi, which the ancients believed could predict the future, the Delphi technique is a way of reaching a consensus about the future among a number of "experts". The first step is to ask the experts to write down their own predictions on a given topic. The collated responses are then returned to them for comment and further written proposals. The process continues, often through many stages, until an acceptable degree of consensus is achieved. Viv Shackleton suggests (1992) that: "In the context of future-oriented competencies, these ideas might be concerned with the impact of new technologies, or working practices, or consumer demand, on job requirements. From this lengthy and extensive process, competencies which many people feel are the key ones for the future can emerge."

Presumably, the technique can also be used by organisations that are uncertain about what the future holds, to gain an insight into what exactly the key factors of the future environment are likely to be. This could precede or accompany consideration of the likely impact of these factors on people's jobs, though this could well make an already time-consuming process even more so.

Visioning workshops

The last of this group of techniques is usually referred to as the "visioning" or "subject-matter expert" workshop. Professor John Sparrow, whose book (Sparrow, 1998) includes a review of this technique, told us that: "Visioning workshops use guided imagery to help participants form a view of what the organisation will look and feel like in the future. The idea is to form a clear picture or 'prototype' in your mind. Once it is a nearly-living thing in your imagination, it then becomes reasonable to ask about the competencies that might be needed."

A visioning workshop is typically run for a group of senior managers or strategists. It can also include technical experts, such as economists or demographers and, if the workshop is to focus on a particular work role or business function, job incumbents, their managers, and human resource specialists. Using a variety of group techniques, most notably brainstorming, the idea is to take the participants through a series of logical stages, tackling questions about various aspects of the future environment, planned changes to the organisation, and their impact on people's roles.

The composition of the group is a matter of great importance, according to Rosemary Boam. She said to us: "You need to make sure that you include the kind of people who can form a vision of the future organisation and those who can focus on the more concrete problem of future job requirements. You can think of it in terms of two Myers-Briggs psychometric types: the 'intuitives' and the 'sensers'. While the intuitives are good at getting the overall vision, you need the sensers to get the behaviours out, and stop the whole thing becoming too woolly."

John Sparrow suggests that a visioning workshop can be used to build up a picture of the future organisation that can then be interrogated using techniques like the repertory grid, in order to get at the competencies that will be required. Presumably, the most obvious way to do this is to conduct group discussions or one-to-one interviews with the participants in the visioning workshop, since these people are likely to have the clearest idea of the suggested future organisation.

Using the techniques

There are differing views on how the various techniques for forecasting competency requirements can be combined in use. For instance, Gareth Morgan (1988) suggests a technique that he calls the "C-plan" process (the "C" stands for competency). This method aims to help senior managers tackle the complex and intangible question of future competencies without becoming completely overwhelmed by it. The C-plan process has affinities with a number of the techniques described above, in particular scenario planning, benchmarking and visioning workshops. Morgan's distinctive contribution is the idea that there are certain "fracture lines" in the environment facing organisations that have the potential to alter the nature of whole industries.

The C-plan process involves bringing together small groups of executives who use the idea of fracture lines to discuss the trends facing their organisation and identify key strategic issues. Further groups can bring together executives from different organisations to provide a wider perspective. The insights gained are synthesised into discussion documents, assessed by a small group of top executives, and converted into agendas for short-term, "line-driven" task forces. Each task force – which may also forge links with external organisations – is asked to provide details of the competencies required to address a particular strategic issue.

Another method is described by Paul Sparrow and Rosemary Boam (1992). They, too, suggest starting with "top-down clarification" of the organisation's strategy, using visioning workshops where managers discuss a particular aspect of the organisation, its structure, or particular job roles. At the same time, "hierarchical business modelling" can be used to establish the key functions and tasks necessary for effective performance in new business areas, and/or a "cultural analysis" survey can be carried out. Business scenarios and benchmarking can also be used at this stage. Sparrow and Boam suggest that the information gleaned from these "top-down" techniques can then be used "to create a sharper set of questions for jobholders" in competency interviews. For instance, repertory-grid questions may be designed to tap particular features of work or new definitions of performance, and the critical incident technique can investigate areas that are felt to reflect more likely events in the future.

Finally, Sparrow and Boam suggest that the emerging competency framework should be subjected to expert interrogation and validation. This might involve collecting evidence from business sector research reports and lists of competencies used in other organisations in order to "assess, question and challenge" the organisation's own emerging framework, to make sure it takes account of new trends. Intriguingly, they also suggest taking this process a step further by comparing the "top-down, future-oriented" data with the information they call "bottom-up, past-oriented" (that is, information derived from classical competency interviews), so as to identify those competencies that will become more, or less, important in the future. In this way, they suggest, a competency framework can "weight" each competency according to its future relevance and its likely "shelf-life".

In conclusion

It is a common theme of discussions about future competencies that much more work needs to be done. But even those ideas that exist tend to be speculative: there is little evidence that organisations are putting into practice even the limited range of techniques available. That is not to say, however, that many users of competencies are unaware of the crucial importance of incorporating a degree of resilience to change in their frameworks. Given that rapid change is now a fact of organisational life, with conditions seemingly fluctuating to even greater extents than in the past, finding an effective way of forecasting competency requirements should become a top priority for users.

So far, the most common means of identifying future competencies involves canvassing the views of board members. In many organisations, members of the competency-development team interview some or all of the main-board directors, chairs and chief executives to gain an insight into their strategic viewpoint at the apex of the organisation. This is often an important process in its own right, as it involves senior management in the competency initiative, and exposes the development team to directors' priorities and concerns. But it can also be a reasonably effective means of incorporating future competencies in a new framework. Even if a board is sometimes less than proactively strategic, its members will be those in the organisation who take the decisions about reactive responses to external events. In either case, the board's decisions will set the agenda for changes to competency requirements.

Case study: remedying earlier defects at Barclays Contact Centres

John Warner

Through its contact centres, Barclays Bank provides a complementary telephone banking service to the service offered by the branch network. This gives its customers a choice in how they conduct their banking for most transactions. It has been providing this service since 1993 when it conducted a pilot, followed by a full UK-wide launch the following year. It has contact centres in Coventry, Manchester, Sunderland (and an associated centre in Liverpool), and employs about 2,800 staff.

The current competency framework (see box 12.1) was introduced in 1997 and replaced an earlier one that was considered complicated, not representative of all roles and not linked to the organisation's mission, values, or strategy. The earlier framework was designed as a tactical solution to challenges of the rapid expansion of the telephone banking service.

12.1. Barclays Contact Centres competencies

People focus

Working with others

Influencing

Developing people

Continuous-improvement focus

Concern for efficiency

Thoroughness

Concern for standards

> **Future focus**
>
> Creativity and innovation
>
> Vision and strategic direction
>
> **Business focus**
>
> Delivering results
>
> Problem-solving and decision-making
>
> Customer focus
>
> Taking initiative
>
> **Personal**
>
> Self-control
>
> Self-confidence
>
> Flexibility
>
> Organisational commitment
>
> Self-development
>
> **Business and technical skills**

In reviewing the earlier competency framework, Barclays aimed to:

- fine-tune the behavioural indicators;
- clarify the skills, knowledge and competencies necessary for roles;
- make links between the skills required for a job and the underpinning behaviours; and
- develop indicators for competencies that were not covered in the earlier framework.

The new framework addresses the deficiencies of earlier provision. It has reduced the number of competencies and clustered them in a more focused way, clearly links behaviours to the achievement of company objectives, provides a common competency language for assessment purposes, and creates a better mechanism for determining training and development needs.

The revisions to the former framework were achieved with wide involvement, including consultations with heads of department, line managers and jobholders, and by gathering data using a variety of means such as critical incident interviews and competency questionnaires. The latter were issued to line managers to assess the roles within their remit. Managers were asked to comment on the behaviours of employees who displayed outstanding performance and to contrast this with employees at more modest performance levels. Jobholders were also invited to make a self-assessment of successful behaviours to provide a comparative view. All of the findings were analysed and taken into account when formulating the new framework.

The gathering of evidence produced a diversity of responses, including:

- examples of highly effective and ineffective behaviours in each of the roles;

- specific situations that individuals are required to handle well in the role;

- contextual-based information about the behaviours that are required of an individual, in words that are specific to the organisation;

- quantitative information in the form of frequency counts of incident types; and

- clarification of the gap between what managers do now and what will be required in the future.

All of this information and evidence for clarification has helped to shape the new competency framework, which takes the form of six clusters containing 18 competencies.

Bands and dimensions

For each competency, examples of behaviours are described in three "performance bands": "needs development; fully effective; and outstanding". Brief descriptive statements for each band give greater clarity of meaning. The lowest band descriptors are negative examples of the type of behaviours that are expected of employees such as "takes constructive criticism poorly, becomes defensive, looks for sympathy or blames others for the situation".

The framework also draws a distinction between "uni-dimensional" competencies (where each role requires a similar level) and multidimensional competencies (where different roles require different levels). Examples of uni-dimensional competencies are "self-confidence; flexibility; and thoroughness". Examples of multidimensional competencies are "influencing; customer focus; and vision and strategic direction". As part of the documentation supporting the framework, employees are issued with a glossary of these and the other terms used.

References

Miller, Linda, Rankin, Neil and Neathey, Fiona (2001), *Competency frameworks in UK organisations*, Chartered Institute of Personnel and Development.

Morgan, Gareth (1988), *Riding the waves of change: developing managerial competencies for a turbulent world*, Jossey-Bass.

Rankin, Neil (2001), "Raising performance through people: the eighth competency survey", *Competency & Emotional Intelligence Benchmarking*, 2000/01, pp.2–23.

Shackleton, Viv (1992), "Using a competency approach in a business change setting", in *Designing and achieving competency: a competency-based approach to developing people and organisations*, Rosemary Boam and Paul Sparrow, McGraw-Hill.

Sparrow, John (1998), *Knowledge in organisations*, Sage.

Sparrow, Paul and Boam, Rosemary (1992), "An assessment of the strengths and weaknesses of existing competency-based approaches: where do we go from here?", in *Designing and achieving competency: a competency-based approach to developing people and organisations*, Rosemary Boam and Paul Sparrow, McGraw-Hill.

Wack, Pierre (1985), "Scenarios: uncharted waters ahead", *Harvard Business Review*, September–October, pp.73–89; and "Scenarios: shooting the rapids", Pierre Wack, *Harvard Business Review*, November–December, pp.139–150.

Learning points

Overview

- It is vital that competency frameworks are maintained and kept up to date. Despite this, many organisations give this process insufficient attention and resources. Difficulties in keeping their competencies up to date are widely reported by users.

- The way that competencies are designed is often the key to keeping competencies up to date.

Forward-looking competencies

- Most organisations use techniques to develop their competencies that are based on interviewing staff and managers about how they perform their current jobs. This approach may be backward-looking, based on behaviour that has proved successful in the past.

- Most solutions to this fall into three categories. The first is an extension of the "benchmarking" idea used in much competency design work; the second is to give competency interviews a more forward-looking focus; and the third is to use a variety of forecasting techniques.

Case study of Barclays Contact Centres

- A competency framework can become completely out of date in less than four years, particularly in a fast-developing sector.

- In Barclays Contact Centres, the initial framework's defects included being over-complex, unrepresentative of all roles and not being derived from the company's strategy and values.

- Initial aims for the review of the framework should be established, based on business needs and the known weaknesses of the current competencies.

- It is usually necessary to involve as many staff and line managers as possible in the review process. More than one method of gathering feedback and information on competencies may be useful.

Index